Praise for *Pope Francis and the Caring Society*

"We are all called to serve and care humbly for others, especially those most in need, but how we do so is crucial in guiding our moral responsibility. Firmly rooted in our Christian tradition, the incisive and timely book *Pope Francis and the Caring Society* carefully examines this vital issue by applying natural-law ethical and economic principles. Instead of command societies, cooperative, virtuous systems of enterprise, creativity, and charity are crucial to uplift people out of poverty, marginalization, and hopelessness; dignify people as purposeful beings through work and families; protect our environment for future genera-tions; and bring us all into closer harmony with one another and to God."
—**Michael C. Barber**, S.J., Bishop, Roman Catholic Diocese of Oakland, California

"The authority of the pope is regarded by many as grounded in essentially spiri-tual sources of wisdom and inspiration. Non-Catholics may stand aloof to such considerations but nonetheless acknowledge the great influence of papal thought on the social and moral dimensions of our time. In light of this, the pope's teach-ing warrants respectful but critical appraisal and receives it in the important book *Pope Francis and the Caring Society*. If what the pope teaches is influential, competent critics must test the teaching, often under the light of history. Under that light, Pope Francis's blueprint for 'caring' draws support from the notoriously failed theories on which socialism erects barriers to human freedom, creativity, and well-being."
—**Daniel N. Robinson**, Faculty Fellow of Philosophy, Linacre College, University of Oxford; Distinguished Professor Emeritus of Philosophy, Georgetown University

"At a time when those today most responsible for transmitting Catholic social teaching need urgently to be reminded of some cause-and-effect realities essen-tial to it, *Pope Francis and the Caring Society* provides us with many necessary reminders, readably and soundly."
—**John M. Finnis**, Biolchini Family Professor of Law, The Law School, University of Notre Dame

"*Pope Francis and the Caring Society* responds to Pope Francis's call for dialogue with a clarion critique of redistributive bromides and bureaucracies. Grounded in the Judeo-Christian principles of liberty, subsidiarity, and civic virtue, this luminous work shines through and shrivels the sanctimonious smog of socialist levelers who wreak demoralization and poverty wherever they rule."
—**George Gilder**, bestselling author, *Wealth and Poverty*, *Knowledge and Power*, *The Spirit of Enterprise*, *Microcosm*, and other books

"The dialogue that the book *Pope Francis and the Caring Society* has initiated is of great importance. The authors, citing numerous examples from world history, assert a fundamental economic truth: that societies with open markets, private property, democratic accountability of public officials, and the rule of law are superior at promoting human flourishing to societies where centralized planning, collective ownership of the means of production and state control over economic activity prevail. That is, democratic capitalism has been shown by history to be superior to socialist collectivism. We economists have known this for some time now, but it is a truth worth reiterating. And yet, it is not the only truth. And this is why the dialogue which Pope Francis has invited, and which this impressive volume pursues is so crucial. For, the fact is that modern economics is incomplete. It shows us how to get more of what we want, but it cannot teach us what we should want. It says little about our obligations to the poor, to the refugee, or to future generations. It is silent on the soul-corrupting influences of naked materialism. It concerns itself with means, not with ends. And yet, as Pope Francis has made clear, a single-minded focus on profit and loss is a profoundly impoverished way of thinking about how we should live together in society. Such a focus lacks moral resonance and spiritual depth. Thus, this dialogue between our spiritual imperatives and our economic realities must continue. I am confident it will."
—**Glenn Cartman Loury**, Merton P. Stoltz Professor of the Social Sciences, Department of Economics, Brown University

"The important book *Pope Francis and the Caring Society* makes a crucial point: It is not enough to have good intentions. How one attempts to fulfill them may override."
—**Rodney Stark**, Distinguished University Professor of the Social Sciences and Co-Director of the Institute for Studies of Religion, Baylor University

"*Pope Francis and the Caring Society* offers novel, balanced, and constructively critical insights into the historical interpretations and empirical assumptions which have informed many of the pope's most important pronouncements on economic development, environmental protection, and other issues. On topics ranging from the pope's precepts regarding how to strengthen the family to his prescriptions for how best to promote charitable giving, reduce poverty, and cope with climate change, this volume is hardly 'for Catholics only,' and it will stimulate and challenge readers of diverse intellectual, theological, and ideological stripes."
—**John J. Dilulio, Jr.**, Frederic Fox Leadership Professor of Politics, Religion, and Civil Society and Professor of Political Science, University of Pennsylvania; first Director, White House Office of Faith-Based and Community Initiatives

"In a manner graceful and civil—and with a proper respect for the Holy Father *Pope Francis and the Caring Society* speaks some bracing truths about economics that Pope Francis, with all his large, encompassing nature, does not seem to understand. In that respect, the authors not only teach lessons that all of us should know; they also show the deep strength of the body of the Church: they treat the Holy Father with reverence and they are inclined to put the most charitable constructions on his sweeping commentaries on inequality and capitalism. The pope's concern for the caring society and the uplifting of the poor is a concern that the authors share. But they also respect truth, and they see no conflict for Christians to convey to Pope Francis the serious things that he must understand when he has the attention of the world for his commentaries. What he doesn't understand are the pitfalls of a 'managed economy,' a scheme of political control that purports to rescue the poor, but delivers instead an economy of rationing, shortages, a diminished standard of living and the pervasiveness of political controls. Some of this misunderstanding may be traced to the pope's lifetime spent in the 'crony capitalism' and 'corporatism' of Argentina. But the volume, in a generous spirit, finds hope that Francis will come to understand far more about the forces at work in the economy as he simply comes to know more about a larger world, extending far beyond his native ground. *Pope Francis and the Caring Society* could not have come at a more timely moment, and in tone and substance, it delivers a worldly lesson that more of the world needs to know."

—**Hadley P. Arkes**, Edward N. Ney Professor of Jurisprudence and American
    Institutions Emeritus, Amherst College; Founder and Director, James Wilson Institute
    on Natural Rights and the American Founding

"*Pope Francis and the Caring Society* is a rich and engaging discussion of the role of religion in civil society. The book helps establish a foundation for productive and mutually beneficial dialogue between supporters and critics of Pope Francis's economic policies. Highly recommended!"

—**Peter G. Klein**, W. W. Caruth Chair, Professor of Entrepreneurship, and
    Senior Research Fellow in the John F. Baugh Center for Entrepreneurship and
    Free Enterprise, Hankamer School of Business, Baylor University

"It is not counter-intuitive to suggest that the superbly conceived, clear, cogent, and convincing book, *Pope Francis and the Caring Society*, introduced by the economist-theologian Michael Novak, has the potential to reconcile the distinctive and contrasting modalities for human flourishing propagated by Pope Francis and advocated by free-market economists aiming to liberate further millions of people from debilitating poverty. The axioms of free-market economics are simple, straightforward, and un-charismatic. Cast in a missionary key, Christian evangelization is loving, affirming, and hopeful. Would that these distinctive and contrasting modalities for human flourishing be reconciled by friendly and truthful intellectual exchange—by the grace of God."

—**Herman J. Belz**, Professor Emeritus of History, University of Maryland

"In the brief years since he was elected to the throne of St. Peter, Pope Francis has captivated the minds and hearts of millions of people both inside and outside the Catholic Church. But what Pope Francis wants is more than captivation. He has repeatedly urged serious, frank and honest conversation on vital matters impacting on the planet and the well-being of the most vulnerable in our midst. *Pope Francis and the Caring Society* responds to that invitation by providing a non-polemical, serious and accessible set of commentaries with which anyone, regardless of religious or political orientation, will want to be acquainted."

—**Father Robert A. Sirico**, President and Co-Founder, Acton Institute; Pastor, Sacred Heart Catholic Church, Grand Rapids, Michigan

"The way in which an economy does its characteristic work of providing goods and services through organized human effort is an issue that inescapably has extensive religious ramifications, and no contemporary religious leader has probed these issues more deeply than Pope Francis. His deliberations shed a constructive and kindly light into many corners of this complex and convoluted domain. *Pope Francis and the Caring Society* examines the pope's contributions to the ethics of markets, the functioning of capitalism, the economic dimensions of social organization, and the economics of family life. In putting these issues into their wider context, this book makes an instructive contribution to the Christian appreciation of economic processes."

—**Nicholas Rescher**, Distinguished University Professor of Philosophy, University of Pittsburgh; former Editor, *American Philosophical Quarterly*

"For two thousand years, Christianity has scrambled conventional categories. The truths of the faith, including the tenets of Catholic social teaching, defy the world's political preconceptions and cut across earthbound ideologies. *Pope Francis and the Caring Society* is an important new book that gives the Church's teachings the deep consideration that they deserve."

—**Arthur C. Brooks**, President, American Enterprise Institute

"*Pope Francis and the Caring Society* is a much-needed volume. The questions of capitalism and socialism, and of how— indeed, whether—markets and morality can mix, could not be more timely. Pope Francis's frequent and powerful statements of concern not only about the poor generally but about how their lives might be negatively affected by market-based economies have thrust these questions into the world's consciousness. The volume's editor Robert Whaples has assembled an all-star group of thinkers to address Francis's thought on everything from poverty relief to the family to climate change. The chapters in turn explain Pope Francis's thought, explore its implications, and evaluate it critically yet charitably. Francis has rightly refocused our attention on the least among us, and the eminence of his position, as well as the depth of his thought, make his work

worthy of careful consideration. This terrific book shows his thought the respect it deserves by examining it carefully, not just interpreting it but offering judicious emendations and even corrections where warranted. For anyone interested not only in understanding the Supreme Pontiff's thought and its significance, but in seeing learned and distinguished commentators display both its strengths and its weaknesses, this volume is a must-read."
—**James R. Otteson**, Thomas W. Smith Presidential Chair in Business Ethics
    and Professor of Economics, Wake Forest University

"*Pope Francis and the Caring Society* is not only about Pope Francis, but even seems in some sense to have been written for him. As the first pope to come from the developing world, and the first from Latin America, Francis brought to his pontificate quite a few immense strengths, including an acute and affecting concern for the many millions all over the world who are trapped in grinding poverty and hopelessness, and a gently Franciscan persona of gracious and unpretentious humility. Yet he has, like his predecessors, had to learn many things on the job; and his understanding of economics needs to catch up with the promptings of his generous heart, if his pontificate is to fulfill its transformational potential. Francis will find no more generous critics or more respectful guides in these matters than the authors whose essays are contained in this wise and helpful volume."
—**Wilfred M. McClay**, Blankenship Chair in the History of Liberty and
    Director, Center for the History of Liberty, University of Oklahoma

"*Pope Francis and the Caring Society* answers the pope's call for engagement on the timely questions of consumerism, inequality and capitalism. Though the authors generally disagree with Francis from a policy perspective, they share both his theology and his understanding that the questions we face are, at bottom, spiritual. The result is a respectful and illuminating dialogue which should serve as a model for how a divided polity can address its most contentious issues."
—**Chaim N. Saiman**, Professor of Law, Villanova University

"In *Pope Francis and the Caring Society*, the authors explore the complexities of Pope Francis's thinking on the market, poverty, and the environment. Part explanation of the pope and part exhortation to the pope, the book examines where he stands relative to the Catholic tradition, to mainstream economics, and to his own personal experience as an Argentinian. The authors have provided an illuminating, important, and broadly accessible conversation between and integration of economics and religion."
—**Andrew E. Busch**, Crown Professor of Government and George R. Roberts
    Fellow, Claremont McKenna College

"Since his elevation to the papacy four years ago, Pope Francis has challenged both Catholics and non-Catholics alike to pay special consideration to the needs of the poor around the world. In the magnificent volume, *Pope Francis and the Caring Society*, scholars from a range of disciplines elucidate the current pontiff's views on the roles of businesses, markets, and the profit motive in contemporary society with particular focus on economic development and ecology. This book is a must-read for anyone who wishes to go beyond media sound bites to understand how Pope Francis regards authentic human development in the context of global poverty alleviation and preservation of the environment, and how his thinking connects to the ongoing Apostolic Mission of the Church."
—**Michael L. Troilo**, Wellspring Associate Professor of International Business, University of Tulsa

"Although it might be nice if God gave us all knowledge about how the world works, the Bible is silent on many areas in economics and environmental science. *Pope Francis and the Caring Society* provides incisive analysis of what Pope Francis believes on many policy issues and why. While praising Francis's theological views, this superb volume suggests that his musing on economics are not infallible. Economics in no way supersedes religion, but it is vitally important for many crucial questions including how best to serve the poor and uplift their lives worldwide."
—**Edward Peter Stringham**, President and Director of Research and Education, American Institute for Economic Research; K. W. Davis Professor of Economic Organizations and Innovation and Deputy Director of the Shelby Cullom Davis Endowment, Trinity College

"*Pope Francis and the Caring Society*, is a greatly-needed engagement with Pope Francis's thought. Critical while respectful, the authors support many of the objectives of the Franciscan pontificate, while questioning the means he proposes. This book is an important work both for college courses and anyone on Christian social thought."
—**Jennifer Roback Morse**, President and Founder, Ruth Institute

"*Pope Francis and the Caring Society* is outstanding and absolutely essential reading for those seeking to engage the theology and values of Pope Francis on the issues of our day: the economies in contemporary democratic republics, the wealth and poverty of peoples, the political implications of a Christian theology of care and compassion, the values of liberty and family, and, of increasing importance for national and international relations, the challenge of addressing climate change. It will also be of great interest for non-Catholic and general readers seeking an intelligent, critical guide to the interrelationship of politics, economics, and religious faith."
—**Charles Taliaferro**, Professor of Philosophy, St. Olaf College

"*Pope Francis and the Caring Society* is a brilliant book laying out both Christian and economic principles side by side in dialogue with Pope Francis's *Laudato si'*. The authors are careful to lay empirical data alongside the claims and historical experiences of Pope Francis and current efforts to help the poor, in which they share a common goal. The various chapters contain a wealth of history, theory, and facts in the context of the Christians' call to serve the poor. Committed Christians who are nonetheless neophytes to economic theory, like myself, will get a thorough education in economics and reality. It is a timely and critical book for our age and for anyone who seriously wants to understand and participate in effectual service to the poor."

—**Mary S. Poplin**, Professor of Educational Studies, Claremont Graduate University; author, *Is Reality Secular?*

"*Pope Francis and the Caring Society* delineates the tension felt and expressed by many economists, business people, and civic and religious leaders with the pronouncements in the encyclical, *Laudato si'*, by Pope Francis. This book would be especially useful in courses on business ethics and bioethics as well as classes taught by theologians, philosophers, law professors, and economists. I recommend the book to Christian colleges and universities, including those where Catholic Social Thought has a presence in the core curriculum. A wide range of topics are covered concerning Francis's views on global environmental issues, capitalism, poverty, consumerism, the role of government including global authority, property rights, and private versus compulsory charitable giving. Attention is also given to the longitudinal evolution of the pope's views on the role of market economies to solve problems of scarcity."

—**Gary M. Quinlivan**, Dean and Professor of Economics, Alex G. McKenna School of Business, Saint Vincent College

"Even those of us who are not Roman Catholics can hardly fail to notice when a pope speaks on immensely important issues on an international stage and with great media fanfare. The contributors to the impressive volume *Pope Francis and the Caring Society* have taken up Francis's call to dialogue on economic and environmental issues and provide a model of charitable, fair, and nuanced scholarly engagement. While exposing many shortcomings in Francis's thought, they also sympathetically embrace his concern for the well-being of the poor and the natural world and quite successfully show better ways to achieve these noble goals. But one of the real strengths of this work is that its relevance extends far beyond contemporary debates about a particular pope: it eloquently unfolds many perennial themes of a humane political economy that will remain timely for many years to come—for Catholics and non-Catholics alike."

—**David M. VanDrunen**, Robert B. Strimple Professor of Systematic Theology and Christian Ethics, Westminster Seminary California

"*Pope Francis and the Caring Society*'s examination of subjects ranging from the family to the environment to capitalism to philanthropy to the Argentinian experience is indispensable reading for anyone interested in understanding and constructively engaging the social vision of Pope Francis."
—**Kenneth L. Grasso**, Professor of Political Science, Texas State University

"Pope Francis has raised important and challenging questions about capitalism, consumerism, poverty, inequality, environmental stewardship, and other concerns arising out of our economic practices and institutions. The wonderful book *Pope Francis and the Caring Society* addresses those concerns without trivializing them, yet also moves the discussion in hopeful and productive directions. The authors demonstrate thorough understanding of the tradition from which Pope Francis draws to critique market economies, the influences upon him, and the economic realities with which Francis seems less familiar. This book is a worthy contribution to the dialogue that Pope Francis has invited."
—**Adam J. MacLeod**, Associate Professor of Law, Faulkner University

"As political discourse in today's culture becomes increasingly partisan and adversarial, *Pope Francis and the Caring Society* is a refreshing model of what proper civil and religious discourse should look like. It is not only a magnificent expression of what the Second Vatican Council called 'the special vocation' of the laity to order temporal affairs according to the Gospel, it is also a richly illuminating response to Pope Francis's call in *Laudato si'* for fruitful dialogue between science and religion. Nowhere is that dialogue more necessary, and more consequential for human welfare, than in the area of economics. Written by ten experts in economics and religion, this book is a must-read for every Catholic who desires a faithful engagement with Catholic Social Teaching, from laypersons to the highest reaches of the Vatican."
—**Nathan W. Schlueter**, Professor of Philosophy and Religion, Hillsdale College

"*Pope Francis and the Caring Society* is a stunning achievement. . . In a fair and careful way, the book brings conceptual economic clarity to those who often speak to and for the church about matters economical without the training to do so. One main purpose of the book is to clarify and defend the proposition that the teachings of Jesus . . . set the ends for Christians . . . regarding a cluster of related issues taken up within its pages, but it is the science of economics that provides knowledge of the best means to reach those ends. Much—usually unintentional—harm has been done by people who have failed to learn the economic justification for those means, but with the publication of *Pope Francis and the Caring Society*, that problem can now be laid to rest. A marvelous book."
—**J. P. Moreland**, Distinguished Professor of Philosophy, Biola University

"The very fine book *Pope Francis and the Caring Society* contains helpfully sympathetic and constructively critical reflections on Pope Francis's environmental and economic views. That judicious combination seems to me exactly what the Holy Father's invitation to dialogue on these topics asks for, and the authors and editor are to be commended for their learned response to that invitation."
—**Christopher O. Tollefsen**, College of Arts and Sciences Distinguished
   Professor of Philosophy, University of South Carolina

"*Pope Francis and the Caring Society* is an outstanding contribution to the dialogue on social and economic policy that Pope Francis has called for."
—**Paul Moreno**, William and Berniece Grewcock Chair in Constitutional History
   and Dean of Social Sciences, Hillsdale College

"*Pope Francis and the Caring Society* re-examines the merits of free markets in the light of Pope Francis's views about the economy, charity, and the environment. The book's measured discussions carefully explain and often defend Francis's opinions, but they also make clear the benefits capitalism offers for reducing poverty, advancing charitable giving, and dealing with today's environmental issues."
—**Mark Blitz**, Fletcher Jones Professor of Political Philosophy and Director,
   Henry Salvatori Center for the Study of Individual Freedom in the Modern
   World, Claremont McKenna College

"*Pope Francis and the Caring Society* is an outstanding book challenging the flawed economics behind Francis's simplistic view that 'capitalism' is evil and government redistribution of income is good. On the contrary, true charity is only possible when it flows from individuals, not governments. Capitalism enriches societies and enables individuals to act more, not less, charitably. This great book demonstrates that government aid is 'dead aid'—it perpetuates dependence, robs the working poor of their dignity, and deadens the charitable impulse by crowding out private efforts which are far more effective. In short, capitalism is an expression of giving, first in the marketplace, then in civil society where individuals and associations are remarkably generous in their giving. If I could put one work in the hands of Pope Francis, it would be this outstanding volume."
—**Jonathan Bean**, Professor of History, Southern Illinois University

"Ever since the publication of Pope Francis's quite lengthy encyclical, we have needed a careful look at its suppositions, economic, ecological, and philosophical. *Pope Francis and the Caring Society* more than meets that need. *Laudato si*'s concerns can mostly be met but usually by means other than those suggested in the document. At bottom, the real question this book clearly addresses is, What is the 'practical reasoning' about man's ability to exercise 'dominion' over the earth?"
—**James V. Schall**, S.J., Professor Emeritus of Political Philosophy, Department of
   Government, Georgetown University

POPE FRANCIS
and the
CARING SOCIETY

POPE FRANCIS
—— and the ——
CARING SOCIE†Y

Edited by ROBERT M. WHAPLES

Foreword by MICHAEL NOVAK

INDEPENDENT
I N S T I T U T E

OAKLAND, CALIFORNIA

Independent Institute
100 Swan Way, Oakland, CA 94621-1428
Telephone: 510-632-1366
Fax: 510-568-6040
Email: info@independent.org
Website: www.independent.org

Cover Design: Denise Tsui
Cover Photo: Stefano Spaziani

Library of Congress Cataloging-in-Publication Data

Names: Whaples, Robert M., editor.
Title: Pope Francis and the caring society / edited by Robert M. Whaples.
Description: Oakland, Calif. : Independent Institute, 2017.
Identifiers: LCCN 2017006606 | ISBN 9781598132878 (hardcover) |
    ISBN 9781598132885 (pbk.) | ISBN 9781598132915 (mobi)
Subjects: LCSH: Christian sociology—Catholic Church. | Economics—
    Religious aspects—Catholic Church. | Catholic Church—Doctrines. | Francis, Pope, 1936–
Classification: LCC BX1753 .P685 2017 | DDC 261.8/5—dc23
LC record available at https://lccn.loc.gov/2017006606

Contents

Acknowledgments

THIS BOOK, *Pope Francis and the Caring Society*, has grown out of a special Symposium, "Pope Francis and Economics," that I had the pleasure and privilege of organizing for the quarterly journal *The Independent Review* as its managing editor. I am very grateful to the enthusiastic sponsorship and support of the Independent Institute for this work, including President David J. Theroux, Research Director William F. Shughart II, Senior Vice President Mary L. G. Theroux, and Acquisitions Director Roy M. Carlisle. I also want to especially thank Cecilia Santini, Denise Tsui, and Barbara Genetin for their exceptional handling of the many details of the book's editing and publication at Independent.

All of the contributing authors to the book deserve special thanks for their superb chapters in addressing very important, sensitive, and complex issues, and I want to particularly express our gratitude to the late Michael Novak for his wonderful support, learned advice, and encouragement throughout, including preparing the splendid and incisive Foreword for the book, even during his final illness. He will be deeply missed by us all.

As a clarification in the book's references, please note that all citations to papal encyclicals and other papal documents in the chapters refer to paragraph rather than page numbers.

—*Robert M. Whaples*

Foreword*

Michael Novak

THIS MARVELOUS BOOK, *Pope Francis and the Caring Society*, is much needed and could not have come at a better time. Completed in response to Pope Francis's invitation in *Laudato si'* to a dialogue on the economy, the environment, and charity, the book shares his commitment to Judeo-Christian teachings and institutions. In the process, the book's authors are seeking constructively to engage and educate civic and business leaders and the general public to understand the legacy and meaning of the natural law, moral and economic principles of liberty, personal responsibility, enterprise, civic virtue, family and community, and the rule of law.

The education of each pope begins anew when he is elected to office. For he is no longer a member of one nation only, but now of a universal community. He must learn, for example, about economics as practiced in other parts of the world besides his own. Notably, Pope John Paul II spent his youth under Nazism and then Communism and was not familiar with how life was lived under other economic and political systems. It took him a while to develop a universal vision in these arenas. Most of the Italian popes before him had similar experiences. Likewise, it would be odd if Pope Francis were not now expanding his own view of political and economic affairs.[1]

Note: I adapted material in this Foreword from Michael Novak and Paul Adams, "Saint Francis in America," *National Review*, October 2, 2015, and Michael Novak, "Agreeing with Pope Francis," *National Review*, December 7, 2013. ©2015 & 2013 *National Review*. Used with permission.

1. Adapted from Michael Novak, "What Will Pope Francis Say?," *Washington Examiner*, September 22, 2015.

I have closely studied the early writings of Pope John Paul II (born Karol Wojtyła), which grew out of long experience of an oppressive Communist regime that pretended to be wholly devoted to "equality," yet enforced total control over polity, economy, and culture by a thorough and cruel state. From 1940 (under the Nazi/Soviet occupation) until 1978 (when he moved to the Vatican), Karol Wojtyła had virtually no experience of a capitalist economy and a democratic/republican polity.

Year by year into his papacy, John Paul II learned how differently things looked in other nations in other parts of the world. He learned the difference between being an archbishop in one locality and becoming a universal pastor. A profound social thinker himself, he gradually developed a new vocabulary for illuminating the new social possibilities of our time.[2]

Pope Francis seems to be following the same trajectory. Year by year, his wisdom seems to grow. On a great many matters, he is in alignment with the principles of St. John Paul II and Pope Benedict XVI. Gradually he has been adjusting his language to realities, especially economic realities outside his lifetime experience in Argentina. For example, at first he often said, "the poor always get poorer," but slowly he is becoming aware that in many advanced countries, people who were poor only two or three generations ago are no longer poor. There is a fact described as "upward mobility." It happens faster and more securely in economies based on the freedom of initiative, creativity, invention, and discovery. Such economies highly value human capital over material capital, because only humans invent and create.[3]

As I found that John Paul's early writings reflect the influence of his pre-papal life under Nazism and Communism, I also found that, having spent not a little time lecturing in Argentina and in Chile since the late 1970s, it is helpful to read Francis's writings with an ear for echoes of daily economic and political life in Argentina.

In my visits to Argentina, I observed a far sharper divide between the upper middle class and the poor than any I had experienced in the United States. In Argentina, I saw very few paths by which the poor could rise out of poverty.

---

2. Adapted from "The Virtue of Social Justice: An Interview with Michael Novak," *The Stream*, January 18, 2016. At https://stream.org/virtue-social-justice-interview-michael-novak/.
  3. Ibid.

In the U.S., many of those who are now rich or middle class had come to America (or their parents had) dirt poor, many of them not speaking English, with minimal schooling and with mainly menial skills. But before them lay many paths upward. As Peru's Hernando de Soto has stressed, the U.S. has the rule of law and clear property rights, on which one can safely build over generations.

Virtually all my acquaintances while I was growing up had experienced poverty in their families. Our grandfathers were garment workers, steel-workers, store clerks, gardeners, handymen, blue-collar workers of all sorts, without social insurance, food stamps, housing allowances, or the like. But they labored and somehow were able to send their children to colleges and universities. Now their children are doctors, lawyers, professors, editors, and owners of small businesses all over the country.

In his *Inquiry into the Nature and Causes of the Wealth of Nations* (1776), Adam Smith compared the economic history of Latin America with that of North America. He noted that in Latin America there were still many institutions of feudal Europe—large landholders, plantations, and plantation workers. In North America, only the southern United States had a similar system.

At the time Smith wrote, throughout Latin America many economic powers and permissions were doled out by government officials in far-off Spain or Portugal. In the Dominican Republic, for example, a farmer who wanted to build a small iron foundry had to wait months or years until a decision came back from Spain. Trading with pirates was easier. In the English-speaking colonies of North America, however, a farmer could just build his foundry without asking anybody. And even after the various Latin American countries achieved independence, habits of state direction were still entrenched, as if by immemorial habit.

Besides, the experience of the former British colonies had led to a distrust of monarchs and their courts, and later of barons and dukes and the aristocracy as a whole, since these people could not be counted on either to see or to serve the common good. By contrast, the opposite habit of mind had grown throughout the Latin world.[4] There, officials of the state were regularly entrusted with minding the common good, despite a long record of official

---

4. Vargas Llosa, *Liberty for Latin America.*

betrayals of duty, outbreaks of tyranny, and the use of economic resources to enrich successive leaders of the state. In Latin America, the pluralistic private sector was mistrusted, but not the state.

As the twentieth century began, Argentina was ranked among the top fifteen industrial nations, and more and more of its wealth was springing from modern inventions rather than farmland. Then a destructive form of political economy, just then spreading like a disease from Europe—a populist fascism with tight government control over the economy—dramatically slowed Argentina's economic and political progress. Instability in the rule of law undermined economic creativity. Inflation blew to impossible heights. (I brought home from Argentina in the early 1980s a note for a million Argentine pesos that had declined in worth to two American pennies.)

Over three generations, very little of the nation's natural wealth and opportunity for social advancement have overflowed into the upraised buckets of the poor. Upward mobility from the bottom up was (and is) infrequent. Today, the lot of Argentina's poor is still static. The poor receive little personal instruction in turning to independent creativity and initiative, and few laws, lending institutions, and other practical arrangements support them in moving upward. Human energies are drained by dependency on state benefits. The visible result has been a society with little opportunity for the poor to rise out of poverty. A great inner humiliation comes over the poor as they see their lack of personal achievement and their dependency.

By contrast, in the U.S., under a government strictly limited by law, there grew up almost universal property ownership by individuals (except under the evil institution of slavery, America's primal sin), a large swath of small enterprises, and a huge base of prospering small farms. Smith described the creation of wealth in North America as welling up from below, from the prosperity at the bottom, where frugal habits led to wise investments in railroads, canals, and other large business corporations.

Less than seventy years after Adam Smith wrote *The Wealth of Nations,* a son of the frontier farm country of central Illinois, Abraham Lincoln, spoke eloquently about the evidences of global trade visible in homes across the prairie—tobacco, cotton, spices, whiskey, sugar, tea, glassware, silverware. He attributed this enprospering trade to the daring of American seamen (as Tocqueville also did).

Lincoln also wrote about the patent-and-copyright clause of the U.S. Constitution, which guaranteed to inventors the right to the monetary fruit of their inventions. Lincoln thought this small clause one of the six greatest contributions to liberty in the history of the world. He thought it critical to liberating human beings everywhere from misery and tyranny.

That single clause—the only time the term "right" is used within the body of the Constitution—launched a wholly new economic model for the world, based not on land (as it had been for thousands of years) but on creative ideas, inventions, and discoveries, which greatly speeded up a cascade of new improvements and new products to enrich the lives of ordinary citizens. The more people these improvements helped, the higher the inventors' royalties. By serving others, they reaped rewards. These rewards furthered the common good.

John Paul II recognized this huge social change in *Centesimus annus (On the Hundredth Anniversary of* Rerum novarum, 1991), paragraph 32 of which opens: "In our time, in particular, there exists another form of ownership which is no less important than land: the possession of know-how, knowledge, and skill. The wealth of the industrialized nations is based much more on this kind of ownership than on natural resources." The rest of this paragraph is concise in its penetration of the causes of wealth and the role of human persons and associations in the virtue of worldwide solidarity, of which globalization is the outward expression.

John Paul II quickly recognized that today "the decisive factor [in production] is increasingly man himself, that is, his knowledge, especially his scientific knowledge, his capacity for interrelated and compact organization, as well as his ability to perceive the needs of others and to satisfy them."[5]

Then in paragraph 42, John Paul II defined his ideal capitalism, succinctly, as that economic system springing from creativity, under the rule of law, and "the core of which is ethical and religious." In his first social encyclical ten years earlier, *Laborem exercens* (*On Human Work,* 1981), directly rejecting orthodox Marxist language about labor, the pope had already begun to project "creation theology" as a replacement for "liberation theology." A bit later, he reached the concept of "human capital." Step by step, he thought his way to

---

5. John Paul II, *Centesimus annus*, 32.

his own vision of the economy best suited to the human person—not perfectly so, in this vale of tears, but better than any rival, Communist or traditional.

Despite the fact that Francis of Assisi (1180–1225) has been for eight centuries, all around the world, the most beloved saint of all, Francis is the first pope to choose the name. He is most known for his concern for the poor, and is widely beloved because he is seen by some as the best model of Jesus Christ anywhere on earth today.[6] The image of the poor and humble Christ is brought to the fore wherever Francis goes. But I am worried whether he has a very good theory for how you get the poor out of poverty. And the main practical task of our generation is breaking the last round of chains of ancient poverty.

In 1776, there were fewer than one billion people on Earth. A vast majority of them were poor, and living under tyrannies. Just over two centuries later, there are more than seven billion human beings. Rapid medical discoveries and inventions have helped to more than double the average lifespan, vastly reduce infant mortality, and provide relief for hundreds of diseases. Thanks to economic progress, six-sevenths of the greatly expanded human race have now broken free from poverty—over a billion people from 1950 to 1980, and another billion since 1980. But there are another billion more still in those chains. The Jewish, Christian, and humanist task is to break them free as well.

Whatever Christians pray in worship on Sunday gets its truthfulness from what Christians actually do in their daily lives to help the poor. If one does not come to the aid of the poor, one does not love God. Francis has done a very good job humanizing Christianity and giving it a distinctive, down-to-earth voice of a sort that no pope, even John Paul II, has expressed before.[7]

As Francis grows in his knowledge of the world beyond Argentina, he will hopefully better understand the political economy that best helps the poor to move out of poverty. A fine place to start would be in the well-reasoned pathway of paragraph 42 of John Paul II's *Centesimus annus:*

> Can it perhaps be said that, after the failure of Communism, capitalism is the victorious social system, and that capitalism should be the

---

6. Adapted from Michael Novak, "Why the Name Francis?," *The Huffington Post*, March 14, 2013.

7. Bowyer, "Scholar Who Taught John Paul II to Appreciate Capitalism Worries About Pope Francis."

goal of the countries now making efforts to rebuild their economy and society? Is this the model which ought to be proposed to the countries of the Third World which are searching for the path to true economic and civil progress?

To this John Paul II answered, in effect, "Yes and no." He wrote:

> The answer is obviously complex. If by "capitalism" is meant an economic system which recognizes the fundamental and positive role of business, the market, private property and the resulting responsibility for the means of production, as well as free human creativity in the economic sector, then the answer is certainly in the affirmative, even though it would perhaps be more appropriate to speak of a "business economy," "market economy" or simply "free economy." But if by "capitalism" is meant a system in which freedom in the economic sector is not circumscribed within a strong juridical framework which places it at the service of human freedom in its totality, and which sees it as a particular aspect of that freedom, the core of which is ethical and religious, then the reply is certainly negative.
>
> The Marxist solution has failed, but the realities of marginalization and exploitation remain in the world, especially the Third World, as does the reality of human alienation, especially in the more advanced countries. Against these phenomena the Church strongly raises her voice. Vast multitudes are still living in conditions of great material and moral poverty. The collapse of the Communist system in so many countries certainly removes an obstacle to facing these problems in an appropriate and realistic way, but it is not enough to bring about their solution. Indeed, there is a risk that a radical capitalistic ideology could spread which refuses even to consider these problems, in the a priori belief that any attempt to solve them is doomed to failure, and which blindly entrusts their solution to the free development of market forces.[8]

Although economic growth falls far short of being the only goal of free societies, its blessings in terms of education, medical improvements, the prospering

---

8. John Paul II, *Centesimus annus*, 42.

of freedom of conscience, and the private financing of civic life and multiple philanthropies are not inessential to the common good.

Further, it is not market systems alone that produce upward mobility, economic progress for all, and wide economic opportunity. Argentina has always had a market economy. So, too, have almost all the peoples in human history. Jerusalem in the biblical period cherished private property ("Thou shalt not steal,"[9] "Thou shalt not covet thy neighbor's goods"[10]), and it lived by a vital market (as the commercial interface of three continents). But for the 1,800 years after Christ, none of the world's markets—nor the aggregate thereof—produced much economic development. The world's economies remained relatively static, as they faced a merciless cycle of "fat" years followed by "lean" ones. Before the rise of capitalism, traditional market systems experienced famines and massive outbreaks of deadly diseases in nearly every generation.

Pope John Paul II came to see this historical reality. We might expect Francis to turn more attention to John Paul II's prescient passages as he continues to tour all the economic alternatives on this planet.

On another matter, Pope Francis sometimes talks with great certainty about matters he has not been trained to deal with. He sometimes allows close advisers to disparage those who are not intimidated by a highly politicized scientific "consensus." Can there be "science" where there is so much political pressure and public mockery? Is the pope alert to the fact that to put climate control into the hands of a world government is to create a center of enormous power, able to bring on world decline by wildly erroneous miscalculations? He has not yet indicated that.

As some in Europe have already learned to joke, Greens are like tomatoes. They begin the spring green, but by late summer have turned very red. All movement is toward the state. Consider, then, that in any likely world government, cultures that are growing fastest and are most inimical to the West—and to Jews and Christians in particular—are most likely to predominate and to dictate terms.

And climate has always been a fickle master. Climate history is complex, tangled, and not easy to explain: warm, even hot weather (when Greenland

---

9. Exodus 20:15 (King James Version).

10. Excerpted from Kinkead, *Baltimore Catechism No. 4 (of 4) An Explanation of The Baltimore Catechism of Christian Doctrine*, Lesson 34, 386 Q.

was not yet covered with ice), then a thousand-year Ice Age, and then a "global warming" that also does not show up as predicted. Time spans are long and changeable. There have been cosmic forces at play, from giant meteorites to solar explosions. Breakthroughs in science regularly overturn the conventional "consensus," but the conventional wisdom at any one time is seldom questioned. If Francis turns out to be wrong on climate control, his mistake may end as a far greater blow to the Church than the Galileo Affair.

Finally, I would like to offer a bet: More human beings by far will move out of poverty by the methods of democracy and capitalism than by any other means.

Following his first visit to the U.S., Pope Francis joked with reporters about how fallible he is in economic matters, and he admitted that he has erred by largely ignoring the middle class while he has much to say about the poor. Let us hope that as he continues to serve, he and others learn from the phenomenal worldwide growth of the middle class the lessons that will best serve the poor he cares so deeply about.

Now with *Pope Francis and the Caring Society* we have the essential and enlightening book to equip us all to understand the crucial issues of economics, the environment, and charity in order to serve and uplift the lives of others.

References

John Paul II. *Centesimus annus: On the Hundredth Anniversary of Rerum Novarum.* Boston, Mass.: Pauline Books and Media, 1991.

John Paul II. *Laborem exercens: On Human Work: Encyclical Letter of John Paul II.* Boston, Mass.: Pauline Books and Media, 1981.

Kinkead, Thomas L. *Baltimore Catechism No. 4 (of 4) An Explanation of The Baltimore Catechism of Christian Doctrine.* 2006.

Smith, Adam. *An Inquiry into the Nature and Causes of the Wealth of Nations.* Chicago: University of Chicago Press, [1776] 1977.

Vargas Llosa, Alvaro. *Liberty for Latin America: How to Undo Five Hundred Years of State Oppression.* New York: Farrar, Straus and Giroux; Oakland, CA: Independent Institute, 2005.

Introduction

The Economics of Pope Francis

Robert M. Whaples*

Responding to Pope Francis's Call for Dialogue

POPE FRANCIS HAS invited those concerned about the economy, the environment, and the destiny of the world—everyone—to join a
dialogue.[1] And there is a clear need for dialogue between Francis and economists because the pope and many in the economics profession do not see eye
to eye at a fundamental level on many issues.[2] The purpose of this book is to

---

1. Francis uses the term dialogue twenty-five times in *Laudato si'*, and he adds a special
plea to economists for an "economic ecology": "We urgently need a humanism capable of
bringing together the different fields of knowledge, including economics, in the service of a
more integral and integrating vision" (141).

2. One might complain that there is no possibility that economists and Pope Francis will
ever see eye to eye because they have different goals in analyzing the economy. Maciej Zieba
argues that some popes (e.g., Leo XIII, Pius XI, and John Paul II) follow the tradition of
Thomas Aquinas and Antoninus of Florence in taking a "holistic" approach that offers a realistic depiction of the social situation and tries to diagnose causes and suggest ways to eliminate problems (an approach that economists tend to take), whereas others (e.g., Paul VI)
follow the tradition of John Chrysostom and Bernard of Clairvaux in taking a "pastoral" approach that focuses on exposing situations that need redress, identifying injustices, and not
pointing the way toward realistic remedies (*Papal Economics*, 196). Francis seems to take this
second approach. Anthony Waterman writes: "Francis, like all popes before him . . . judges
the validity of behavioral assumptions by their conformity with Christian anthropology as
viewed from the Vatican. Therefore, it seems to me impossible that . . . Francis could ever
'see eye to eye at a fundamental level' with economists. The modern social scientific method
of explaining social phenomena by means of abstract models based on methodological individualism is utterly alien and unwelcome to traditional papal thinking. For the latter is based
on . . . [an] organicist conception of society; its purpose is always normative (to identify the

---

*Acknowledgments: I thank A. M. C. Waterman and J. Daniel Hammond for comments.

I

advance the dialogue at a critical juncture when Francis's encyclical *Laudato si'*, other writings, and public comments have called into question the benefits of free markets and advocated measures to protect the environment from excessive consumption and harmful production practices.

The book begins with my own examination of what Pope Francis—"who credits his father, an overworked accountant, with imparting to him 'a great allergy to economic things'"[3]—says about the economy, especially about the poor and the rich. Then I juxtapose his first principles with those used by economists and attempt to put his ideas into the terms economists use. I close by broadly exploring the strengths and weaknesses of capitalism as seen by economists and by Pope Francis—points that each can reflect upon as the dialogue continues.

In the next essay in this book, "Pope Francis, His Predecessors, and the Market," Andrew M. Yuengert outlines the evolution of Catholic social teaching, demonstrating that Pope Francis's statements—including his conviction that markets are instruments of an inequality that "kills" and his rejection of the "magical conception" of the power of markets to solve social problems easily—fit into a long tradition within the Catholic Church. He shows that over the past half-century Popes Paul VI, John Paul II, and Benedict XVI credited markets with the potential to serve as an outlet for human creativity and promote the efficient provision of goods but that they always warned that markets could not be left to function without the constraints of a healthy culture and governments able to place markets at the service of the common good. "Where his predecessors warned of the danger that markets might overrun culture and political control, Francis asserts that they have in fact done so." He concludes that Francis's alarm about the dismal social facts of today's world—especially in developing countries—makes "the previous popes' analy-

---

need for distributive justice); and its philosophical basis in the Neo-Thomism of Leo XIII excludes any possibility of a Hayekian 'spontaneous order' which at least since Adam Smith has been fundamental to 'the economic way of thinking.' [Francis] and 'economists' must always be at cross-purposes in this matter. They cannot 'disagree' because there is no common ground. To attempt a comparison of their incommensurable views is like comparing chalk with cheese" (personal correspondence to the author, July 25, 2016). Despite these points, I believe that dialogue can be fruitful.

3. Schneider, "How Pope Francis Is Reviving Radical Catholic Economics."

sis somewhat irrelevant, in the way that advice for keeping a car on the road does not help someone whose car is in a ditch." However, although Yuengert agrees that in some important ways Francis's evaluation is not too extreme, he fears that Francis's most extreme statements will close off real dialogue with conscientious businesspeople and sincere advocates of free markets—thus simply moving the car from one ditch to another.

In "Understanding Pope Francis: Argentina, Economic Failure, and the *Teología del Pueblo*," Samuel Gregg emphasizes that Pope Francis is much more hostile to the market and capitalism than his predecessors and explains that to understand Francis one must consider his background in Argentina, a country in which a relatively free economy has over the past seventy years decayed into corporatism and cronyism due to populist political forces embodied in Peronism. Thus, when Francis envisions capitalism, it is the dysfunctional capitalism of Argentina that most informs his thinking—a model of capitalism that friends of free markets rightly reject as capitalism at its worst, which isn't reflective of how capitalism generally works in the places our readers will know best, especially the United States. Gregg also explains how Francis's affection for the *teología del pueblo*, "theology of the people," which attributes much power to lowly people in forming the church, in shaping its ideas, and even in directing its doctrine, has influenced much of his outlook. This theology is not Marxist, but it unfortunately has particular problems of its own. In the first place, although the church is Christ and His people and has always had a special care for those on society's margins, it also holds that its sacred doctrines come from divine revelation and two millennia of careful, well-informed discernment of that revelation's meaning. Popular movements have had a history—from biblical times to the present—of pulling away from these truths. (One example would be the church's clear teaching on sexuality and birth control in encyclicals such as Paul VI's *Humanae vitae* from which so many in the restive flock have wandered.) Second, many of the ideas that emerge from the peripheries of society are, like ideas that emerge elsewhere, often unaware of facts, illogical, and sometimes simply wrong. The fact that an idea emerges on the periphery does not mean it is without flaws. Third, the *teología del pueblo* has been influenced by Peronist ideas and priorities. That means it is influenced by populism, and populist movements have never been especially good at reducing material poverty.

Pope Francis has been dismissed as a "socialist" by some adherents of free markets. In "Uneven Playing Fields: Markets and Oligarchy," Gabriel Martinez aims to explain how this dismissal misreads both Francis and the realities of markets in many societies. A good market, like a good athletic competition, is contingent on a level playing field. But in reality, market players do not begin with clean-slate starting positions and incumbent winners try to protect their position and ensure future victories by muscling competitors out of the way, changing the rules, and directing public resources to their own benefit. In *Evangelii gaudium* Francis warns: "In this game, the powerful benefit at the expense of the weak, and so a large part of the population is excluded and marginalized." Martinez tests this point by statistically examining the relations between barriers to entering business and inequality—finding that these barriers are positively correlated with a higher share of income going to those at the top and a smaller share going to those at the bottom. He warns that often plans for market "liberalization" are actually designed to help the oligarchs who already have power and concludes that the pope is right to attack "trickle down" explanations that misappropriate the free market as a cover in order to rationalize indifference towards the excluded and the dispossessed.

Lawrence J. McQuillan and Hayeon Carol Park write their contribution, "Pope Francis, Capitalism and Private Charitable Giving," with a passionate directness akin to that of Pope Francis. They embrace his emphasis on everyone's moral responsibility to help those who are less fortunate but question his tactics. They call Francis's attention to the clear historical fact that capitalism has a unique, unrivaled history of lifting the poorest of the poor out of their desperate, absolute poverty. The pope is simply too pessimistic about the facts on the ground, and his embrace of forced redistribution through the state forgets how wealth is created—by giving people incentives to be productive, not by robbing Peter to pay Paul. Forced redistribution ultimately isn't real charity; it instead crowds out the true charity to which all are called and serves primarily to make people more accepting of the use of force to achieve ends they consider worthy. McQuillan and Park question Francis's claims that "'unbridled capitalism . . . has taught the logic of profit at any cost, of giving in order to receive, of exploitation without looking at the person'"[4] because they believe

---

4. Quoted in Wooden, "Pope Francis Warns of the Dangers of 'Unbridled Capitalism.'"

this vision of capitalism is a caricature—the reality is that businesspeople are real people and have learned that the ethic of "profit at any cost" is generally bad for business. They go a further step and empirically document the strong positive relationship between charitable activities and both economic freedom and secure property rights across countries, drawing on a wide range of studies that support the conclusion that free markets bring forth greater charity. Economic freedom has not turned people into monsters; it has enabled them to be generous in new, powerful ways.

In the fifth essay in this book, A. M. C. Waterman turns to Pope Francis and the environment in "Pope Francis on the Environmental Crisis." He begins by explaining the key arguments of Francis's encyclical *Laudato si'* —its enumeration of environmental problems that have escalated to the level of a crisis that is a "matter of life and death"; its rebuttal of the hollow charge that the "dominion" granted to humankind in Genesis has encouraged the unbridled exploitation of nature; its explanation that sin is the true cause of the crisis; its call for a global political response; and its conclusion that it is we human beings who need a deep conversion, a new lifestyle "free of the obsession with consumption" so that "at the end, we will find ourselves face to face with the infinite beauty of God."[5] Next, Waterman examines the intellectual context of the encyclical—the science, papal social doctrine, and nonofficial influences from Aristotle to Romano Guardini—before providing his own learned analysis of the document. Despite harsh criticisms from some economists that *Laudato si'* is "economically flawed," Waterman concludes that "[o]n careful examination . . . some of the pope's strictures turn out to contain valid criticisms" of the "'deified market,'"[6] although they are sometimes "undermined or weakened by hyperbolic language." He closes with worries that Francis wants to rely too much on virtue for solving these problems and has ignored traditional church concerns that original sin has corrupted the state, too, thus "turning a blind eye to 'the proper economic function' of the market"[7] and its potential to mitigate the problems it has helped unleash. Original sin makes it necessary to supplement virtue with

---

5. Francis, *Laudato si'*, 222, 243.

6. Quoting ibid., 56.

7. Quoting ibid., 171.

self-interest, but Francis ignores this key insight as well as the relevance of the market economy as a potent instrument for recruiting self-interest to the common good.

Philip Booth continues this theme in "Property Rights and Conservation: The Missing Theme of *Laudato si'*" and points out that economists and other scholars have much to teach about how to protect the environment, citing research that should ease the worries about property rights that Pope Francis seems to express in the encyclical. The church has in the past stressed the social functions of private property, and much recent economic work suggests that this social usefulness applies also to the conservation of the natural environment. Booth discusses how Nobel Prize winner Elinor Ostrom stresses some important ways in which property rights can promote conservation, and these forms of community-controlled property seem especially well aligned with church teaching. In *Laudato si'*, says Booth, the church has "missed an opportunity to enable its faithful to contribute in a positive way to a debate with long-term consequences for the environment and for social policy."

Allan Carlson concludes the volume by examining "The Family Economics of Pope Francis." He finds a unity in Francis, whose critique of individualism is relentless, as is his critique of the urban-industrial revolution and its "consumerism." Consumerism has infected all of human life, devastating marriage and families. Instead, "the family—understood as one man bound to one woman in a sacramental indissoluble union and their children—rests at the center of the whole of Creation" and should rest at the center of the economy. Francis celebrates the beautiful complementarity of men and women and embraces traditional teachings that feminine and masculine roles are grounded in human nature, with mothers called upon to labor within the family and fathers naturally serving as workers and breadwinners. Children are to be embraced as gifts from God, as a means of salvation and the very purpose of human history rather than as consumption choices. Critics of this teaching point toward dire Malthusian consequences arising from the resultant "overpopulation," but Francis rebuts these worries by rejecting consumerism and emphasizing the "capacity to be happy with little" and a "sobriety," which "when lived freely and consciously, is liberating." Rejecting consumerism—and economists' assertion that "more is better"—is the key both to solving ecological problems and to recapturing the integrity of the family in Francis's unified vision.

These summaries give a hint of the need for dialogue between the thousands of economists in the world and Pope Francis. There is much room for healthy discussion—for learning in both directions—but there is also a gulf, a veritable chasm, to be bridged.

Pope Francis's View of the Economic World

> [G]ive me neither poverty nor riches;
> provide me only with the food I need;
> Lest, being full, I deny you,
> saying, "Who is the LORD?"
> Or, being in want, I steal,
> and profane the name of my God.
> —Proverbs 30:8–9

As Pope Francis sees it, the purpose of the economy, like the purpose of everything else in the world, is to lead all people to God. In this section, I focus on three major pillars of his view: the idea that poverty is bad for the poor not simply for material reasons but also because it marginalizes them; the warning made emphatically by Jesus against the seduction of riches, against worshipping mammon, and against denying the Lord; and the idea that business is a noble profession that needs to be charitable, to create work, and to be generous with employees rather than merely to focus on profits.[8] Francis's encyclicals and press interviews are laden with these ideas, but even more so are the homilies that he gives at daily mass in his role as a "parish priest," upon which I also draw.[9]

---

8. My coverage of Francis's ideas on the environment is minimal here because Waterman and Booth thoroughly explore these ideas elsewhere in this book.

9. In fact, looking at homilies may give a better sense of what Francis thinks. These pastoral homilies are almost certainly composed by Francis himself, whereas the encyclicals are drafted by committees of expert advisers, with the pope authorizing the end product—though often adding his own flavor in some passages.

The Poor and Marginalization

Francis's concern for the poor is obvious. He chose his papal name after St. Francis of Assisi, whom he sees as "the example par excellence of care for the vulnerable."[10] Even in his "environmental" encyclical, *Laudato si'*, his focus is as much on the poor as on the environment: "Today . . . we have to realize that a true ecological approach *always* becomes a social approach; it must integrate questions of justice in debates on the environment, so as to hear *both the cry of the earth and the cry of the poor*."[11] He decries the fact that "we are all too slow in developing economic institutions and social initiatives which can give the poor regular access to basic resources"[12] and affirms that, especially in the poorest countries, "the priorities must be to eliminate extreme poverty."[13] But his is principally a "summons to solidarity and a preferential option for the poorest of our brothers and sisters . . . [that] demands before all else an appreciation of the immense dignity of the poor."[14] He closes *Laudato si'* with a prayer that implores, "O God of the poor, help us to rescue the abandoned and forgotten of this earth, so precious in your eyes. . . . Touch the hearts of those who look only for gain at the expense of the poor and the earth. Teach us to discover the worth of each thing."[15]

Helping "the poor financially must always be a provisional solution in the face of pressing needs. The broader objective should always be to allow them a dignified life through work."[16] And caring for the poor isn't simply a matter of alleviating material want, it is also a matter of care and closeness: *Closeness* is a "beautiful word, for each of us. . . . Do I know how to draw near?" Francis asks elsewhere. "Do I have the strength, do I have the courage to touch those who are marginalized? . . . Do I have the courage to draw near or do I always keep my distance? Do I have the courage to close the distance, as Jesus did?

---

10. Francis, *Laudato si'*, 10.
11. Ibid., 49; emphasis added.
12. Ibid., 109.
13. Ibid., 172.
14. Ibid., 158.
15. Ibid., 246.
16. Ibid., 128.

. . . I think that it may be . . . very difficult to do good without getting our hands dirty. . . . Jesus got dirty" with His "closeness."[17]

The Rich and Excessive Consumption

For all Francis's tender attention to the poor, it's easy to overlook his attention to the rich. And here his message is that wealth and abundant consumer goods and services are *dangerous*—mainly because they separate us from God, from our brothers and sisters, and from our true nature. "There are three things . . . that separate us from Jesus: wealth, vanity and pride. . . . Possessions are so dangerous: they lead you immediately to vanity, and you believe you are important," but "when you believe you are important, your head swells and you become lost."[18] The solution is the "path of divesting"—literally taking off our garments, giving away our cloaks. By becoming poor, we may become rich: this happens "each time I strip myself of something, but not only of the excess, to give to a poor person, to a poor community, to so many poor people who lack everything," because "the poor enrich me" insomuch as "it is Jesus who acts in him."[19]

This theme bears repetition here because Francis himself often repeats it. "[T]hose who cling to riches are not concerned with either the past or the future. . . . Wealth is an idol . . . [that] needs nothing. . . . What do these riches and concerns do to us? They merely cut us out of time." Those attached to wealth therefore "cut off their relationship with the future," with God.[20] "Each and every one of us needs to examine our conscience and find out what riches keep us from approaching Jesus on the road of life. They are the riches that come from our culture. The first is well-being or comfort or luxury. The culture of well-being that . . . makes us lazy and selfish."[21] We think comfort is enough. Our concern for material well-being leads us to make bad choices. Francis refers to a possible dialogue between spouses. "No, no, no more than

---

17. Francis, "Let Us Close the Distance."
18. Francis, "Our Wage from Jesus."
19. Francis, "Wealth and Poverty."
20. Francis, "The Pillars of Christian Salvation."
21. Francis, "God's Time."

one child, no? Because then we can't go on vacation, we can't go here, we can't buy a house. . . . We are in love with temporal things, while what Jesus offers is infinite. We like the temporary because we are afraid of God's time, the end of time."[22] The riches of the market seduce us into settling for too little—for vacations rather than for children, for an earthly paradise walled away from humanity instead of for God. "There is a mystery in the possession of wealth. Riches have the capacity to seduce . . . to make us believe we are in an earthly paradise. I recall that in the 1970s I saw for the first time a closed community, of people who were wealthy; it was closed to protect against thieves, to be secure." The desire of these people was to be enclosed in that sort of "earthly paradise." When this happens, we close ourselves off "to protect possessions." We lose "the horizon," and "living without a horizon is sad."[23] We need to put on the brakes: "we need to grow in the conviction that a decrease in the pace of production and consumption can at times give rise to another form of progress and development."[24]

Putting one of the Gospel parables into modern terms, Francis asks how the rich man didn't notice the poor beggar Lazarus suffering at his door step. "When the rich man left the house, perhaps the car he left in had darkly tinted windows so he couldn't see out." But "surely . . . the eyes of his soul were tinted dark so he couldn't see." And thus the rich man "saw only his life and didn't realize what was happening" to Lazarus. Francis notes that three men are named in this parable—Lazarus, Abraham, and Moses—but the rich man "had no name, because the worldly lose their name," which is merely a feature "of the well-off crowd who need nothing" more and therefore who lose out on an eternity with God.[25] Beware, says Francis, your riches may cause you to lose everything.

In *Laudato si'*, Francis argues that this excessive, self-destructive consumption on the part of the rich is partly the fault of markets. "[T]he market tends to promote extreme consumerism in an effort to sell its products, [and] people can easily get caught up in a whirlwind of needless buying and spending. Compulsive consumerism. . . . This paradigm leads people to believe that

---

22. Francis, "God's Time."
23. Francis, "Beguiled by the Serpent."
24. Francis, *Laudato si'*, 191.
25. Francis, "Nameless."

they are free as long as they have the supposed freedom to consume."[26] The market caters to people's emptiness: "When people become self-centered and self-enclosed, their greed increases. The emptier a person's heart is, the more he or she needs things to buy, own and consume. It becomes almost impossible to accept the limits imposed by reality. In this horizon, a genuine sense of the common good also disappears. . . . Obsession with a consumerist lifestyle . . . can only lead to . . . mutual destruction."[27] So many of the rich "have not the faintest idea of what to do with their possessions, vainly showing off their supposed superiority and leaving behind them so much waste."[28] So, as we must do with other addictions, we need to acknowledge the problem, reject the lures of the market, and kick the habit: "Many people know that our current progress and the mere amassing of things and pleasures are not enough to give meaning and joy to the human heart, yet they feel unable to give up what the market sets before them."[29] "Happiness means knowing how to limit some needs which only diminish us."[30] But this is hard for individuals because a "constant flood of new consumer goods can baffle the heart and prevent us from cherishing each thing and each moment."[31] "It is not easy to promote this kind of healthy humility or happy sobriety when we consider ourselves autonomous, when we exclude God from our lives or replace Him with our own ego, and think that our subjective feeling can define what is right and what is wrong."[32] The solution is to turn to the Christian Church and to God: "Christian spirituality proposes a growth marked by moderation and the capacity to be happy with little. It is a return to that simplicity which allows us to stop and appreciate the small things."[33] "Such sobriety, when lived freely and consciously, is liberating."[34]

As Andrew Yuengert emphasizes in his essay, this conviction that many are now consuming too much is not novel to Pope Francis. In the encyclical *Sollic-*

---

26. Francis, *Laudato si'*, 203.
27. Ibid., 204.
28. Ibid., 90.
29. Ibid., 209.
30. Ibid., 223.
31. Ibid., 222.
32. Ibid., 224.
33. Ibid., 222.
34. Ibid., 223.

itudo rei socialis, St. John Paul II referred to this excess as "super-development," which consists in an excessive availability of every kind of material good for the benefits of certain social groups" and which

> easily makes people slaves of "possession" and of immediate gratification, with no other horizon than the multiplication or continual replacement of the things already owned with others still better. This is the so-called civilization of "consumption" or "consumerism," which involves so much "throwing-away" and "waste." All of us experience firsthand the sad effects of this blind submission to pure consumerism: in the first place a crass materialism, and at the same time a radical dissatisfaction, because one quickly learns—unless one is shielded from the flood of publicity and the ceaseless and tempting offers of products—that the more one possesses the more one wants, while deeper aspirations remain unsatisfied and perhaps even stifled.[35]

Business and Employees

Some observers have detected in Pope Francis a deep hostility to business, citing, for example, a statement in which he uses Basil of Caesarea's words to describe "the unfettered pursuit of money" as the "dung of the devil";[36] a homily that "money is the enemy of harmony; money is selfish";[37] and a warning that "[w]ar . . . is an act of faith in money.[38] However, he clearly distinguishes business from money.

Pope Francis instead affirms that "business is a noble vocation, directed to producing wealth and improving our world. It can be a fruitful source of prosperity for the areas in which it operates, especially if it sees the creation of jobs as an essential part of its service to the common good."[39, 40] But hiring workers

---

35. John Paul II, *Sollicitudo rei socialis*, 28.

36. "Pope Francis: Speech at World Meeting of Popular Movements," Vatican Radio.

37. Francis, "How Harmony Is Created."

38. Francis, "Where Is Your Brother?"

39. Francis, *Laudato si'*, 129.

40. Every month the pope announces a set of prayer intentions. It is interesting to note that, despite the elevated importance of businesspeople in the affairs of the world, Francis has yet to offer an intention for them. Prayer intentions have included those for "[s]mall

must be about more than profit; it cannot lead to abuse of workers, which Francis refers to hyperbolically as "slave labor," as he did when he mourned the deaths of more than seven hundred workers when a factory building collapsed in Bangladesh. This "slave labour exploits the most beautiful gift which God gave man: the ability to create, to work, to discover our dignity. How many of our brothers and sisters in the world are in this situation at the hands of these economic, social and political attitudes!"[41]

Though Francis sees business as noble, he stridently condemns "the principle of profit maximization" because it "reflects a misunderstanding of the very concept of the economy."[42] He warns that "[t]he economy accepts every advance in technology with a view to profit, without concern for its potentially negative impact on human beings,"[43] and he chastises those "obsessed with profits."[44] "We need to reject a magical conception of the market, which would suggest that problems can be solved simply by an increase in the profits of companies or individuals."[45] When he meets with business groups, he calls on them to make the jobs of their employees—and the lives of these workers' families—secure and stable rather than to focus solely on the bottom line. He exhorts them to relieve "mothers and fathers of families [of] the worry of not being able to give a future, or even a present, to their children" and to act "in such a way that one task creates another, one responsibility creates other responsibilities, hope generates other hopes."[46]

---

[f]armers, that small farmers may receive a just reward for their precious labor" (United States Conference of Catholic Bishops, "The Pope's Monthly Intentions for 2016"); for scientific researchers; for people involved in sports (in both 2014 and 2016); journalists, the media, artists, and workers; and the unemployed. Some may doubt the sincerity of this characterization of business as noble and point to contrary statements, such as Francis's homily warning that "the Church must 'let herself be startled by the newness of God' . . . . Otherwise she risks becoming barren, afflicted by . . . the desire to . . . become an 'entrepreneur'" ("The Time of Re-creation").

41. Francis, "No to Slave Labour."

42. Francis, *Laudato si'*, 195.

43. Ibid., 109.

44. Ibid., 190.

45. Ibid.

46. "Pope Francis to Confindustria Business People: 'Justice Excludes Every Favoritism,'" Vatican Radio.

How Pope Francis and Economists Disagree

It is clear that Pope Francis and many in the economics profession do not see eye to eye at a fundamental level.[47] This is immediately obvious if one examines the core microeconomic principles on which most of modern economics rests. Standard intermediate microeconomics textbooks explicitly state what most economists assume is true about individuals' preferences in most of their teaching and research:

> The theory of consumer behavior begins with three basic assumptions about people's preferences for one market basket versus another. We believe that these assumptions hold for most people in most situations. . . . [1] Preferences are assumed to be complete. In other words, consumers can compare and rank all possible baskets. . . . [2] Preferences are transitive. Transitivity means that if a consumer prefers basket A to basket B and basket B to basket C, then the consumer also prefers A to C. . . . [3] More is better than less. . . . [C]onsumers always prefer more of any good to less . . . [and] are never satisfied or satiated; more is always better, even if just a little better.[48, 49]

The third assumption is also known as "nonsatiation."[50]

After describing preferences, the standard intermediate microeconomics textbook turns to the consumer's budget constraint and the maximization

---

47. The reader will note that most people accept economists' key assumption that Pope Francis rejects, so economists are part of a much larger group that does not see eye to eye with the pontiff.

48. Pindyck and Rubinfeld, *Microeconomics*, 66.

49. It's not just textbooks that buy this assumption. In a recent survey, only 2 percent of professional economists disagreed with the statement that "[e]conomic growth in developed countries like the U.S. leads to greater levels of well-being" (Whaples, "The Policy Views of American Economic Association Members," 341).

50. Pindyck and Rubinfeld follow this explanation by saying that "[t]his assumption is made for pedagogic reasons; namely, it simplifies the graphical analysis. Of course, some goods, such as air pollution, may be undesirable, and consumers will always prefer less. We ignore these 'bads' in the context of our immediate discussion because most consumers would not choose to purchase them" (*Microeconomics*, 66). In terms of my discussion, this is not much of a caveat. It divides the world into "goods" (of which more is always better) and "bads," without a hint that having more of something you like can also be bad for you or, in other words, that the nonsatiation assumption may not be correct or benign.

problem that the consumer solves, showing that budget constraints and a set of indifference curves generate individual consumers' demand curves and ultimately the market demand curve. These demand curves reflect the marginal benefit consumers receive from the various goods they may buy, while supply curves reflect the marginal costs to profit-maximizing firms of producing goods.[51] When self-interested consumers and producers come together in markets, the equilibrium quantity—at which supply and demand are equal—is also the efficient quantity—at which the upward-sloping marginal cost curve equals the downward-sloping marginal benefit curve. Thus, the market does exactly what so many want it to do. The amount the market actually produces *equals* the efficient quantity—the quantity that maximizes the total value of all the resources used in the economy—unless one of the assumptions we have just made is invalid.

Unless one of the assumptions is invalid? As shown earlier, Pope Francis's view of the world is that one of these foundational assumptions is assuredly invalid. This simply isn't how God made people. Christianity holds that God made man in His own image. In many cases, this relationship can make man capable of the rationality that goes into the first two assumptions about consumer choice—that preferences are complete and transitive—but the third assumption is fundamentally flawed, says Francis. More material possessions and greater consumption aren't always or even generally better. A consumer who never feels satisfied with his material life—who always wants more—is not on the path to God. Christian teaching has always been that God made people to have an infinite desire for Him, *not* to have an insatiable desire for the things of this world.

---

51. One can also question the assumption that firms attempt to maximize profits. As noted earlier, Francis condemns "the principle of profit maximization." I would wager that if pushed most economists would back off the firms-maximize-profits assumption before the consumer nonsatiation assumption. In fact, the principal-agent problem explains why it is so hard for firms to maximize profits, even if their owners desire it. But some businesspeople explicitly state that their goal is to maximize profits. A fitting example is candy-magnate Forrest Mars, who when he became CEO is reported to have told executives, "I'm a religious man," and then sank to his knees to recite the following litany: "I pray for Milky Way. I pray for Snickers. . . . That's what the consumer buys . . . that's what creates profit. And profit is our single objective" (qtd. in Brenner, *The Emperors of Chocolate*, 177).

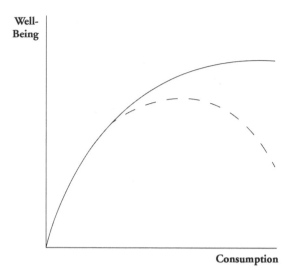

Figure 1. Two Views of Consumption and Well-Being

The avowedly utilitarian approach at the core of economics is certainly useful in some contexts but is no firm foundation for making choices in Francis's view. "Since the world has been given to us, we can no longer view reality in a purely utilitarian way, in which efficiency and productivity are entirely geared to our individual benefit."[52] Relentless utility maximization and this entire way of approaching the world, as Francis sees it, are flawed: "Rather than a problem to be solved, the world is a joyful mystery to be contemplated with gladness and praise."[53] In response to the claim that economics "often teaches [its] students to demoralize choices through an emphasis on consumer sovereignty and the subjectivity of value,"[54] Francis counters that "[p]urchasing is always a moral—and not simply [an] economic—act."[55] "Isolated individuals can lose their ability and freedom to escape the utilitarian mindset, and end up prey to an unethical consumerism,"[56] so we need to turn to faith to help

52. Francis, *Laudato si'*, 159.

53. Ibid., 12.

54. Shields and Dunn, *Passing on the Right*, 144.

55. Francis, *Laudato si'*, 206.

56. Ibid., 219.

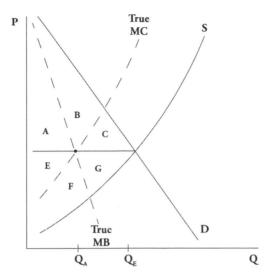

Figure 2. Two Views of the Optimal Amount of Production

us "devise models of development which are based not simply on utility and profit."[57]

The typical economists' view of the utility function is graphically shown in figure 1. As the level of income or consumption rises, the consumer's utility or well-being always rises—although inevitably the additions to well-being get smaller as one consumes more, which is one facet of the law of diminishing returns. But Pope Francis's critique of market outcomes is much deeper than the law of diminishing returns. He argues that the well-being of the rich *falls* as they consume more and more, as shown along the dashed curve. From this perspective, the utility of the rich rises when they divest themselves of possessions. This is the advice that Jesus gives and that Francis often repeats.

Economists argue that because demand reflects marginal benefits and supply reflects marginal costs, a competitive market will maximize the total gains to society. This outcome is shown in figure 2, a staple of introductory economics textbooks, which shows that the sum of the gains to consumers (consumer surplus, area ABC) and producers (producer surplus, area EFG) is maximized at the competitive market's equilibrium, QE. Any other level

57. Francis, *Lumen fidei*, 55.

of production creates a deadweight loss—a loss of surplus, a loss of the gains from trade between buyers and sellers. Economists acknowledge that this fortuitous outcome will be blocked if there are third-party costs or benefits (externalities) that are not captured in the supply or demand curves, and they advocate solutions to this problem such as enforcement of property rights and pollution taxes. But Pope Francis says this view is much too simple. He not only sees ubiquitous hidden costs—especially costs that suppliers impose on others—but also questions the true benefits of much consumption. If so, the true marginal benefits (MB) of consumption—especially high levels of consumption—are low or nonexistent, and the true marginal costs (MC) are higher than those in the supply curve. In this case, the market-output level is excessive—greatly excessive. Thus, the level of output produced in markets, QE, isn't the optimal amount. In this view, the true optimal amount—perhaps we should call it the adequate amount, QA—is much less.

Because almost all of the public-policy advice that economists offer starts from ideas similar to the outline presented here, much of that advice will be at odds with Francis's point of view. But a tree must be judged by its fruit. Despite beginning from different premises, there may be room for agreement if the market—we buyers and sellers coming together and trading—bears good fruit. What are the fruits of the market? Here, too, there is much room for debate.

The Strengths and Weaknesses of Capitalism

No system of human interaction can be perfect, especially if we live in a fallen world. But how well does flawed capitalism[58] stack up against other flawed systems, such as socialism?[59]

---

58. Some defenders of capitalism are wary of using the very term *capitalism* because of its Marxist pedigree and negative connotations in some circles. But the Latin root *cap* means "head" (as in head of cattle), so it strikes me that the term is quite apt if capitalism is largely about us using our heads.

59. To most Americans, even posing this question might be considered odd or a complete waste of time, but not for the students in the sustainability program in which I teach. Accordingly, we open the semester with Jason Brennan's *Why Not Capitalism?* (2014), which is an answer to George Cohen's *Why Not Socialism?* (2009), and then consider the strengths and weaknesses of capitalism as outlined later in this introduction.

A textbook definition says that capitalism is "a socioeconomic system in which resources (land, labor, and capital) are owned, operated, and traded for the purpose of generating profits by private individuals acting either singly or jointly. Investment, production, pricing, and the distribution of resources, goods, and services are determined by the decentralized choices of individuals in a market economy. In a capitalist system the private rights and property relations of individuals are protected by the rule of law."[60] This system can be contrasted with the centrally planned allocation of scarce resources and government ownership or control of various combinations of land, labor, and capital under socialism or communism. This definition of capitalism isn't perfect—many economists will question, for example, the assertion that profits are the sole purpose in capitalism because the motives of actors within the system are much broader (on both the supply side and the demand side), and one should probably add a mention of freedom of entry into markets (hence, exiling extreme crony capitalism from the land of true capitalism). An alternative definition says that capitalism is a "system based on consumer sovereignty, animated by the responses of owners of resources to prices, and by entrepreneurs to prospects of profit and loss. That is, the pursuit of profits is a consequence of the primacy of serving consumer wants, with profits demonstrating that more value is being created than is being used up in resources."[61] I'm not sure which definition Pope Francis has in mind when he critiques market capitalism, but using either definition we can outline the strengths and weaknesses that friends and foes of capitalism offer.

Here's the vision of capitalism at its best, according to its champions—informed by the research and reasoning of many economists.

1. Most fundamentally, capitalism and markets help solve three big problems: *(a)* the knowledge problem (no one in isolation knows the costs and benefits of the many resources they possess or the best way to fulfill their own needs and wants, but information about all of this is pooled and communicated to everyone when prices emerge from trades); *(b)* the incentive problem (scarce resources are often wasted or used inefficiently if no one owns them or they are owned collectively,

---

60. Hackett, *Environmental and Natural Resources Economics*, 35.
61. Munger, "Tomorrow 3.0."

but owners have a strong personal incentive to use resources efficiently and add value to them); and *(c)* the learning problem (by providing feedback, especially in the form of profits and losses, everyone learns how to better allocate resources).

2. Because capitalism solves these problems so well, it accelerates technological improvements, eliminates absolute poverty, and generates rising standards of living, life expectancy, education, leisure, and more. The rich have gotten richer *and* the poor have also gotten much richer because of capitalism.[62]

3. Capitalism increases freedom because it achieves its ends without coercion. It is less violent than other economic systems. It promotes cooperation and harmony of interests—not only between buyers and sellers but also within firms.

4. Capitalism democratically diffuses power rather than concentrating it in the hands of central authorities. Although it sometimes seems that big businesses are "all powerful," in fact most of the power is in the hands of consumers—the people rule—because businesses can't force consumers to buy and so must compete for their business. Therefore, almost all of the gains from innovations ultimately go to consumers, not to businesses.[63] Capitalism handles fraud and deception well because people have the option to stop buying from those who defraud them. It *doesn't* tend toward monopoly—unless the state blocks entry into markets—and workers don't get exploited because they are mobile or have multiple options or both.

5. Capitalism incentivizes people to think in the long term—assets are worth less now if their future value is ignored, so owners of resources naturally pay close attention to conserving them. In addition, capitalism has brought higher levels of wealth, which allows people to be more patient. The starving man cannot wait; the well-fed one can.

---

62. See, for example, the historical statistics in van Zanden et al., *How Was Life?*

63. In fact, William Nordhaus estimates that from 1948 to 2001 only about 2.2 percent of the returns from technological gains were captured by producers—the other 97.8 went to consumers (*Schumpeterian Profits in the American Economy*, 22).

6. Capitalism gives people the incentive to be more virtuous and to serve each other. There is a payoff to acting kind, caring, decent, and prudent—and practicing these virtues in the market can actually help turn us into better persons.

7. Capitalism enables greater philanthropy and charity. It makes us richer so we can and do give away more to those in need.[64]

8. Capitalism unleashes creativity—it is the essence of creativity. We celebrate creativity in the arts, literature, science, and other fields, but capitalism means creativity, too. Joseph Schumpeter likened successful entrepreneurs to Enrico Caruso, the great opera singer.[65] Think about the creativity of Steve Jobs in the capitalist United States versus his father's life in socialist/totalitarian Syria. Problem solving, creativity, philanthropy, and service to others add meaning to people's lives.

9. As capitalist markets set an example of how people can work together to solve problems, everyone is encouraged to act in a more trustworthy manner, thus improving social ties and harmony.

10. Capitalism makes people wealthy enough to demand improvements in environmental quality and to create technologies to solve these problems—in the most significant ways (for example, the air we breathe), the environment is *cleaner* in the richest countries.[66]

11. Capitalism leaves room for people to behave socialistically (for example, families, communes, and convents), but socialism doesn't return the favor.[67]

Here are the downsides of capitalism emphasized by skeptics who agree that business can be noble.[68]

---

64. See McQuillan and Park's essay in this book.

65. Schumpeter, *The Theory of Economic Development*.

66. See Yandle, Vijayaraghavan, and Bhattarai, *The Environmental Kuznets Curve*.

67. As John Paul II put it, the right "to take initiatives in economic matters" is a human right. Does not depriving people of this right (and of other rights, such as the right to religious freedom and freedom to organize unions) "impoverish the human person as much as, if not more than, the deprivation of material goods?" (*Sollicitudo rei socialis*, 15).

68. I have omitted sweeping condemnations by critics, such as Marxists, who deliberately ignore capitalism's strengths.

1. Capitalism incentivizes people not only to reduce *private* costs but also to ignore *social* costs and to push those costs onto others—it doesn't solve very well problems of externalities (such as pollution) or common-pool resources (such as overfishing) or the underprovision of public goods.[69]

2. Because capitalist economies produce so much, external damages often rise as output rises (for example, more automobiles mean more pollution). Because of capitalist economies' unslakable thirst, common-pool resources are drained more quickly (for example, better fishing boats and relentless competition mean there are dwindling stocks of fish in the oceans).

3. Capitalism is producing more than the earth can sustain. We're using up resources and leaving too few for the future. As Francis puts it, "We all know that it is not possible to sustain the present level of consumption in developed countries and wealthier sectors of society, where the habit of wasting and discarding has reached unprecedented levels."[70]

4. Even if excess production didn't damage the earth, capitalism has gotten so productive that many people simply have too much for their own good. The problem of obesity is an example, but the problem is much deeper. Almost everybody is getting spoiled now. Gluttony abounds.

5. Capitalism can generate high levels of economic inequality. Even if the poor get richer along with the rich, wealth and income gaps are much, much wider than they would be under other arrangements, and the rich

---

69. Pope Francis puts this point (and some of those that follow) this way: "The principle of the maximization of profits, frequently isolated from other considerations, reflects a misunderstanding of the very concept of the economy. As long as production is increased, little concern is given to whether it is at the cost of future resources or the health of the environment; as long as the clearing of a forest increases production, no one calculates the losses entailed in the desertification of the land, the harm done to biodiversity or the increased pollution. In a word, businesses profit by calculating and paying only a fraction of the costs involved. Yet only when 'the economic and social costs of using up shared environmental resources are recognized with transparency and fully borne by those who incur them, not by other peoples or future generations,' can those actions be considered ethical" (*Laudato si'*, 195, quoting Benedict XVI, *Caritas in veritate*, 50).

70. Francis, *Laudato si'*, 27.

flaunt their wealth, marginalizing those at the bottom. The rich "are far removed from the poor, with little direct contact with their problems."[71]

6. Capitalism encourages and feeds on envy—one of the (deadly) cardinal sins. Advertisements celebrate consumers for outdoing the Joneses and play on anxieties about keeping up with them—setting up zero-sum status competition. They make envy the norm.[72]

7. Capitalism can lure people into focusing on crass material things and "frenetic activity" rather than on more important things, especially spiritual matters and personal relationships. For example, in a study of people in forty-two countries, the Pew Research Center finds a *strong negative* correlation between income per capita and the importance of religion to people.[73] The lesser material light distracts us from the true light: "[H]ow can we listen to [words of love] amid constant noise, interminable, and nerve-wracking distractions?"[74]

8. Capitalism often panders to our worst nature. Advertisements focus on whatever is cool and whatever sells (especially sex), a focus that permeates and degrades society. It enables people to buy bad things for bad reasons.

9. Capitalism overemphasizes the individual to the detriment of the collective. It erodes social capital and communal bonds. Markets increase anonymous interaction, and people become part of a commodity chain instead of building purposeful relationships with their neighbors. (Note that this point directly contradicts point 9 on the previous list.) Its "emphasis on success and self-reliance . . . does not appear to favour an investment in efforts to help the slow, the weak or the less talented to find opportunities in life."[75]

---

71. Ibid.

72. Francis warns that when "media . . . become omnipresent, their influence can stop people from learning how to live wisely, to think deeply and to love generously" (*Laudato si'*, 47).

73. Theodorou, "Americans Are in the Middle of the Pack Globally When It Comes to the Importance of Religion."

74. Francis, *Laudato si'*, 225.

75. Ibid., 196.

10. Capitalism and markets tend to put a price tag on everything. When someone asks, "How much is Warren Buffett worth?" they think about his net worth and put a dollar sign in front. When they ask how much a minimum-wage worker is worth, the dollar sign is followed by a lot fewer zeros—as if that person is actually worth less. Putting a price tag on everything means that nothing is sacred. But there are many things that should never be bought and sold.

11. Workers are often exploited by capitalism. They don't get their fair share. Employers begin to view them as mere objects, dismissing them when they are no longer needed, paying them the lowest wages possible, and subjecting them to harsh and unsafe working conditions.

12. Capitalism is often perverted by cronyism and rent seeking (capturing the state to do one's bidding).

13. Capitalism is plagued by booms and busts. It's unstable.

I'm sure that others would prune some items from my two lists or add some to them or do both. And friends of markets will quickly add rebuttals to this second list. For example, they might say that the booms and busts of capitalism would be much milder if ill-advised government policies didn't destabilize markets so much; that although it might appear that workers are being "exploited," competition among employers means that they have to pay employees roughly the value of their productivity, which keeps rising over time as working conditions improve;[76] that we're not actually running out of resources—the scarcity of resources is best measured by their real prices, which are not generally headed up;[77] that proven global reserves of key natural resources such as petroleum, natural gas, and coal are rising, not falling;[78] and that it appears that in most places around the world consumption is not unsustainably high because physical capital, human capital, and technology add to productive capacity faster than natural-resource use subtracts from it.[79]

But, of course, foes of capitalism will do the same for the list of its strengths.

---

76. Powell, *Out of Poverty.*

77. Jacks, *From Boom to Bust.* Jacks finds that the real prices of most commodities has not been upward in the long run. The exceptions are precious metals (not a vital resource from Francis's point of view) and petroleum.

78. Covert, Greenstone, and Knittel, "Will We Ever Stop Using Fossil Fuels?"

79. Arrow et al., "Are We Consuming Too Much?"

Conclusion

Pope Francis has a much lower opinion of capitalism and market economies than most economists. He especially emphasizes the problems on the list of capitalism's weaknesses—many of which he has seen firsthand. But most economists would argue that he has some blind spots that lead him to miss (or simply ignore) many things mentioned on the list of strengths—and this is a loss. Perhaps, the most baffling of these blind spots is his contention that levels of poverty—absolute poverty—are not diminishing around the world. In *Laudato si'*, he speaks of "growing poverty" and says that "[t]he exploitation of the planet has already exceeded acceptable limits and we still have not solved the problem of poverty."[80]

According to economists, however, the numbers simply don't support this position. Branko Milanovic has traced out the worldwide income distribution in recent decades as people in countries around the world have used markets to expand trading and as technology—largely developed by the world's profit-driven firms—has spread to poorer countries.[81] His numbers are stunning and show that the whole world is getting richer. Most importantly, the stark poverty of the left tail of the worldwide income distribution has fallen substantially. He estimates, for example, that from 1988 to 2008 real incomes of those incredibly poor people living at the fifth percentile of the world's income distribution rose by about 15 percent, by 40 percent at the tenth and twentieth percentiles, and by more than half at the thirtieth to the fiftieth percentile.[82]

Another empirical fact that most economists accept but Pope Francis does not mention is the vast improvement in the quality of the environment in many places throughout the world. For many pollutants, economists have identified a pattern in which emission levels rise as countries begin developing economically but then peak once the countries pass a middle economic level and begin to fall as they become richer. The good news is that overall levels of pollution now peak at lower levels than in earlier decades—largely because of cleaner technologies developed in the most advanced market economies.[83]

---

80. *Laudato si'*, 25, 27.

81. Milanovic, *Global Inequality*.

82. Ibid., 11.

83. Yandle, Vijayaraghavan, and Bhattarai, *The Environmental Kuznets Curve*.

But the differences between Francis and most economists (as well as most non-economists) are far greater than these numbers can reconcile. Even if he were to concede that they are correct, his values are simply not aligned with the world's way of thinking. He turns the logic of the world on its head. "When someone is given a higher position—in the world's eyes—we say, 'ah, that person has been promoted.' . . . Yes, that's a lovely phrase and we in the Church should use it, yes: this person was promoted to the cross; that person was promoted to humiliation. That is true promotion. It is what makes us more like Jesus."[84]

The golden rule of the economy seems to be "I will serve you if you pay me—and we both will be better off." But Francis argues that "[h]umility is the 'golden rule.'"[85] The golden rule becomes "I will serve you because you are in need." If this view is correct, it's not about bettering ourselves in this world—it's about humbling ourselves, recognizing that we all are lowly and that true power comes from humility.

References

Arrow, Kenneth, Partha Dasgupta, Lawrence Goulder, Gretchen Daily, Paul Ehrlich, Geoffrey Heal, Simon Levin, Karl-Goran Maler, Stephen Schneider, David Starrett, and Brian Walker. "Are We Consuming Too Much?" *Journal of Economic Perspectives* 18, no. 3 (2004): 147–72.

Benedict XVI. *Caritas in veritate* (authorized English translation). Vatican: Libreria Editrice Vaticana, June 29, 2009. At http://w2.vatican.va/content/benedict-xvi /en/encyclicals/documents/hf_ben-xvi_enc_20090629_caritas-in-veritate.html.

Brennan, Jason. *Why Not Capitalism?* New York: Routledge, 2014.

Brenner, Joel Glenn. *The Emperors of Chocolate: Inside the Secret World of Hershey and Mars.* New York: Broadway Books, 2000.

Cohen, Gerald A. *Why Not Socialism?* Princeton, N.J.: Princeton University Press, 2009.

---

84. Francis, "True Power Is Service."
85. Francis, "The Golden Rule of Humility."

Covert, Thomas, Michael Greenstone, and Christopher Knittel. "Will We Ever Stop Using Fossil Fuels?" *Journal of Economic Perspectives* 30, no. 1 (2016): 117–38.

Francis. "God's Time." May 27, 2013. At https://w2.vatican.va/content/francesco /en/ cotidie/2013/documents/papa-francesco-cotidie_20130527_god-time.html.

———. "The Golden Rule of Humility." April 8, 2013. At https://w2.vatican.va /content/francesco/en/cotidie/2013/documents/papa-francesco-cotidie_20130408 _rule-humility.html.

———. *Lumen fidei* (authorized English translation). Vatican City: Libreria Editrice Vaticana. June 29, 2013. At http://w2.vatican.va/content/francesco/en/encyclicals /documents/papa-francesco_20130629_enciclica-lumen-fidei.html.

———. "No to 'Slave Labour.'" May 1, 2013. At http://w2.vatican.va/content/ francesco/en/cotidie/2013/documents/papa-francesco-cotidie_20130501_slave -labour.html.

———. "The Pillars of Christian Salvation." June 22, 2013. At http://w2.vatican .va/content/ francesco/en/cotidie/2013/documents/papa-francesco-cotidie _20130622_christian- salvation.html.

———. "True Power Is Service." May 21, 2013. At http://w2.vatican.va/content /francesco/en/cotidie/2013/documents/papa-francesco-cotidie_20130521_service -power.html.

———. "Where Is Your Brother?" June 2, 2013. At http://w2.vatican.va/content /francesco/ en/cotidie/2013/documents/papa-francesco-cotidie_20130602_war -madness.html.

———. "The Time of Re-creation." December 19, 2014. At http://w2.vatican.va /content/francesco/en/cotidie/2014/documents/papa-francesco-cotidie _20141219_the-time-of-re- creation.html

———. "Beguiled by the Serpent." May 25, 2015. At http://w2.vatican.va/content /francesco/en/cotidie/2015/documents/papa-francesco-cotidie_20150525 _beguiled-by-the-serpent.html.

———. *Laudato si'* (authorized English translation). Vatican City: Libreria Editrice Vaticana. May 24, 2015. At http://w2.vatican.va/content/francesco/en/encyclicals /documents/papa-francesco_20150524_enciclica-laudato-si.html.

———. "Let Us Close the Distance." June 26, 2015. At http://w2.vatican.va/content /francescomobile/en/cotidie/2015/documents/papa-francesco-cotidie_20150626 _let-us- close-the-distance.html.

———. "Nameless." March 5, 2015. At https://w2.vatican.va/content/francesco/ en/ cotidie/2015/documents/papa-francesco-cotidie_20150305_nameless.html.

———. "Our Wage from Jesus." May 26, 2015. At https://m.vatican.va/content /francescomobile/en/cotidie/2015/documents/papa-francesco-cotidie_20150526 _our-wage- from-jesus.html.

———. "Wealth and Poverty." June 16, 2015. At http://w2.vatican.va/content /francesco/ en/cotidie/2015/documents/papa-francesco-cotidie_20150616_wealth- and-poverty.html.

———. "How Harmony Is Created." April 5, 2016. At https://w2.vatican.va/content /francesco/en/cotidie/2016/documents/papa-francesco-cotidie_20160405_how -harmony-is- created.html.

Hackett, Steven C. *Environmental and Natural Resources Economics: Theory, Policy, and the Sustainable Society.* 4th ed. Armonk, NY: M. E. Sharpe, 2011.

Jacks, David. *From Boom to Bust: A Typology of Real Commodity Prices in the Long Run.* NBER (National Bureau of Economic Research) Working Paper no. 18874. Cambridge, MA: NBER, 2013.

John Paul II. *Sollicitudo rei socialis* (authorized English translation). Vatican City: Libreria Editrice Vaticana, December 30, 1987. At http://w2.vatican.va/content/ john-paul-ii/ en/encyclicals/documents/hf_jp-ii_enc_30121987_sollicitudo -rei-socialis.html.

Milanovic, Branko. *Global Inequality: A New Approach for the Age of Globalization.* Cambridge, MA: Harvard University Press, 2016.

Munger, Michael. "Tomorrow 3.0: Surviving in the Middleman Economy." Unpublished book manuscript, n.d.

Nordhaus, William. *Schumpeterian Profits in the American Economy: Theory and Measurement.* NBER (National Bureau of Economic Research) Working Paper no. 10433. Cambridge, MA: NBER, 2004.

Paul VI. *Humanae vitae* (authorized English translation). July 25, 1968. Vatican City: Libreria Editrice Vaticana. At http://w2.vatican.va/content/paul-vi/en/encyclicals /documents/ hf_p-vi_enc_25071968_humanae-vitae.html.

Pindyck, Robert S., and Daniel L. Rubinfeld. *Microeconomics.* 6th ed. Upper Saddle River, NJ: Pearson, 2005.

"Pope Francis: Speech at World Meeting of Popular Movements." Vatican Radio, July 9, 2015. At http://www.news.va/en/news/pope-francis-speech-at-world-meeting -of-popular-mo.

"Pope Francis to Confindustria Business People: 'Justice Excludes Every Favoritism.'" Vatican Radio, February 27, 2016. At http://en.radiovaticana.va/news/2016 /02/27/pope_francis_ meets_with_confindustria_business_people/1211545.

Powell, Benjamin. *Out of Poverty: Sweatshops in the Global Economy.* New York: Oxford University Press, 2014.

Schneider, Nathan. "How Pope Francis Is Reviving Radical Catholic Economics." *The Nation*, September 9, 2015.

Schumpeter, Joseph A. *The Theory of Economic Development: An Inquiry into Profits, Capital, Credit, Interest, and the Business Cycle.* New Brunswick, N.J.: Transaction Books, [1911] 1983.

Shields, Jon A., and Joshua M. Dunn Sr. *Passing on the Right: Conservative Professors in the Progressive University.* New York: Oxford University Press, 2016.

Theodorou, Angelina E. "Americans Are in the Middle of the Pack Globally When It Comes to the Importance of Religion." Pew Research, December 23, 2015. At http://www.pewresearch.org/fact-tank/2015/12/23/americans-are-in-the-middle -of-the-pack-globally-when-it- comes-to-importance-of-religion/.

United States Conference of Catholic Bishops. "The Pope's Monthly Intentions for 2016." 2016. At http://www.usccb.org/prayer-and-worship/prayers-and-devotions /the-popes-monthly-intentions-2016.cfm.

Van Zanden, Jan Luiten, Joreg Baten, Marco Mira d'Ercole, Auke Rijpma, Conal Smith, and Marcel Timmer, eds. *How Was Life? Global Well-Being since 1820.* Paris: Organization for Economic Cooperation and Development, 2014.

Whaples, Robert. "The Policy Views of American Economic Association Members: The Results of a New Survey." *Econ Journal Watch* 6, no. 3 (2009): 337 48.

Wooden, Cindy. "Pope Francis Warns of the Dangers of 'Unbridled Capitalism.'" *Catholic Herald*, May 22, 2013.

Yandle, Bruce, Maya Vijayaraghavan, and Madhusudan Bhattarai. *The Environmental Kuznets Curve: A Primer.* Property and Environment Research Center (PERC) Research Study no. 02-1. Bozeman, Mont.: PERC, 2002.

Zieba, Maciej. *Papal Economics: The Catholic Church on Democratic Capitalism.* Paperback ed. Wilmington, Del.: ISI Books, 2014.

I

Pope Francis, His Predecessors, and the Market

Andrew M. Yuengert

"JUST AS THE COMMANDMENT 'Thou shalt not kill' sets a clear limit in order to safeguard the value of human life, today we also have to say 'thou shalt not' to an economy of exclusion and inequality. Such an economy kills."[1] "Once more, we need to reject a magical conception of the market, which would suggest that problems can be solved simply by an increase in the profits of companies or individuals."[2] You do not have to look hard to find passages like these two in the latest pope's written exhortations. He expresses a conviction that markets are instruments of an inequality that "kills" and that those who defend markets have an unreasonable, "magical conception" of markets' power to solve social problems. It certainly seems that Pope Francis, compared to his predecessors, is a harsher critic of markets and is friendlier to statists and socialists who would suppress markets in the name of some state-defined common good.

It is difficult, however, to separate his opinions from how those opinions are reported by a left-leaning press eager to recruit and promote a hoped-for ally to progressive causes. To be sure, Pope Francis's large personality, his pastoral experience among the poorest of the poor, and his Argentine roots shine through in his writings. He is less cautious in his language and less careful in his distinctions. He speaks passionately in simple and direct phrases.

Despite his open and unguarded style, however, Pope Francis is still a *pope*, writing from within a centuries-old social tradition. Even in the area

---

1. Francis, *Evangelii gaudium*, 53.
2. Francis, *Laudato si'*, 190.

of ecology, he can cite "Green Pope" Benedict XVI[3] and John Paul II, from whom he gets the term *ecological conversion.*[4] The most natural interpretation of Francis's contributions to the Catholic Church's teaching and analysis is through what Benedict XVI called the hermeneutics of continuity (or reform), not the hermeneutics of rupture.[5] To do Francis full justice, we must place his economic analysis in the context of his predecessors, whose documents he generously quotes and in whose footsteps he conscientiously treads.

Sam Gregg has respectfully but forcefully criticized Pope Francis's economic worldview.[6] My primary purpose in this article is not to critique the pope's economics but to highlight the continuities and discontinuities of his economic opinions with those of his predecessors. Modern Catholic social teaching covers a vast range of topics stretching back 125 years. I cannot hope to keep the comparison of Francis with his predecessors manageable except by sharply limiting the range of the comparison. At this point in his papacy, Francis has almost entirely confined his economic analysis to global poverty and the ecological crisis. Although ecological questions have become increasingly important in Catholic thought, concerns about poverty in the developing world have a richer pedigree and provide a richer backdrop for a comparison.

The poverty of the developing world took center stage with John XXIII's encyclical *Mater et magistra* and the Pastoral Constitution *Gaudium et spes,* developed at the Second Vatican Council, in which Paul VI gave it his full attention. I begin with Paul VI's analysis and trace papal teaching on development through John Paul II and Benedict XVI to Francis. As a basis of comparison, from the writings of each of these popes I formulate answers to the following questions:

1. What are the causes of the deep poverty in the developing world?
2. What is true development, and where do material goods fit in?
3. What role should markets play in development?
4. How should markets be regulated so that they can promote full human development?

---

3. Stone, "The Green Pope."
4. John Paul II, "General Audience."
5. Benedict XVI, Address to the Roman Curia Offering Them His Christmas Greetings.
6. Gregg, "*Laudato si*': Well-Intentioned, Economically Flawed."

When Francis is read in light of his predecessors' analysis and concerns, his own survey of the economic terrain can be seen to follow in paths they laid. Paul VI, John Paul II, and Benedict XVI developed an account of development in which markets can serve as an outlet for creative human agency in promoting the efficient provision of goods. Markets cannot, however, be left to function without the constraints of a healthy culture and a government able to place markets at the service of the common good. All three popes warned that markets should not be allowed to function autonomously, and, if unchecked, markets might undermine both culture and politics. Where his predecessors warned of the danger that markets might overrun culture and political control, Francis asserts that they have in fact done so. As a result, he pays less attention to the role of markets in a healthy social order and more attention to their bad effects in an unhealthy social order.

The Predecessors

Paul VI and the New Developing Nations

Pope Paul VI wrote two documents commonly listed in the canon of Catholic social teaching: *Populorum progressio* (1967) and *Octogesima adveniens* (1971). In the post–World War II era, the "social question" expanded worldwide to include relations between wealthy Western countries and the extremely poor countries of the Third World, many of which were newly independent.[7] Paul VI called for a coordinated effort to help impoverished nations, which would require contributions from the wealthy nations.[8]

The Causes of Poverty. Paul VI suggested a range of causes for the "flagrant inequalities . . . in the economic, cultural, and political development of the nations."[9] He blamed primarily the lack of economic and political institutions capable of supporting economic growth and integration into the world economy.[10] He was reluctant to blame the colonial era for all of the problems of the

---

7. John XXIII, *Mater et magistra*.
8. Paul VI, *Populorum progressio*, 13, 44, 49.
9. Ibid., 2.
10. Ibid., 8.

developing world; there were real abuses but also some institutional benefits.[11] He did not mention corruption directly, although one might interpret his call for better institutions as an oblique reference to it. He placed greater blame on fluctuations of prices in commodities and agricultural export markets.[12] The pope also expressed a growing concern about "new economic powers emerging," multinational corporations. These new entities were difficult to regulate by national governments; they were "not subject to control from the point of view of the common good."[13] Their unregulated power was leading to a "new and abusive form of economic domination on the social, cultural, and even political level."[14]

True Development and the Economy's Role in It. Paul VI was careful to distinguish mere economic growth, as important as it is to human well-being, from what he called "a full-bodied humanism"[15] capable of satisfying spiritual as well as material needs. He expressed concern that economic prosperity is a "two-edged sword: . . . necessary if man is to grow as a human being; yet it can also enslave him, if he comes to regard it as the supreme good and cannot look beyond it."[16] Along with economic growth should come "social progress"; developing nations should seek to "reduce inequities, eliminate discrimination, free men from the bonds of servitude, and thus give them the capacity, in the sphere of temporal realities, to improve their lot, to further their moral growth and to develop their spiritual endowments."[17] Paul VI highlighted the crucial role of both equality and participation in social progress.[18]

Markets and Development. Paul VI enunciated an already-established principle in Catholic social teaching: that market exchange (including free trade) can be just and beneficial when it is between equally situated agents but results in unjust and unequal outcomes when the parties to exchange are unequal in

---

11. Paul VI, *Populorum progressio*, 7.
12. Ibid., 57–58.
13. Paul VI, *Octogesima adveniens*, 44.
14. Ibid.
15. Paul VI, *Populorum progressio*, 42.
16. Ibid., 19.
17. Ibid., 34.
18. Paul VI, *Octogesima adveniens*, 22.

power: "The principle of free trade . . . can work when both parties are about equal economically; in such cases it stimulates progress and rewards effort. . . . But the case is quite different when the nations involved are far from equal. Market prices that are freely agreed upon can turn out to be most unfair."[19] This judgment—that market exchange can lead to injustice when one of the parties is more vulnerable than the other—leads to a respect for markets tempered by an insistence that they cannot be free of government regulation and that the poor need support beyond access to markets. This qualified respect for markets is closely related to Catholic teaching on private property. Just as markets should not be fully autonomous of government, private property is not a principle of personal autonomy but a practical tool by which access to the goods of the earth (and the creative initiative those goods make possible) can be guaranteed to all.[20]

Because the church rejects the autonomy of markets, along with any right to private property free from social obligation, it also firmly rejects the ideology of liberalism, which promotes a reliance on "profit as the chief spur to economic progress, free competition as the guiding norm of economics, and private ownership of the means of production as an absolute right, having no limits nor concomitant social obligations."[21] Paul VI did not attribute the abuses of capitalism to business enterprise itself but to the ideological promotion of a reliance on markets and an ideological hostility to market regulation.

Similarly, the pope qualified his support for technological advances by insisting that they also must serve human development. When technology becomes an end and not a means, we ask of it, "What can we do?" not "What should we do?" Without guidance from ethics, technology can become a barrier to development: "The reign of technology—technocracy, as it is called—can cause as much harm to the world of tomorrow as liberalism did to the world of yesteryear. Economics and technology are meaningless if they do not benefit man, for it is he they are to serve."[22] This concern about technocracy would be taken up by Paul VI's successors.

---

19. Paul VI, *Populorum progressio*, 58.
20. Ibid., 22–24.
21. Ibid., 26.
22. Ibid., 34.

Markets and Government. Because markets can promote or impede full "social progress," market competition must be evaluated in light of and placed at the service of the common good, which is the sphere of politics.[23] At the international level, this placement will require some sort of world political and regulatory authority to make sure the globalizing economy serves the full human good.[24] Paul was somewhat vague about what form regulation should take. Like many of his contemporaries in the 1960s, he was confident that once the world committed itself to development, the details of the appropriate regulation could be left to technical experts (working closely with ethical and religious leaders).

Urgency and Optimism. Rereading this pope's social teaching five decades after his papacy, one is struck by the sense of urgency that pervades his discussion of the challenges facing poor countries: "We must make haste. Too many people are suffering. While some make progress, others stand still or move backwards; and the gap between them is widening."[25] "The matter is urgent, for on it depends the future of world civilization."[26] The suffering of the poor in developing nations, when other countries had generated such prosperity, was intolerable.

The grievances of ongoing poverty and powerlessness presented both dangers to world peace as well as moral challenges.[27] If they were not addressed, the pope feared that revolution and violence would make the poor nations vulnerable to revolutionary ideology, which would lead not to real reform but to "new injustices, introduce new inequities and bring new disasters,"[28] merely "a change of masters."[29] His concern was an echo of a common theme going back to the beginnings of modern Catholic social teaching: that failure to reform the economy would tempt the poor to believe what Leo XIII called

---

23. Paul VI, *Octogesima adveniens,* 46.
24. Paul VI, *Populorum progressio,* 78.
25. Ibid., 29.
26. Ibid., 44.
27. Ibid., 55.
28. Ibid., 31.
29. Paul VI, *Octogesima adveniens,* 45.

"the lying promises" of socialist revolutionaries, which "will only one day bring forth evils worse than the present."[30]

At the same time that Paul VI expressed a sense of urgency, he expressed confidence that problems of extreme poverty would yield to coordinated programs crafted by experts motivated by solidarity.[31] His optimism would give way to disappointment in the writings of future popes, including Francis.

John Paul II and the Persistence of World Poverty

John Paul II continued the Catholic analysis of poverty in the developing world in three social encyclicals: *Laborem exercens* (1981), *Sollicitudo rei socialis* (1987), and *Centesimus annus* (1991). In spite of the urgency that saturated Paul VI's pleas and after two decades of development initiatives, John Paul II noted an air of disappointment and frustration in his time: "the hopes for development, at that time so lively, today appear very far from being realized."[32] He contrasted the continuing poverty in many countries with "superdevelopment" in Western economies, driven by empty consumeristic desires.[33]

Twenty years after Paul VI, John Paul II had to reiterate the intolerability of the ongoing problem. However convincing the excuses and explanations, and however difficult the ongoing challenges, the continuing delay was unacceptable, "a betrayal of humanity's legitimate expectations . . . a harbinger of unforeseeable consequences . . . a real desertion of a moral obligation."[34] Against this backdrop, he reexamined the persistence of underdevelopment. In doing so, he formulated a richer description of a healthy social order and of the place of markets, culture, and politics in that order.

The Causes of Poverty. John Paul II was clear-eyed about the responsibilities of the developing countries themselves for their predicament. Those holding economic and social power in developing nations often serve their own

---

30. Leo XIII, *Rerum novarum*, 18.
31. Paul VI, *Populorum progressio*, 79.
32. John Paul II, *Sollicitudo rei socialis*, 12.
33. Ibid., 28.
34. Ibid., 23.

interests.[35] As a result, there are few competent and trustworthy people to govern and administer the state.[36] These elites set up political institutions that violate the rights of their citizens, especially the rights of free initiative so crucial for a vibrant, innovative society.[37]

That being said, John Paul did not exonerate the developed nations of responsibility for developing nations' poverty. Developing-country debt, undertaken on easy terms but poorly invested, resulted in crippling debt-service burdens.[38] The Cold War had made the developing nations a battleground in the service of the competition between the United States and the Soviet Union.[39] Finally, a lack of equal access to the international trade system, particularly in agricultural products, harmed developing-country economies.[40]

True Development and the Economy's Role in It. John Paul II situated the economic sector within a larger model of society in which the cultural and political sectors are crucial.[41] In the arena of politics, the common good is formulated and pursued through governing structures; in the cultural arena, answers to the deeper questions of meaning and purpose are formulated; in the economic arena, goods are exchanged and material needs are met in an efficient way. A thriving society requires that all three of these sectors be healthy, each able to shape and constrain the others.

The most important human goods are produced and nurtured in the culture; although the economic and political sectors have their own goods (even spiritual goods), their primary purpose is to support community and culture. Life in healthy human societies is lived in a network of interlocking communities, including (most importantly) the family. These "networks of solidarity"[42] generate many important human goods (love and support, growth in virtue and trust, the goods of cooperation) and are critical arenas in which people live out their freedom in community. They are also important preconditions

---

35. John Paul II, *Sollicitudo rei socialis*, 16.

36. John Paul II, *Centesimus annus*, 20.

37. John Paul II, *Sollicitudo rei socialis*, 44; John Paul II, *Centesimus annus*, 47.

38. John Paul II, *Sollicitudo rei socialis*, 19; John Paul II, *Centesimus annus*, 35.

39. John Paul II, *Sollicitudo rei socialis*, 22.

40. Ibid., 43.

41. John Paul II, *Centesimus annus*, 34–40.

42. Ibid., 49.

for robust and sustainable economic growth—John Paul II attributed the economic failure of communism in eastern Europe to the destruction of these networks.[43]

The pope's diagnosis of the evil of consumerism located its ultimate source in the culture. A materialistic secular culture provides neither sources of meaning nor spiritual goods. Without any "other horizon than the multiplication or continual replacement of the things already owned with others still better," the free market and the goods it delivers will move into the spiritual vacuum to provide an alluring but unsatisfying alternative.[44] An abundance of goods leads to a "throw-away culture" that fails to liberate the spirit.

The Free Market and Development. John Paul II expressed a genuine appreciation of the benefits of the free market, but his support for it should not be overstated; he did not represent a rupture with the tradition of previous popes. He did not abandon the Catholic tradition's insistence that the market cannot be left to operate autonomously, with the state doing no more than guaranteeing property rights and enforcing contracts. He accepted both the promise and the limits of the market: "It would appear that . . . the free market is the most efficient instrument for utilizing resources and effectively responding to needs. . . . But there are many human needs which find no place on the market."[45]

The pope's respect for market exchange was so strong that he urged action to equip the poor and marginalized "to enter the circle of exchange."[46] Nevertheless, his support for markets was not absolute. Like the right to property in the Catholic tradition, markets are supposed to serve the common good and ought to be regulated to that end. John Paul II, like his predecessors, rejected radical liberal theories in which the problems of poverty can be solved only by "blindly [entrusting] their solution to the free development of market forces."[47]

Markets and Government. John Paul II's reflections on the relations between economy and state were informed by his three-part model of society because

---

43. Ibid., 13.
44. Ibid., 36, 39.
45. Ibid., 34.
46. Ibid.
47. Ibid., 42.

"there are human needs which find no place on the market."[48] In what he called "a society of free work, of enterprise and participation," John Paul demanded that "the market be appropriately controlled by the forces of society and by the State, to guarantee that the basic needs of the whole of society are satisfied."[49]

The tasks of the state are determined by the limits and the promise of markets.[50] First and principally, the state should provide a stable juridical framework for exchange. Second, it should (along with the business sector) promote rights in the economic sector. In protecting these rights, it should be careful not to usurp the crucial functions of civil society. Finally, it should safeguard the human and natural environments.[51]

Benedict XVI and the Worldwide Crisis

Benedict XVI wrote one social encyclical, *Caritas in veritate* (2009), analyzing the continued problems of development amid an increasingly global economy and a financial crisis and offering a rich description of the three-part structure of society and of the place of love in its operation. His treatment of the problem of development and the constitution of a healthy society followed along lines laid down by his predecessors, Paul VI and John Paul II.

Although *Caritas in veritate* gave significant attention to the financial crisis of 2008, its main focus was to mark the fortieth anniversary of Paul VI's encyclical *Populorum progressio* (1967). Benedict noted the decidedly mixed record on development in poorer nations: "More than forty years after *Populorum Progressio,* its basic theme, namely progress, remains an open question."[52] Although there were some successes (notably India and China, both of which still have a long way to go), "other zones are still living in a situation of deprivation comparable to that which existed at the time of Paul VI, and in some cases one can even speak of a deterioration."[53]

---

48. John Paul II, *Centesimus annus*, 34.
49. Ibid., 35.
50. Ibid., 48.
51. Ibid., 40.
52. Benedict XVI, *Caritas in veritate*, 33.
53. Ibid., 33.

The Causes of Poverty. Benedict did not shy away from pointing out the developing countries' own responsibility for their failure, citing the "corruption and illegality" all too evident both inside and outside of those nations,[54] and he pointed out that a crucial portion of development aid must go toward developing institutions that can establish a stable rule of law.[55] As willing as he was to place some blame on developing countries themselves, he also placed significant blame on international aid agencies and developed-world agricultural policies. He warned against poorly designed aid programs that produce passivity among impoverished populations and argued for greater access to Western agricultural markets.[56]

He placed the bulk of the blame for continued poverty in developing nations, however, at the feet of the increasingly globalized markets that engulf developed nations. Within John Paul II's three-part structure (politics, culture, and economics), politics is limited by national boundaries, culture is increasingly homogenized by world media, and the economy is international. The result is a market that has escaped any bounds that culture and politics might place on it. John Paul II described a weakened culture unable to resist a market-driven consumerism. Benedict described the weakening of the political order in the face of global competition in all markets, which undermines the state's ability to impose labor standards and to protect its citizens from the risks and instability of the global financial system.[57]

True Development and the Economy's Role in It. Because *Caritas in veritate* was a celebration of *Populorum progressio*, it repeated Paul VI's call for true development and seconded John Paul II's analysis of the proper place of the economy in human flourishing. Benedict added to this established tradition a discussion of the place of gratuitous giving (love and friendship) in society, including within economic relationships. His analysis called on society both to recognize the role already played by friendship and love in business enterprises and to make more room for human values to operate in the economy: "The Church's social doctrine holds that authentically human social relationships of

---

54. Ibid., 22.
55. Ibid., 41.
56. Ibid., 47, 58.
57. Ibid., 24–25.

friendship, solidarity, and reciprocity can also be conducted within economic activity, and not only outside it or 'after' it. The economic sphere is . . . part and parcel of human activity[,] and precisely because it is human, it must be structured and governed in an ethical manner."[58]

The Market and Development. Benedict XVI accepted John Paul II's respect for markets and his insistence that markets must be intentionally put at the service of society. If markets are unregulated, they generate inequality and marginalize the weak: "Grave imbalances are produced when economic action, conceived merely as an engine for wealth creation, is detached from political action, conceived as a means for pursuing justice through redistribution."[59] According to Benedict, the practical dominance of global markets is reinforced by ideological currents that justify the market's autonomy from government control. "The conviction that the economy must be autonomous, that it must be shielded from 'influences' of a moral character, has led man to abuse the economic process in a thoroughly destructive way. In the long term, these convictions have led to economic, social and political systems that trample upon personal and social freedom."[60] The autonomy of markets is allied with a technocratic confidence that society and economies can be engineered: "the development of peoples is considered a matter of financial engineering, the freeing up of markets, the removal of tariffs, investment in production, and institutional reforms—in other words, a purely technical matter."[61]

Markets and Government. Because development can never be a purely technocratic process, in which questions of what ought to be are driven off the stage by questions of what can be, crucial to Benedict XVI's social vision is the restoration of politics' ability to regulate the market in view of the common good, to encourage a longer-term view in financial markets, and to keep inequality from marginalizing those who are left out of economic growth. "Economic activity . . . needs to be directed towards the pursuit of the com-

---

58. Benedict XVI, *Caritas in veritate*, 36.
59. Ibid.
60. Ibid., 34.
61. Ibid., 71.

mon good, for which the political community in particular must also take responsibility."[62]

It is in light of the need to embed the operations of the market within a political framework capable of making use of and shaping it that Benedict's proposals for a world governing authority and for new ways of thinking about the moral nature of business and economy make sense. A global market needs a global political order capable of both using and resisting its logic: "The integrated economy of the present day does not make the role of States redundant, but rather it commits governments to greater collaboration with one another."[63] However naive it is to expect much embodied wisdom from a worldwide government (one with "real teeth," as Benedict alarmingly called for[64]) or even from coordinated government action, the need for a more effective international authority is a logical consequence of markets' inability to bring about by themselves the full human good of society.

Pope Francis and Markets Unbound

Pope Francis came to the papacy nearly fifty years after Paul VI had written about the urgent problems of world poverty and nearly thirty years after John Paul II had declared the delays in development intolerable. Having spent his pastoral career among the marginalized poor, he approaches the problems of poverty with an impatience born of fifty years of frustrating failure. His inflamed tone reflects in part dismay that the world has become too comfortable with the intractable problems of poverty—problems that Paul VI was optimistic could be addressed.

Francis is also a citizen of Argentina—a country that is without political institutions capable of putting the economy at the service of the common good and that instead uses and is used by business and political interests to increase the power of business and political elites. It is a prime example of how crony capitalism and statist control of the economy can wreck a country

---

62. Ibid., 36.
63. Ibid., 41.
64. Ibid., 67.

that deserves better. It is thus not surprising that a pope from this part of the world emphasizes the dangers of markets over their potential contributions (see Samuel Gregg's chapter in this book, which focuses on Francis and Argentina).

Causes of Poverty. The ongoing poverty of the Third World is due, according to Francis, to a combination of weak states and powerful global business. In *Laudato si'*, he assigns some blame to corrupt government elites who fail to enforce the rule of law,[65] but even the corruption of government he attributes to powerful business interests that foster and then take advantage of this corruption. As a result, government is helpless to regulate markets to limit environmental damage,[66] to limit financial instability,[67] and to pursue peace.[68] International debt burdens render developing nations more helpless.[69]

In short, poor nations are at the mercy of the global economy and those business interests that benefit from it. According to Francis, liberal theories in the developing world, whereby unregulated markets operate according to their own logic, are anything but theoretical. Lightly regulated markets govern finance, technology, employment, consumption, and the environment. The logic of efficiency justifies reductions in employment to cut costs and increase profits, without regard for the human costs.[70] The financialization of the economy reinforces the temptation to see people as consumers and income streams, not as persons.[71] The increasing marginalization of those left out of markets leads to exclusion, a situation in which the poor become invisible, and their suffering goes unnoticed.[72] To all of this is added profit-driven environmental degradation, which imposes further burdens on the poor.[73]

---

65. Francis, *Laudato si'*, 142, 179, 197.
66. Ibid., 54, 169.
67. Ibid., 56.
68. Ibid., 57.
69. Ibid., 52.
70. Ibid., 128, 141.
71. Francis, *Evangelii gaudium*, 55.
72. Ibid., 53–54.
73. Francis, *Laudato si'*, 16.

True Development and the Economy's Role in It. Francis's predecessors acknowledged the value of material goods, even as they warned of the dangers of idolatry and consumerism. Perhaps because his main writing on social matters concerns dangers to the environment, Francis says very little about how material goods fit into a good human life. Of the twelve uses of the term *goods* in *Laudato si'*, none emphasizes the goodness of material goods or their place in a flourishing life.[74]

It is difficult to give an account of the place of markets in development without an account of the place of material goods in a good life and the place of the economy in meeting human needs and providing human work. The account of markets in Francis's work is entirely negative: a healthy social order must put markets in their place, reducing their outsized influence on consumption choices, government policy, and labor markets in poor countries. Francis does not give an account of markets that is capable of placing them properly in a well-functioning economy that fully respects "human ecology."

Markets and Development. In Pope Francis's encyclicals, the effects of markets are uniformly bad, and arguments for competition are mere cover for exploitation: "Today everything comes under the laws of competition and the survival of the fittest, where the powerful feed upon the powerless. As a consequence, masses of people find themselves excluded and marginalized: without work, without possibilities, without any means of escape."[75] Markets harm local agriculture.[76] They harm the environment, failing to take into account the intrinsic value of creation and our duties toward it.[77] They foster a selfish consumerism, distracting people from spiritual goods and their duties toward the poor.[78] There is no balance in his account—no description of the role

---

74. The term *goods* is used five times to emphasize the connection between the consumption of goods and the degradation of the environment; three times as part of the phrase *universal destination of goods*; once to indicate inequality in consumption; once to explain the dangers of consumerism; and twice in a neutral way.

75. Francis, *Evangelii gaudium*, 53.

76. Francis, *Laudato si'*, 51, 129.

77. Ibid., 56, 123, 190.

78. Ibid., 55, 203, 209, 210, 215.

that market exchange plays in a healthy social order or of the efficiencies and virtues that might be realized in the proper operation of market exchange.[79]

In Francis's judgment, market forces corrupt not only government but also the truth. Arguments for free markets and for market solutions to the problems of poverty and the environment are not simply the mistaken or misguided opinions of ideologues; according to Francis, these arguments are offered in bad faith by people rendered untrustworthy by greed and power. Examples of this frank suspicion are easy to find: "Many of those who possess more resources and economic or political power seem mostly to be concerned with masking the problems or concealing their symptoms,"[80] and "[i]t sometimes happens that complete information is not put on the table; a selection is made on the basis of particular interests, be they politico-economic or ideological."[81] I know of no other social encyclical, going back to *Rerum novarum* by Leo XIII in 1891, in which the truthfulness and motives of any party were questioned as relentlessly as the honesty of businesses and market advocates is impugned here.[82]

Markets and Government. In light of the overwhelming power of economic forces to undermine government structures and foster a culture-deadening consumerism, the only possible practical course of action, according to Francis, is to restore government's power to rein in out-of-control markets to protect the common good:

> We can no longer trust in the unseen forces and the invisible hand of the market. Growth in justice requires more than economic growth, while presupposing such growth: it requires decisions, programs, mechanisms and processes specifically geared to a better distribution of income, the creation of sources of employment and an integral promotion of the poor which goes beyond a simple welfare mentality. I am far from

---

79. The only hint that markets might be a positive good is in the lone assertion that access to markets would be good for rural farmers (Francis, *Laudato si'*, 180), but from Francis's treatment of markets it is not clear how markets could ever be a blessing and not a curse to the rural poor.

80. Francis, *Laudato si'*, 26.

81. Ibid., 135.

82. For other examples from *Laudato si'*, see paragraphs 59, 132, 138, 188.

proposing an irresponsible populism, but the economy can no longer turn to remedies that are a new poison.[83]

Stronger and more effective government constraints on business and the economy are needed both at the nation-state level and at a global level to address continued underdevelopment and the challenge of global ecological degradation.[84]

Francis and His Predecessors: A Summary

For fifty years, Catholic social teaching has moved from an attitude of caution to increasing unease about the functioning of markets in society. Francis's analysis of markets represents a movement from unease to alarm. Paul VI was optimistic about the prospects for the developing world but warned about the danger that wealth might lead to consumerism and that international firms were unaccountable to national governments. John Paul II noted the decline of culture and the movement of markets into the culture vacuum. Benedict XVI cautioned that an increasingly globalized market was undermining the political sector. Francis describes a developing world in which both culture and politics are weak and unable to regulate markets. What his predecessors warned about, Francis claims has come true.

At the beginning of the apostolic exhortation *Evangelii gaudium* (2013), Francis embraces the social analysis of his predecessors: "I take for granted the different analyses which other documents of the universal magisterium have offered, as well as those proposed by the regional and national conferences of bishops."[85] We must take him at his word that he accepts the accounts of the economy and its role in a well-functioning social order that are found in the writings of Benedict XVI, John Paul II, and Paul VI. Nevertheless, his reading of the social facts, especially in the developing world, make the previous popes' analyses somewhat irrelevant, in the way that advice for keeping a car on the road does not help someone whose car is in a ditch. Perhaps Francis agrees that there should be a healthy balance among the economic,

---

83. Francis, *Evangelii gaudium*, 204.

84. Francis, *Laudato si'*, 173–75.

85. Francis, *Evangelii gaudium*, 50.

cultural, and political orders, but, from his point of view, business reigns like a tyrant, not like a partner, running roughshod over the other sectors, causing harm to the poor, deadening culture through consumerism, and destroying the natural and human environments. If this is the case, the first priority, he claims, is to restore (or perhaps to establish for the first time) effective government at the local and international levels that is capable of rescuing society from the depredations of world markets and putting economics at the service of human flourishing.

Francis is the first pope from the developing world and the first from Latin America. His immediate predecessors, all native Europeans, experienced functioning markets within societies that constrained those markets and provided labor protection and safety nets. It is not surprising that a Latin American from a small economy in a global market, burdened by external debt and cursed with poor economic management, might see the market as an oppressive force rather than as an engine of growth. Is Francis's evaluation too extreme? In some important ways it is not: billions of people *are* still stuck in grinding poverty fifty years after Paul VI raised the alarm. There are many plausible reasons for the ongoing failure, including massive institutional failures in developed countries, predatory elites, disastrous socialist experiments, destructive wars, as well as indifferent or exploitative foreign business and political powers. Francis's absolute impatience with explanations that excuse inaction is healthy and warranted. Even those of us who do not share his suspicion of markets and in whose opinion the problems of development can be solved by less crony capitalism and more property rights, by respect for the rule of law, and by access to markets for the poor ought to heed his call to work harder and not to tolerate failure.

It is not enough to be right in our analysis when billions are still poor.

However, even if for the sake of argument we grant the pope's contention that, in Latin America at least, the market is holding down the poor, we must nevertheless acknowledge that his deep hostility to markets poses two dangers. One is his oft-expressed judgment that business interests and market advocates are dishonest and offer only sham arguments and slanted analysis. It is impossible to hold a real dialogue with those whose integrity you publicly and repeatedly doubt. Surely international businesspeople and market advocates should be kept in the conversation?

There is a second danger from the pope's tone of relentless suspicion. If the pope is right that politics and the culture have been pushed into a ditch by economic forces, we should not forget that once balance has been restored between the three sectors, there will be a crucial place for markets and competition in a healthy social order. Recent social revolutions in Latin America, like those by Evo Morales in Bolivia and Rafael Correa in Ecuador, are responses to problems of the sort the pope raises: persistent inequality, unequal standing before the law, and helplessness in the face of the global economy. Unfortunately, these reformers provide little space for markets in their visions of a reformed economy. Getting yourself out of a ditch is not enough to keep your car functioning and on the road. These revolutions will be sustainable only if they find a balance between market, culture, and the state. If they do not seek a balance, they will simply move out of one ditch and into another.

In 1891, Leo XIII was concerned that those who were oppressed in the factories would turn to socialist solutions that would bring forth worse evils. In 1967, Paul VI was concerned that the poor countries of the world would lose patience and embrace socialist revolution, exchanging one master for another. Even if Francis's bracing diagnosis of the current societal sickness is correct, his predecessors described what a healthy social order looks like. Their analysis should keep us from moving from one unhealthy state to another. The danger is real. The revolution in Venezuela did not restore markets in their proper place. It abolished them, and its people are now starving.

References

Benedict XVI. Address to the Roman Curia Offering Them His Christmas Greetings. December 22, 2005. At http://w2.vatican.va/content/benedict-xvi/en /speeches/2005/ december/documents/hf_ben_xvi_spe_20051222_roman-curia .html.

———. *Caritas in veritate* (authorized English translation). Vatican City: Libreria Editrice Vaticana, June 29, 2009. At http://w2.vatican.va/content/benedict-xvi /en/encyclicals/ documents/hf_ben-xvi_enc_20090629_caritas-in-veritate.html.

Francis. *Evangelii gaudium* (authorized English translation). Vatican: Libreria Editrice Vaticana, November 24, 2013. At http://w2.vatican.va/content/francesco /en/apost_exhortations/ documents/papa-francesco_esortazione-ap_20131124 _evangelii-gaudium.html.

————. *Laudato si'* (authorized English translation). Vatican City: Libreria Editrice Vaticana, May 24, 2015. At http://w2.vatican.va/content/francesco/en/encyclicals /documents/ papa-francesco_20150524_enciclica-laudato-si.html.

Gregg, Samuel. "*Laudato si'*: Well-Intentioned, Economically Flawed." *American Spectator*, June 19, 2015.

John XXIII. *Mater et magistra* (authorized English translation). Vatican City: Libreria Editrice Vaticana, May 15, 1961. At http://w2.vatican.va/content/john-xxiii /en/encyclicals/ documents/hf_j-xxiii_enc_15051961_mater.html.

John Paul II. *Laborem exercens* (authorized English translation). Vatican City: Libreria Editrice Vaticana, September 14, 1981. At http://w2.vatican.va/content/john -paul-ii/en/encyclicals/ documents/hf_jp-ii_enc_14091981_laborem-exercens .html.

————. *Sollicitudo rei socialis* (authorized English translation). Vatican City: Libreria Editrice Vaticana, December 30, 1987. At http://w2.vatican.va/content /john-paul-ii/en/encyclicals/ documents/hf_jp-ii_enc_30121987_sollicitudo -rei-socialis.html.

————. *Centesimus annus* (authorized English translation). Vatican City: Libreria Editrice Vaticana, May 1, 1991. At http://w2.vatican.va/content/john-paul-ii/en /encyclicals/ documents/hf_jp-ii_enc_01051991_centesimus-annus.html.

————. "General Audience." January 17, 2001. At http://w2.vatican.va/content /john-paul-ii/ en/audiences/2001/documents/hf_jp-ii_aud_20010117.html.

Leo XIII. *Rerum novarum* (authorized English translation). Vatican City: Libreria Editrice Vaticana, May 15, 1891. At http://w2.vatican.va/content/leo-xiii/en /encyclicals/ documents/hf_l-xiii_enc_15051891_rerum-novarum.html.

Paul VI. *Populorum progressio* (authorized English translation). Vatican City: Libreria Editrice Vaticana, March 26, 1967. At http://w2.vatican.va/content/paul-vi /en/encyclicals/ documents/hf_p-vi_enc_26031967_populorum.html.

————. *Octogesima adveniens* (authorized English translation). Vatican City: Libreria Editrice Vaticana, May 14, 1971. At http://w2.vatican.va/content/paul-vi /en/apost_letters/ documents/hf_p-vi_apl_19710514_octogesima-adveniens .html.

Second Vatican Council. *Pastoral Constitution on the Church in the Modern World: Gaudium et spes.* Vatican City: Libreria Editrice Vaticana, December 7, 1965. At http://www.vatican.va/archive/ hist_councils/ii_vatican_council/documents /vat-ii_cons_19651207_gaudium-et-spes_en.html.

Stone, Daniel. "The Green Pope." *Newsweek*, April 16, 2008.

2

Understanding Pope Francis

Argentina, Economic Failure,
and the Teología del Pueblo

Samuel Gregg

SINCE THE ELECTION of Jorge Bergoglio to the Chair of St. Peter in 2013, much has been written about the views of economic life expressed in many of his speeches as well as in his apostolic exhortation *Evangelli gaudium* (2013) and his encyclical *Laudato si'* (2015). Although many have applauded the evident skepticism of free markets and economic globalization that pervades these texts, others, including many practicing Catholics, such as myself,[1] have taken issue with aspects of Pope Francis's critiques of the market economy. These aspects range from significant omissions in his analyses, such as the connection between economic globalization and widespread reductions in poverty, to the manner in which he characterizes the arguments of those who favor economic liberty and its associated institutional supports as the optimal way for realizing worthy Christian goals such as substantially reducing absolute poverty.

Pope Francis's views on these questions did not emerge in a vacuum. Like all those elected to the papacy before him, Jorge Mario Bergoglio brought a range of ideas, convictions, and experiences to the exercise of the teaching office of the papacy, or what the Catholic Church calls its *magisterium*. It would be difficult to understand particular emphases of Saint John Paul II's teaching documents, for example, if readers did not know that Karol Wojtyła lived through the agony of Poland during World War II and experienced the denial of freedom that was part and parcel of two totalitarian systems: National Socialism and Marxism–Leninism. Likewise, it is possible to draw

---

1. See, e.g., Gregg, "Pope Francis and Poverty" and "*Laudato si'*: Well-Intentioned, Economically Flawed."

connections between Wojtyła's particular interests as an academic philosopher who had a strong interest in natural-law theory and the way in which particular ideas are expressed in magisterial documents promulgated during his pontificate, especially some of the early encyclicals.

In the case of Jorge Bergoglio, there is less material to survey in this regard. Bergoglio was not and has never claimed to be a theologian, philosopher, or any other form of academic practitioner. Nevertheless, he has brought a distinct set of experiences and ideas to his role as bishop of Rome and universal pastor of the Catholic Church. The purpose of this paper is to identify and briefly elaborate upon the most pertinent of these experiences and ideas inasmuch as they help to explain some of his comments and observations about the economy. The first concerns the particular political and economic experiences of Argentina from World War II on. The second is the influence of what is known as the *teología del pueblo*, "theology of the people."

From Riches to Rags

There is a saying that is often attributed to Peru's Nobel Prize–winning author Mario Vargas Llosa:

> There are countries that are rich
> and countries that are poor.
> And there are poor countries that are growing rich.
> And then there is Argentina.

In the annals of economic decline, Argentina is invariably cited as the twentieth century's textbook case of how a once wealthy, relatively politically stable country moved over a series of decades to being a nation characterized by profound political instability and a steady march toward economic decrepitude. Born in 1936, Jorge Bergoglio lived virtually all his life until his election as pope through this transformation. It is reasonable to suggest that witnessing the effects of this change would affect some of Pope Francis's thinking about economic questions. This is not to claim that there is an immediate and traceable cause-and-effect relationship. Nor am I implying that Pope Francis reflects on economic matters solely through the lens of Argentina's twentieth-century economic ups and downs. To claim that these experiences had no impact whatsoever on the pope's outlook would, however, be a dubious proposition.

The sad economic history of twentieth-century Argentina is well documented. A particularly comprehensive and succinct survey is outlined in Mauricio Rojas's short book *The Sorrows of Carmencita: Argentina's Crisis in a Historical Perspective* (2002). For our purposes, two dimensions of this decline are especially significant. The first is the phenomena of Peronism and its economic expressions. The second is the failure of the economic liberalization program upon which Argentina embarked in the early 1990s: this program resulted in the financial crisis of 1998 to 2001, from which, it is arguable, Argentina is still recovering.

Perón, Peronism, and the Path of Economic Nationalism

Pope Francis is often described as a Peronist when it comes to his political and economic views. This label, however, is not immediately helpful in understanding him inasmuch as Peronism is not a simple movement to interpret. There are, for instance, left-wing and right-wing forms of Peronism, a division that erupted into open and violent conflict in the 1970s in the lead-up to the outbreak of the leftist Montonero insurgency (which combined Marxist and left-wing Peronist elements), a military coup d'état that overthrew President Isabel Perón in 1976, and the Dirty War as the army moved to eliminate an extremely violent and widespread insurgency and deployed extremely brutal methods in doing so. Another complicating factor is that Juan Perón himself adopted a range of positions at different points of his political career.

Despite these complications, broad features of Peronism are relatively simple to identify.[2] In the first place, Peronism has always been reliant on charismatic leaders. All Peronist presidents of Argentina, whether Perón himself or, more recently, Néstor and Cristina Kirchner, have invested considerable resources in developing a cult of personality. This emphasis on "the leader" reflects a second dimension of Peronism, which is populism and the type of

---

2. For comprehensive explanations of these characteristics, see Brennan, *Peronism and Argentina*.

populist rhetoric that goes along with populist movements. Peronist movements have typically sought to appeal to "the people," especially those from working-class and lower-middle-class backgrounds, against the interests of the elite. In Argentina, this orientation meant a hostile view of, among others, employers, the financial sector, and those perceived as adhering to liberal and conservative constitutional principles. To this extent, Peronism relies heavily on an us-versus-them rationale: workers against the middle class, Argentines against foreigners, trade unions against employers, and so on.

Part of this logic plays out in a third feature of Peronism: nationalism of the political and economic type. By the early 1950s, Perón had implemented economic nationalist policies such as intense state-directed industrialization and import-substitution programs, which were accompanied by efforts to minimize foreign investment. The latter goal was realized primarily through the nationalization of British-owned infrastructure and banks. This nationalization is associated with Peronists' tendency to see foreign investment and companies as exploiters and extractors rather than as sources of income and capital for the host nation.[3] Peronism is also characterized by what might be called the economics and policies of clientelism, underlain and often justified by reference to corporatist theory. From its beginning, Peronism has involved creating large constituencies of supporters through disbursement of state largesse, whether in the form of direct welfare payments or government jobs. At the same time, Peronism relies on corporatist organizational theory in which people are corralled into groups recognized by the government, which then seeks to coordinate "capital" and "labor" in ways that promote the common good.

In 1949, Juan Perón oversaw Argentina's adoption of a new corporatist-inclined constitution. He then proceeded to push the policies articulated in this constitution even deeper into the economy. His government forced trade unions, businesses, universities, journalists, and even high school students into state-controlled associations. The associated doubling of public-sector employees, Rojas stresses, "triggered a development that was to lead to one of Argentina's severest problems, namely growing corruption and a contest for

---

3. See Rojas, *The Sorrows of Carmencita*, 49–97.

privilege."[4] Not surprisingly, much business activity ceased being directed by consumer demand and was instead focused on pursuing political favors.

Argentine society became deeply polarized politically between 1946 and 1955 as Perón pursued us-versus-them politics: the pursuit was so extreme that in a speech delivered on August 31, 1955, he called for the killing of any one of his supporters to be met by the killing of five opponents of Peronism. Nineteen days later the Argentine military, with the support of the Catholic Church, removed Perón from power. Successive governments, however, did little to dismantle the economic structures he had put in place, not least because of fears of working-class unrest.[5]

The effects of Perón's agenda as a set of economic policies are well documented. It resulted not only in a redistribution of wealth to the working classes (thus cementing wage earners' loyalty to Perón and the Peronist movement) but also in diminishing exports, declining competitiveness as Argentine industry and agriculture were sheltered behind tariffs, an outflow of foreign capital, rampant inflation, and significant underperformance in per capita gross domestic product (GDP) vis-à-vis other nations. With regard to the latter, Argentina went from having one of the highest incomes per capita in the late 1800s to being nearer the middle of international rankings. In 1890 and 1900, for instance, Argentina's GDP per capita was almost equal to that of Germany. Today, it is less than half as high.[6]

For much of Jorge Bergoglio's life, Peronists were not in control of the government. Peronist political parties were often banned or dissolved by military and civilian governments. That said, however, there is little question that Peronism still commanded the allegiance of millions of Argentines. Pope Francis appears to have some affinity for the types of political culture associated with Peronism, especially the notion that the state should express the ideas and priorities of ordinary people—a point I elaborate when I discuss the influence of *la teología del pueblo* on the pope's thought.

---

4. Ibid., 74.

5. Ibid., 63–76.

6. Van Zanden et al., *How Was Life?*

Free Markets and the Argentine Experience

Although Peronism has certain identifiable characteristics, it is also marked by the type of ideological fluidity often associated with dependence on a charismatic leader. This fluidity is highlighted by the fact that Argentina's effort to pursue a free-market liberalization program was presided over by a Peronist president, Carlos Menem, from the late 1980s on.[7] The program ended, however, in the financial crisis that gripped Argentina from 1998 to 2002, a period in which the archbishop of Buenos Aires was Cardinal Jorge Mario Bergoglio, S.J.

When Menem was elected to office, he was confronted with recession and hyperinflation. Jettisoning traditional Peronist policies, Menem engaged in the wide-scale privatization of many state-owned industries; sought to end subsidies, reduced tariffs, and other forms of protectionism; and, above all, set a fixed one-to-one exchange rate between the U.S. dollar and the new Argentine peso. The program itself was portrayed specifically as one of economic liberalization, especially by Menem's fourth minister for the economy, Domingo Cavallo. Argentina itself was presented as the new posterchild for the benefits of free markets. Between 1990 and 1998, for example, per capita income grew by almost 40 percent, and the Argentine economy was 50 percent larger in 1998 than it was in 1990.[8]

Over time, however, more and more problems with the economic liberalization program surfaced, some of which owed much to the fact that the program was not as free market as many supposed. In the first place, efforts to liberalize the highly regulated labor market were blocked by Argentina's Congress and powerful Peronist trade unions in the mid-1990s, which made it more difficult for Argentina to address its high unemployment levels. The unemployment problem was worsened by the fact that many privatized former state companies laid off large numbers of workers, thereby increasing levels of poverty and extreme poverty, the former reaching approximately 35 percent of the Buenos Aires population by October 2001—approximately

---

7. Rojas, *The Sorrows of Carmencita*, 97–139.
8. Ibid., 111.

1.5 million people—and the latter approximately 12 percent of the Buenos Aires population.[9,10]

Privatization also acquired a bad image in the Menem years. In the first four years of Menem's administration, approximately sixty large publicly owned companies were sold off, and close to eight hundred public properties were sold. Efficiency of services increased, but people were now also charged real costs, which had formerly been hidden by subsidies. The whole process of selling off was also immediately marked by corruption scandals involving politicians, which destroyed the legitimacy of the privatization program in many Argentines' eyes.[11]

Overshadowing Argentina's move toward a free market was the fact that government spending did not substantially decrease (and was fueled by the need to meet the increasing costs of social security, pensions, and unemployment insurance),[12] while public and private indebtedness continued to grow.[13] The straight jacket established by convertibility meant that the government could not embark on measures (such as devaluation) that might have addressed the debt problem. Given the memories of hyperinflation and the fact that the government had invested so much of its credibility in breaking the back of inflation, it was difficult for the government to end convertibility. With international and domestic investors losing confidence in Argentina's capacity to meet its debt obligations, loans to and investment in Argentina increasingly dried up.

Much more could be said about Argentina's experience with what was perceived to be a thorough-going effort to liberalize the Argentine economy. For our particular purposes, however, what matters is the fact that it ended in what Argentines today call their "Great Depression." This outcome inevitably

---

9. Ibid., 128.

10. Poverty is defined here in the terms used by the then Argentine Central Bureau of Statistics: the relation between available income and the cost of a certain quantity of goods and services judged necessary for tolerable living. Extreme poverty is defined as an income that does not give access to an acceptable calorie intake for an adult person (2,700 calories per day).

11. Rojas, *The Sorrows of Carmencita*, 115–17.

12. Ibid., 131.

13. Ibid., 122.

created a jaundiced view of free markets among a population already skeptical of the merits of liberal economies thanks to the powerful influence of Peronism. *Neoliberalismo,* as free-market economics is called in Latin America, continues to carry very negative connotations in Argentina across all sectors of society, including the Catholic Church. One may dispute, of course, the accuracy of this understanding of the nature of a free-market economy and economic globalization. What is not in doubt is that this negative view *is* the image of market economies that prevails in much of Latin America and among many Latin American Catholics.

That Pope Francis in part shares this view is evident from a small book, *Diálogos entre Juan Pablo II y Fidel Castro* (1998), that Bergoglio coordinated or compiled in the aftermath of John Paul II's visit to the Communist dictatorship in 1998 and as the Argentine economic crisis began to unfold. The book shows not only that Bergoglio was at the time of publication deeply critical of communism and socialism, especially in terms of the social damage inflicted by these systems, but also that the future pope disliked *neoliberalismo,* going so far as to say that "no one can accept the precepts of neoliberalism and consider themselves Christian."[14,15] Specifying that he was not opposed to economic productivity or the capital accumulation that is a prerequisite for growth, he criticized what he called "the spirit that has driven capitalism, utilizing capital to oppress and subject people, ignoring the human dignity of workers and the social purpose of the economy, distorting the values of social justice and the common good."[16] Neoliberalism, he added, "brings about unemployment, coldly marginalizing those who are superfluous," and "corrupts democratic values by alienating from them the values of equality of social justice."[17]

On one level, such a critique of capitalism is not unusual in some Catholic social thought and even manifested itself in some earlier social encyclicals, especially *Quadragesimo anno* by Pius XI (1931). That said, some of the language employed in Diálogos and some of the specific issues it highlighted—most

---

14. Bergoglio, *Diálogos entre Juan Pablo II y Fidel Castro,* 7.

15. All translations are mine unless otherwise noted.

16. Bergoglio, *Diálogos entre Juan Pablo II y Fidel Castro,* 7.

17. Ibid.

notably unemployment—reflect the Argentine crisis of the 1990s. Moreover, the contrast between Bergoglio's reflections on capitalism in this book and John Paul II's reflections in his third social encyclical, *Centesimus annus* (1991), are significant.[18] Although John Paul did critique a form of capitalism, *Centesimus annus* made it clear that capitalism properly understood was not simply an economic system that worked better from the standpoint of utility but also part and parcel of a free society and an arena in which people could realize important virtues. On a moral level, by contrast, Bergoglio in 1998 appeared to see fewer redeeming features in a capitalist economic system and to be more skeptical of the market economy's capacity to create real opportunities for human flourishing.

La Teología del Pueblo

During his time as archbishop of Buenos Aires, Cardinal Jorge Bergoglio was censorious, sometimes outspokenly so, of aspects of the populist presidencies of Néstor and Cristina Kirchner. But in July 2015, Pope Francis appeared with Bolivia's left-populist president Evo Morales before the Second World Meeting of Popular Movements. The speech Francis delivered at this meeting had more than a populist edge to it in terms of content and rhetoric. The same may be said of his address to the participants at the (first) World Meeting of Popular Movements in October 2014.

In the numerous addresses, press conferences, and interviews Francis has given since becoming pope, it is difficult to find any criticism of left-populist policies that comes close to matching his impassioned denouncements of market economies. Likewise, Jorge Bergoglio's critiques of the Kirchner regimes were not directed so much at the populist dimension but at generic problems such as the corruption and unemployment that are characteristic of but not specific to populist regimes. What is consistent across all these remarks and statements by Bergoglio as archbishop, cardinal, and pope is an emphasis on *el pueblo*.

The stress on "the people" owes something to particular intellectual currents that have marked Latin American Catholicism since the late 1960s,

---

18. See especially paragraphs 30 and 42 of *Centesimus annus*.

most notably *la teología del pueblo*. The origins of this theology are found in the Second Vatican Council's Dogmatic Constitution on the Church, *Lumen gentium* (1964). In this text, one way in which the council described the church was as "the People of God." As stated in *Lumen gentium*, the phrase "the People of God" expresses the ideas that "[i]n the beginning God made human nature one" and that "all men are called by the grace of God to salvation."[19] The stress is thus on universality—not on sectionalism.

This language acquired rather different meaning in the Latin America of the late 1960s. In the case of Marxist versions of liberation theology, the idea of *el pueblo de Dios* was subsumed into the rationale of class conflict: "the people" against the oppressors, the proletariat against the bourgeoisie, dissenting theologians against the church hierarchy, and so on. A somewhat different take was adopted in what is known as the *teología del pueblo*. This school of thought was developed primarily by three Argentine priests—Rafael Tello, Lucio Gera, and the Jesuit Juan Carlos Scannone—and it certainly influenced Jorge Bergoglio, S.J., from the 1970s on.[20]

The first thing to note about the *teología del pueblo* is that it rejects Marxist categories. As Scannone commented in an interview in 2011, the main difference between his position and that of the Marxist liberationists is that his theology "has used neither Marxist methodology for analyzing reality nor categories taken from Marxism."[21] Another prominent characteristic of the *teología del pueblo* is its deep respect for the popular piety expressed in phenomena such as veneration of local saints, public processions, localized religious art, and specific prayers that draw upon the experience and history from which the prayer emerged. In practical terms, the *teología del pueblo* has inspired many priests and religious to live in and serve the slums of Buenos Aires.[22] Significantly, the *teología del pueblo* has never expressed hostile views of the church's teaching authority, let alone portrayed that authority as an instrument of class oppression. Unlike prominent liberation theologians such

19. Second Vatican Council, *Lumen gentium*, 13.
20. See Scannone, "Papa Francesco y la *teología del pueblo*."
21. Armato, "Teología del pueblo: Parla il gesuita Juan Carlos Scannone."
22. See, e.g., Vedia, "Curas Villeros."

as Leonardo Boff or Jon Sobrino, S.J., no "people theologian" has found his writings subject to investigation by those charged with maintaining the orthodoxy of Catholic teaching on matters of faith and morals.

The *teología del pueblo* does, however, take "the people" as its primary reference point, and it is unclear if "the people" is defined precisely in the same way that Vatican II understood the concept of "the People of God." Gera, for instance, specifically identified *el pueblo* as the "marginalized and scorned majority" in Latin America.[23] This characterization would seem at odds with *Lumen gentium*'s use of the phrase "the People of God" to underscore universality. What Gera's interpretation meant for those Latin American Catholics who were not on society's margins seems unclear.

Unlike Marxists, the theologians promoting *la teología del pueblo* do not believe that *el pueblo* need a Leninist-like vanguard of middle-class intellectuals to lead them out of the darkness. If anything, the *teología del pueblo* is skeptical of *all* elites. In an article published in a collection of essays about Latin American theologies, for example, Scannone wrote that "[w]e must denounce the elitism in the area of knowledge that we now find among the enlightened elites of both the left and the right."[24] This would include, for instance, not just the Argentine liberal and conservative constitutionalists who were Peronism's strongest intellectual opponents but also Marxist thinkers. The people theologians argued instead that the church's focus should be upon *el pueblo:* not so much as a class but rather as the master of their own destiny, liberating themselves over time and without recourse to armed struggle. *El pueblo* are also understood as a cultural reality and movement that show the church how to live the faith. In this sense, *el pueblo* functions as a type of hermeneutical key that allows us to better understand the truth of Catholic faith. "Either theology," Gera wrote, "is the expression of the People of God or it is nothing."[25] In this connection, the people are seen as possessing a special type of prophetic charism, one that is theirs by virtue of their membership in the people of God.

---

23. Gera, "Cultura y dependencia, a la luz de la reflexion teología," 91.
24. Scannone, "Theology, Popular Culture, and Discernment," 201.
25. Gera, "Cultura y dependencia, a la luz de la reflexion teología," 93.

But Who Are the People?

Viewed from this standpoint, the *teología del pueblo* allowed the church to underscore its option for the marginalized and poor without taking sides in the interminable conflict between the Left and the Right that dominated Latin America throughout the Cold War, which often erupted into violence. Notwithstanding this neutrality, however, the *teología del pueblo* has its own problems.

In the first place, there are unanswered theological questions. The manner in which the *teología del pueblo* is presented as a type of hermeneutical key, for example, is somewhat reminiscent of the consistent Catholic teaching that the body of the faithful cannot err on questions of faith and morals. "The faithful," however, in Catholic doctrine are not identified with a specific group in a particular place who happen to have a great deal in common culturally. The term refers to the communion of the living faithful and the dead faithful, a group that transcends differences of material wealth, social class, and even historical period.

A second difficulty is that the *teología del pueblo* was conceived in a political culture soaked in Peronism, a movement that also emphasized the importance and insights of "ordinary people" and that was always much more popular among Argentina's poor, working class, and lower middle class than other political movements. In his biography of Pope Francis, Austen Ivereigh points out that "[a]lthough a non-Peronist could in theory support people-theology. Its adherents were natural Peronists. They identified with the popular Catholic nationalist tradition, as opposed to a liberal, conservative, or socialist viewpoint, and saw their task as walking with the Peronists as the expression of the people."[26] Ivereigh also notes that some people theologians were close to various Peronist movements and that one, Ernesto López Rosas, S.J., even wrote at length on Peronism's Christian values.[27] For people theologians, Peronism was a type of mechanism that gave political expression to the values they associated with *el pueblo*.

Yet, as we have seen, Peronism as a political movement and as a set of specific policies has been a major source of Argentina's economic problems since

---

26. Ivereigh, *The Great Reformer*, 113.

27. See, e.g., López Rosas, "Valores cristianos del Perónismo."

the mid-1940s. Even today, plenty of *el pueblo* in Buenos Aires's *villas miserias* maintain saintlike images of Juan and Eva Perón in their houses and apparently do not see the link between Argentina's precipitous decline and Peronist populism, a blind spot evidenced by the fact that many of them continue voting for Peronist parties and leaders.

The problem for the *teología del pueblo* is that it has difficulty criticizing populist movements such as Peronism that make the people their primary reference point because of the special status accorded to "the people" in this theology and the emphasis it places on the people's wisdom. That difficulty underscores yet another difficulty: the *teología del pueblo* embodies the weaknesses of any set of ideas that makes *el pueblo* its main reference point.

Take, for instance, the reality that you are likely to find different views on numerous subjects among any group denoted as *el pueblo*. Recognizing this multiplicity becomes more difficult if millions of individuals are simply placed into one catch-all category. Then there are the questions surrounding who qualifies as a member of *el pueblo*. If *el pueblo* consist primarily of those on the margins of life, as Gera seemed to suggest, what does this imply for those who are not living in a slum? Does their social and economic status mean that they are somehow "nonpeople" or even "antipeople"? To put the matter another way: Do those who escape poverty or leave the slums cease to be part of the people? Moreover, if those who escape poverty are no longer part of the people, as understood by people theologians, then why would one want the people to escape relative poverty and become part of the middle class? It is also worth considering that if societies are to be free, they require not only restraints on elites' ability to run roughshod over everyone else but also acceptance that preserving and promoting freedom, rule of law, and social justice rightly understood actually require *restraints on the will of the people*. Such a notion is hard to integrate into the *teología del pueblo*'s understanding of the people, not least because it could be dismissed as elitism.

Another difficulty with the internal logic of *la teología del pueblo* is that although those who live on life's margins often possess insights that escape the attention of elites, it is also probable that some of the ideas flourishing among *el pueblo* are simply wrong in terms of facts or reasonability. Not every thought circulating on what Pope Francis often calls life's peripheries is reasonable or coherent. We know, for example, from the Christian scriptures that large numbers of Christ's first followers came from the margins of first-century Judean and Galilean society. Yet the Gospel of John (6:15) also relates that at one point many of them made the error of wanting to make Christ an earthly king.

It may well be, for example, that some Catholics who qualify, from the standpoint of the *teología del pueblo,* as members of "the people" hold that intentional abortion is sometimes acceptable, despite the Catholic Church's teaching that intentional abortion is never a morally licit choice. Or, in another example, some members of *el pueblo* believe that state collectivization of property is a necessary and even good goal despite (1) the clear evidence that such a policy invariably ends in tears and consistent Catholic teachings against economic collectivization. With regard to both questions, it is not immediately clear that the *teología del pueblo* has a way of distinguishing the people's insights from the errors in fact, logic, and doctrine that may be circulating among the people.

Pope Francis and People Theology

It would not be accurate to say that Pope Francis identifies as a people theologian. His respect and even sympathy for this theological outlook is, however, well established. In his time as provincial of the Jesuits in Argentina and as archbishop of Buenos Aires, some of his speeches and a great deal of his practical pastoral work reflected the priorities of the *teología del pueblo.* In the 1970s, for instance, Bergoglio would give retreats in which he sought to distinguish ideologies such as liberalism and Marxism from Christian hope in that the latter is found in the faith of ordinary people.[28] In a speech to Argentine Jesuits in 1974, for instance, he urged his fellow Jesuits to put ordinary people first by embracing ordinary people's ideas, hopes, and worries instead of following revolutionary ideologies.[29]

In practical terms, Bergoglio sent Jesuits to live in those areas that were especially poor. As archbishop of Buenos Aires, he consistently sent diocesan priests to establish missions in those areas. This endeavor involved not only

---

28. See Ivereigh, *The Great Reformer,* 115.
29. See Bergoglio, "Apertura de la Congregación Provincial XIV."

building churches but also encouraging the development of what might be called "bottom-up" economic development, ranging from building schools and vegetable gardens in the barrios to combatting drug abuse and working directly with groups such as drug addicts and prostitutes.[30]

Strong endorsements of this way of proceeding may be found in the two speeches Pope Francis gave to the first and second World Meeting of Popular Movements. "I have seen first-hand," he stated at the second meeting in July 2015, "a variety of experiences where workers united in cooperatives and other forms of community organization were able to create work where there were only crumbs of an idolatrous economy. . . . Recuperated businesses, local fairs and cooperatives of paper collectors are examples of that popular economy which is born of exclusion and which, slowly, patiently and resolutely adopts solidary forms which dignify it. How different this is than the situation which results when those left behind by the formal market are exploited like slaves!" The speech stressed the importance of rootedness in that which is local and the need for governments to "make it their responsibility to put the economy at the service of peoples" by "the strengthening, improvement, coordination and expansion of these forms of popular economy and communitarian production."[31]

Such language and emphases reflect the *teología del pueblo*. These statements are also accompanied by very critical comments about the formal economy, many of which are reminiscent of Peronist ideas and preoccupations. Referring at the second meeting, for instance, to "the new colonialism," Pope Francis commented that "[a]t times it appears as the anonymous influence of mammon: corporations, loan agencies, certain 'free trade' treaties, and the imposition of measures of 'austerity' which always tighten the belt of workers and the poor." He also spoke of "the tyranny of mammon," the manner in which "the unfettered pursuit of money rules," and how "certain interests" manage "to take over, to dominate states and international organizations." Then there was the pope's stress upon the need to look into the eyes of "the endangered *campesino*, the poor laborer, the downtrodden native, the homeless family, the persecuted migrant, the unemployed young person."[32] On

30. See, e.g., Ivereigh, *The Great Reformer*, 180–86.
31. Francis, Address to the Second World Meeting of Popular Movements.
32. Ibid.

one level, the rhetoric of this address reflects the classic Christian emphasis upon the need to encounter Christ in the person of the poor and marginalized. But it is also very reminiscent of Juan Perón, his wife, Eva Perón, and contemporary Peronist leaders.

Conclusion

Much more might be said about the background to many of Pope Francis's pronouncements on economic matters that have puzzled many in economically developed countries. It is also the case that popes' views often change as a result of their being placed in a position where they need to transcend the specifics of their background because they are now head of a truly global entity. Moreover, issues or developments may occur that require otherwise unanticipated responses that mark a break from previous patterns of thought. With regard to capitalism, for instance, John Paul II's first two social encyclicals, *Laborem exercens* (1981) and *Sollicitudo rei socialis* (1987), focused on criticizing aspects of this economic system, though without condemning it outright, as is the case with Catholic teaching about communism and socialism. The collapse of Communist political and economic systems across central and eastern Europe between 1989 and 1990 meant that Catholic social teaching had to engage the question of capitalism's acceptability in a more comprehensive manner than had been done before.

In the case of Pope Francis, these factors appear, at least for the moment, not to be operative. Although substantial criticisms were made of the economic analysis and language in *Evangelii gaudium* (2013), the economic claims made in *Laudato si'* (2015) suggest that these earlier critiques did not result in any significant shifting of the pope's perspective on economic issues. Perhaps Francis's views will change over the course of his papacy. Nonetheless, the ideas he has expressed do appear to echo many aspects of the Argentine experience as well as particular theological emphases. It may well be that Pope Francis considers these insights and concerns to be more universally applicable than others may realize. It may also be the case that the pope regards these concerns as important factors operative in the life of Argentine and Latin American Catholicism that deserve a wider hearing in a church that he and others may believe to be too much influenced by western Europe and the experience of developed economies with regard to economic issues. In that sense, two long-term questions are (1) whether Catholic social teaching and Catholic social thought will more generally assume, under the influence of what Francis emphasizes, a different trajectory and (2) the extent to which these ideas and experiences are indeed universally applicable. The answers to those questions, I suspect, will be found in the next pontificate.

References

Armato, Alessandro. "Teología del pueblo: Parla il gesuita Juan Carlos Scannone." *Mission Online*, November 1, 2011, Speciale 5. At http://www.missionline.org /index.php? l=it&art=4170.

Bergoglio, Jorge, S.J. "Apertura de la Congregación Provincial XIV." In *Meditaciones para religiosos*, 101–20. Buenos Aires: Ediciones Diego de Torres, 1982.

———. *Diálogos entre Juan Pablo II y Fidel Castro*. Buenos Aires: Editorial de Ciencia y Cultura, 1998.

Brennan, James P., ed. *Peronism and Argentina*. Wilmington, Del.: Scholarly Resources, 1998.

Francis. *Evangelli gaudium* (authorized English translation). Vatican City: Libreria Editrice Vaticana, 2013. At http://w2.vatican.va/content/francesco/en/apost _exhortations/ documents/papa-francesco_esortazione-ap_20131124_evangelii -gaudium.html.

———. Address to Participants in the World Meeting of Popular Movements. October 28, 2014. At https://w2.vatican.va/content/francesco/en/speeches/2014/october /documents/ papa-francesco_20141028_incontro-mondiale-movimenti-popolari .html.

———. Address to the Second World Meeting of Popular Movements. July 9, 2015. At http://w2.vatican.va/content/francesco/en/speeches/2015/july/documents /papa-francesco_20150709_bolivia-movimenti-popolari.html.

———. *Laudato si'* (authorized English translation). May 24, 2015. Vatican City: Libreria Editrice Vaticana. At http://w2.vatican.va/content/francesco/en/encyclicals /documents/ papa-francesco_20150524_enciclica-laudato-si.html.

Gera, Lucio. "Cultura y dependencia, a la luz de la reflexion teología." *Stromata* 30, nos. 1–2 (January–June 1974): 90–99.

Gregg, Samuel. "Pope Francis and Poverty." *National Review*, November 26, 2013.

———. *"Laudato si'*: Well-Intentioned, Economically Flawed." *American Spectator*, June 19, 2015. At http://spectator.org/63160_laudato-si-well-intentioned -economically-flawed/.

Ivereigh, Austen. *The Great Reformer: Francis and the Making of a Radical Pope*. New York: Picador, 2015.

John Paul II. *Laborem exercens* (authorized English translation). Vatican City: Libreria Editrice Vaticana, September 14, 1981. At http://w2.vatican.va/content /john-paul-ii/en/encyclicals/ documents/hf_jp-ii_enc_14091981_laborem -exercens.html.

———. *Sollicitudo rei socialis* (authorized English translation). Vatican City: Libreria Editrice Vaticana, December 30, 1987. http://w2.vatican.va/content/john-paul-ii /en/encyclicals/ documents/hf_jp-ii_enc_30121987_sollicitudo-rei-socialis.html.

———. *Centesimus annus* (authorized English translation). Vatican: Libreria Editrice Vaticana, May 1, 1991. At http://w2.vatican.va/content/john-paul-ii/en /encyclicals/documents/ hf_jp-ii_enc_01051991_centesimus-annus.html.

López Rosas, Ernesto, S.J. "Valores cristianos del Perónismo." *Revista CIAS*, no. 234 (August 1975): 7–30.

Pius XI. *Quadragesimo anno* (authorized English translation). Vatican City: Libreria Editrice Vaticana, May 15, 1931. At http://w2.vatican.va/content/pius-xi/en /encyclicals/documents/ hf_p-xi_enc_19310515_quadragesimo-anno.html.

Rojas, Mauricio. *The Sorrows of Carmencita: Argentina's Crisis in a Historical Perspective*. Translated by Roger G. Tanner. Kristianstads, Sweden: Timbro, 2002.

Scannone, Juan Carlos, S.J. "Theology, Popular Culture, and Discernment." In *Frontiers of Theology in Latin America*, edited by Rosino Gibellini, 153–170. Maryknoll, NY: Orbis Books, 1979.

———. "Papa Francesco y la *teología del pueblo*." *Razón y Fe* 271, no. 1395 (2014): 31– 50. At http://www.encuentromundi.org/wp-content/uploads/2015/02/Bergoglio -y-teologia-del-pueblo.pdf.

Second Vatican Council. *Lumen gentium: Dogmatic Constitution on the Church*. 1964. At http://www.vatican.va/archive/hist_councils/ii_vatican_council/documents /vat-ii_const_19641121_ lumen-gentium_en.html.

Van Zanden, Jan Luiten, Joerg Baten, Marco Mira d'Ercole, Auke Rijpma, Conal Smith, and Marcel Timmer. *How Was Life? Global Well-Being since 1820*. Paris: Organization for Economic Cooperation and Development, 2014.

Vedia, Mariano de. "Curas Villeros." *Vida Nueva*, 1, no. 11 (2013): 9–15.

3

Uneven Playing Fields
Markets and Oligarchy
Gabriel X. Martinez

Introduction

PERHAPS NO PARAGRAPH in Pope Francis's apostolic exhortation *Evangelii gaudium* attracted as much international attention as paragraph 54, which begins:

> [S]ome still defend the theories of "trickle down," which suppose that all economic growth, favored by market freedom, manages to provoke by its own power greater equity and social inclusion in the world. This opinion, which has never been confirmed by the facts, expresses an artless and naïve trust in the goodness of those who hold economic power and in the sacralized mechanisms of the ruling economic system. Meanwhile, the excluded continue waiting.[1]

For writing these words, the pope was accused of being a Marxist and of having a blinkered Argentine view. However, the contention of this chapter is that when people criticize paragraph 54 of *Evangelii gaudium*, they read it backwards. The pope does not mean to criticize rising prosperity and economic liberty in general: Francis takes for granted the tradition of Catholic social teaching that has assessed the free market amply, viewing it as ambiguous but highly promising. What Francis criticizes instead is the use of a theory to justify indifference: the view that eventually the poor will be alright if we just leave them alone; the market will take care of them.

The critics believe that the pope is criticizing statements like this one by Bill Clinton: "We have to reaffirm unambiguously that open markets are the

---

1. Francis, *Evangelii gaudium*, 54, author's translation.

best engine we know of to lift living standards and build shared prosperity."[2] The critics think that the pope is against the American experience and the free market system. For example, writing in *National Review* in response to Francis, Michael Novak said, "'Trickle-down' is not an apt description of what has happened here [in the United States]; rather, what has been experienced is wealth 'welling up from below.'"[3] But this disagreement comes from a misreading of *Evangelii gaudium*. Pope Francis, indeed, would agree that American prosperity has not been a result of wealth "trickling down"—sustained, broadly shared prosperity is not built from the top down. Even more deeply, he is not concerned with describing the process of economic growth and development in the United States at all. He is not attempting a description, much less a criticism, of the sources of the high levels of income of democratic-capitalist societies. Rather, what Francis is addressing is our lack of concern: our indifference towards very large concentrations of economic and political resources with a limited group of powerful individuals (and the resulting exclusion of others), in the hope that eventually, somehow, the poor will benefit. The pope is concerned with a politics of indifference to injustice, not with the theoretical or practical advantages of this or that other economic system.

This chapter intends to explain three key aspects of paragraph 54 of *Evangelii gaudium* and describe the economic evidence and theory that supports it. First, the pope is concerned that market competition takes place on an uneven playing field. Second, a society marked by oligarchy cannot simply trust in free-market economic reforms to bring about inclusion: it is very much in the self-interest of a narrow economic and political elite to lobby for policies that benefit them. Focusing exclusively on the "free economy" third of Catholic philosopher Michael Novak's tripartite system of economic freedom, rule of law and inclusive politics, and a moral/cultural system based on virtue[4] only frees the hands of the already powerful and does nothing for the poor. Third, there is no factual evidence that high levels of inequality eventually benefit the poor.

2. William J. Clinton, Remarks to the World Economic Forum in Davos, Switzerland, January 29, 2000, quoted in Dollar and Kraay, "Growth is Good for the Poor," 195.

3. Novak, "Agreeing with Pope Francis."

4. Novak, *The Spirit of Democratic Capitalism*.

Economics: Market Competition and Level Playing Fields

Pope Francis has insisted that *Evangelii gaudium* must be read in the context of Catholic social teaching. The most immediate context is the teaching of John Paul II, which includes the much-celebrated proclamation of the "right to economic initiative" as a fundamental human right:[5] "the denial of this right, or its limitation in the name of an alleged 'equality' of everyone in society, diminishes, or in practice absolutely destroys the spirit of initiative, that is to say the creative subjectivity of the citizen."[6]

The free market has important benefits. It gives agents incentives to satisfy needs and in so doing, to use resources optimally, reduce costs, and expand possibilities, without a government's grandiose plans or the calculations of a rational social engineer. The modern business economy encourages people to work with each other in freedom and commutative justice. It encourages us to "foresee both the needs of others and the combinations of productive factors most adapted to satisfying those needs," to organize, plan, take risks, to be diligent, industrious, prudent, reliable, faithful, and courageous.[7]

A good market, like a good game of sports, allows us to see who is the better team, and in the market we measure excellence in terms of being able to satisfy real human needs while using society's resources frugally and intelligently. A market competitor imbued with the spirit of the game aims to serve customers' needs better by providing a better product and producing it with better methods, by making its benefits better known and more accessible, and by pricing it so that it truly reflects both the cost of producing it and the benefit to be received from it. It requires ingenuity, foresight, ability to see the big picture, perseverance, and courage. The profit statement is the scorecard: "When a firm makes a profit, this means that productive factors have been properly employed and corresponding human needs have been duly satisfied."[8]

In ideal circumstances, the free market generates allocative efficiency (as the marginal benefit of the last unit produced is equal to its marginal cost,

---

5. John Paul II, *Sollicitudo rei sociallis*, 15, 42.

6. Ibid., 15.

7. John Paul II, *Centesimus annus*, 32.

8. Ibid., 35.

society optimally devotes its resources to the satisfaction of human wants) and productive efficiency (no resources are wasted or left unused, and output is produced at its minimum average total cost). A good way to conceptualize the ideal circumstances of market competition is to think of the free and fair play between two evenly matched teams that reveals true excellence. If through virtue and joy one carries the day, we celebrate, justly, the fact that the free market is such an engine of human prosperity and, yes, of human fulfillment.

In the ideal, abstract system that informs our ideology and political advocacy, market competitors face each other as approximate equals, as in sports or board games. They find themselves on a level playing field, made so by clean-slate starting positions, similar starting endowments, a pre-set rule book, and impartial referees. Therefore, much turnover is expected: last year's champion may be this year's worst team. As an example, one can point out that only one of the thirty companies in the 1896 Dow Jones Industrial Average is still on it (General Electric). Inasmuch as reality approaches the ideal abstraction, all that is required for everyone to have a fair shot is for the rule makers to get out of the way.

One way to characterize such a society is to call it an "inclusive society."[9] In such a society, people are free to pursue the vocations that fit their talents because they live and work on a level playing field. There being no massive disparities of relative resources, luck and effort are able to overwhelm whatever differences there may be between market participants, and there is a reasonable assumption that satisfying people's needs at the lowest cost will be rewarded with success. Inequalities are neither so small to discourage effort nor so large as to make effort pointless.[10] Because "inclusive economic institutions require secure property rights and economic opportunities not just for the elite but for a broad cross-section of society," the state must be able to perform its role as "the enforcer of law and order, property, and contracts, and often as the key provider of public services."[11] This requires that no one be so rich as to be able to take over the state, nor so poor as to be effectively excluded from participation.

---

9. Acemoglu and Robinson, *Why Nations Fail.*

10. Leo XIII, *Rerum novarum*, 15.

11. Ibid., 75–76.

In reality, market players do not begin with clean-slate starting positions and identical starting endowments. It is the nature of the game that market incumbents start out with access to established distribution and supply channels, are more attractive employers than other firms, and can provide their employees with higher-quality and more abundant capital. A market incumbent can take advantage of this position to, say, price products below cost to drive out entrants, buy them up before they become a threat, or limit their access to suppliers. Market incumbents can sometimes agree not to compete for customers or for employees (see, for example, Rajan and Zingales[12] and Zaller[13]). In addition, market incumbents will seek and be sought out by politicians willing to sell influence. Naturally, incumbents want to advocate for laws that benefit them (for example, they will make it harder for new businesses to start) and will try to tip the scales of the system of enforcement and adjudication—it is just smart business.

The spirit of the game of market competition also requires personal habits of self-restraint and self-denial. It is the natural tendency of winners to want to continue winning, and to use whatever means they have at their disposal, fair or foul. It takes fortitude and a certain kind of abnegation to want to win fair and square by simply providing better products at a lower cost.

Winners, if not endowed with such levels of virtue, try to protect their position and ensure future victories by muscling competitors out of the way, changing the rules, or directing public energies to their benefit (say, spending initiatives, tax changes or abatements, new legislation, or other ostensibly market-friendly reforms). The free market is threatened by those who covertly or overtly change the nature of the game by regulatory capture (that is, changing rules or their enforcement to favor themselves), or by designing market liberalization to allow them to operate without rules or effective adjudication of claims. The goal of this kind of "business smarts" is to ensure easy victories, perhaps with lip service to the free market and competitiveness.

In short, when economic resources are highly concentrated so that market incumbents are able to guarantee that rules and market pressure prevent "entry of new businesses and [do not] allow people to choose their careers,"

---

12. Rajan and Zingales, *Saving Capitalism from the Capitalists.*
13. Zaller, "Silicon Valley Companies Sued Over Agreements."

then markets do not resemble level playing fields. Economic exclusion and concentration feed into political systems where "the distribution of power is narrow and unconstrained," and instead of being an impartial referee, the state is at the service of "those who can wield this power . . . to set up economic institutions to enrich themselves and augment their power at the expense of society."[14]

The competition that Pope Francis or John Paul II[15] have in mind in their critiques is a world in which entrants with limited political, social, and economic resources coexist with middle-sized firms and with behemoths with enormous human, physical, and financial resources and with unlimited access to the corridors of power. Winning today makes it easier to win tomorrow. Of course, luck and effort and unusual ability always play a role, but insofar as resources (e.g., technical skill, analytical ability, physical and mental health, tools, financing) are necessary for production and successful competition, those who have resources are more competitive and by degrees become entrenched winners.

Conversely, it is a world in which losing today makes it difficult to compete tomorrow. A system that gives primacy to knowledge and organizational ability excludes those who lack the knowledge, the resources, or the skill. The result is a two-tiered society. As Tyler Cowen[16] and Charles Murray[17] warn regarding the United States, society as a whole has benefited tremendously from the "knowledge economy," and those who possess that knowledge lead lives of high quality. But a large segment of the population is caught in a vicious cycle where having lacked access to that knowledge in the past means being stuck in low-wage, low-skill jobs from which exit is improbable.[18] Moreover, the "excluded" lead lives with lower social capital and family stability, fail to acquire good study and work habits, commit crimes and are punished more frequently, go to church less often, and see little hope for a way out.[19]

---

14. Acemoglu and Robinson, *Why Nations Fail*, 75 and 80.

15. Cf. John Paul II, *Centesimus annus*, 34.

16. Cowen, *Average Is Over*.

17. Murray, *Coming Apart*.

18. Cowen, *Average Is Over*.

19. Murray *Coming Apart*.

Politics and Culture:
"An Artless and Simple-Minded Trust in the Powerful"

Put no trust in princes (Psalm 146:3)

In *Evangelii gaudium*, Pope Francis warns: "In this game, the powerful benefit at the expense of the weak, and so a large part of the population is excluded and marginalized: without work, without opportunities, without a way out.[20]

Before we accuse him of socialism, consider that in an article in the *Washington Post*, Charles Koch (no socialist, to be sure) voiced agreement with attacks on:

> a political and economic system that is often rigged to help the privileged few at the expense of everyone else, particularly the least advantaged. . . . we have a two-tiered society that increasingly dooms millions of our fellow citizens to lives of poverty and hopelessness. . . . many corporations seek and benefit from corporate welfare while ordinary citizens are denied opportunities and a level playing field. . . .
>
> Democrats and Republicans have too often favored policies and regulations that pick winners and losers. This helps perpetuate a cycle of control, dependency, cronyism and poverty in the United States. These are complicated issues, but it's not enough to say that government alone is to blame. Large portions of the business community have actively pushed for these policies.[21]

Government overreach is not the only threat to free markets. When an economy is characterized by a large accumulation of economic resources by a few, who also hold a large portion of the levers of political power and who use this political power to protect their wealth, it is no longer appropriate to think of it as a "free market." The proper academic term, with a long intellectual history, is "oligarchy." Societies as diverse as ancient Athens and Rome, medieval Europe, Indonesia and the Philippines, the United States and Singapore are oligarchies of various shapes.[22]

---

20. Francis, *Evangelii gaudium*, 53, author's translation.
21. Koch, "Charles Koch."
22. Winters, *Oligarchy*, 6–7.

The free market depends on open and fair competition, on a level playing field, but it is a natural human propensity that people with economic power will seek political power and that people who have political power will use it to increase their wealth. In a "political and economic system that is often rigged to help the privileged few at the expense of everyone else, particularly the least advantaged,"[23] those privileged few will actively engage in the defense of their wealth and income through political power or monopoly position. It betrays inexperience with the ways of the world to believe that those who hold economic power will simply deny themselves and play nice or that they will not do what they can to protect themselves from market competition.

While market incumbents want to remove rules that restrict their own entry into new markets, they tend to take a dim view of competition. As a concrete example, using the *Doing Business Database*,[24] consider a very unequal country such as Honduras, where the top 10 percent of income earners earn about 43 percent of total income while the bottom 20 percent earn only 2.8 percent of total income. There it takes twelve separate procedures and fourteen days to start a business, and fulfilling the regulatory requirements costs almost 40 percent of a person's average annual income. In contrast, consider a less unequal country such as Slovenia, where the top 10 percent of income earners earn about 20 percent of total income and the bottom 20 percent earn almost 10 percent of total income. There it takes only two procedures and six days to start a business, and the regulatory requirements impose no financial cost.

The following graphs provide tentative evidence. They show the relation between an index for the ease of starting a business across the world (from the World Bank's Doing Business database[25]) against two measures of inequality.

- When plotted against the share of income earned by the top 10 percent of earners, the "starting a business" index exhibits a clear negative relation: the more income earned by the top tenth, the lower the index is; that is, the harder it is to start a business.

- When plotted against the share of income earned by the bottom 20 percent of earners, the "starting a business" index exhibits a clear positive

23. Koch, "Charles Koch."
24. World Bank, *Doing Business*.
25. Ibid.

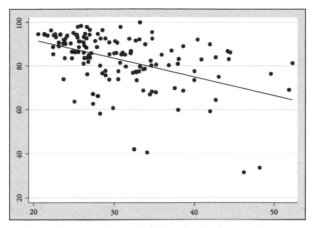

Figure 1. Income Share Held by the Highest 10 Percent
Source: World Bank, *Doing Business: Measuring Business Regulations.*

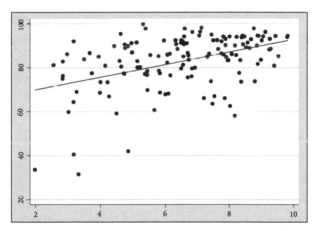

Figure 2. Income Share Held by the Lowest 20 Percent
Source: World Bank, *Doing Business: Measuring Business Regulations.*

relation: the more income earned by the bottom fifth, the easier it is to start a business.

It is hard to establish the direction of causality. Arguably, in unequal countries the very rich defend their position by making it difficult to become a competitor. In the opposite direction, restricting business entry will protect incumbents and produce greater inequality. In all probability, causation runs both ways: incumbent-protecting behavior and inequality are mutually reinforcing.

Why do market incumbents raise obstacles in the way of new entrants? Ultimately, their fear is that competition will put downward pressure on profits, which may reveal that the market incumbent is not, in fact, serving the needs of its customers and/or using society's resources optimally.

> To widen the market and to narrow the competition, is always the interest of the dealers [owners of capital]. To widen the market may frequently be agreeable enough to the interest of the public; but to narrow the competition must always be against it, and can serve only to enable the dealers, by raising their profits above what they naturally would be, to levy, for their own benefit, an absurd tax upon the rest of their fellow-citizens.[26]

As Pope Francis says, it is not true that "economic growth, favored by the free market, leads on its own" to the welfare-optimizing outcome[27] because winners entrench themselves into oligarchies. When an economy exhibits the characteristics of an oligarchy, much political energy will be devoted to "wealth defense."[28] That is, oligarchs will get involved in politics, directly or through surrogates, in order to direct economic activity (which may be sold to the public as "free economic activity") so that it enhances or at least does not "threaten the essentials of wealth defense and accumulation by oligarchs."[29]

Proposals from the winners of market competition are rarely unbiased, as Adam Smith argued:

> The proposal of any new law or regulation of commerce which comes from this order [of merchants and manufacturers], ought always to be listened to with great precaution, and ought never to be adopted till after having been long and carefully examined, not only with the most scrupulous, but with the most suspicious attention. It comes from an

---

26. Smith, *The Wealth of Nations*, 278.
27. Francis, *Evangelii gaudium*, 54, author's translation.
28. Winters, *Oligarchy*, 6.
29. Wescott, "Review of *Oligarchy*," 744.

order of men, whose interest is never exactly the same with that of the public, who have generally an interest to deceive and even to oppress the public, and who accordingly have, upon many occasions, both deceived and oppressed it.[30]

Behind the pope's statement, one can read a concern with how often electorates in South America, North America, Asia, Africa, Europe, Australia and the Pacific have been sold promises of radical social transformation to come from embracing market-liberalizing proposals, and in the absence of accompanying political and cultural reforms. Perhaps somewhat unfairly, this agenda has come to be summarized as "the Washington Consensus," that is, the views held in the early 1990s by the US Treasury, the International Monetary Fund, the World Bank, and the most prestigious think-tanks of the United States capital.[31] These reforms, which can be summarized as macroeconomic stabilization, deregulation, privatization, trade opening, and financial liberalization, were implemented (partially or fully) across the world.[32]

Economic freedom and rational government are undoubtedly desirable. Why, then, be concerned? Acemoglu and Robinson note that democratic-capitalist reforms, in order to be successful, must generate concrete, short-term benefits to an identifiable set of political actors, while operating in a broad coalition against the background of a history of supportive institutions.[33] To implement market-friendly reforms, reformers and their political backers must see themselves as standing to benefit from competition and free entry and exit and creative destruction. For example, Acemoglu and Robinson note that England's seventeenth century Glorious Revolution worked because of the "merchants and businessmen [who wished] to unleash the power of creative destruction from which they themselves would benefit" and because England had a centuries-old tradition of putting limits on those who held economic power.[34] That is, successful inclusive reform is a close thing: a well-designed

---

30. Smith, *The Wealth of Nations*, 278.
31. Williamson, "What Washington Means by Policy Reform."
32. Williamson, *Political Economy of Policy Reform*.
33. Acemoglu and Robinson, *Why Nations Fail*, 362–363.
34. Ibid., 362.

and well-funded reform needs to share the benefits broadly enough, quickly enough; and there must be a history (supported by a credible structure and a strong culture) of forcing winners to "play by the rules of the game," that is, to accept the verdict of the market and to decline to use political power for personal advantage.

However, market liberalization (removing rules and regulations) is not, per se, unfriendly to market incumbents. It can benefit them, depending on the incumbents' political power and economic position at the time of the reform. Acemoglu and Robinson chronicle a multitude of attempted reforms in which market incumbents gain political power and keep the ability to design the new rules, especially when there is little history of keeping the economically or politically powerful in check.[35] If those who hold economic power start out from a strong enough economic position, where they do not need to share the benefits broadly, they may well benefit from and seek market liberalization that will expand opportunities that only they are in a position to exploit. As Bates indicates, "Politicians are likely to come to trust those technocrats whose policies [of macroeconomic stabilization, market liberalization, and economic opening] enhance the economic fortunes of key constituents and thus their own political fortunes as well."[36]

Suppose, then, that a market-liberalizing policy is proposed. Market incumbents hold political and economic power and thus their support is necessary. Their influence is so pervasive that the support of others is not needed, and there is little history or culture of putting limits on the holders of economic power. They are in a position to design the reform and to be harmed (or to benefit) from alternative designs. Is it not "an artless and naïve trust in the goodness of those who hold economic power"[37] to believe that the reform will not be biased in their favor? Insofar as one of the objectives of oligarchs (those who hold economic power) is to protect their social and political position and their exclusive access to resources, it is remarkable that we should simply trust that the invisible hand will be able to defeat the very visible power of those who hold it.

---

35. Acemoglu and Robinson, *Why Nations Fail*, 362.

36. Bates, "Comment," 32.

37. Francis, *Evangelii gaudium*, 54.

Trickle down theories

Against the preceding arguments, one may answer that while today some may benefit from large accumulations of economic and political resources, market freedom will ensure that the benefits will eventually become diffused across society. This can be taken to be the claim of "trickle down" theories: that distributing income more unequally (or tolerating highly unequal distributions) will eventually help the poor.[38] As the rich accumulate, they consume and create jobs, the economy grows, and as long as market participants are unconstrained, the poor benefit. Therefore, the possession of great wealth and purchasing power by a few (perhaps in the face of great material deprivation by the many) should not be a cause of concern. The "theory" would predict that

(A) periods of great income inequality should be followed by an acceleration of economic growth and

(B) economic growth, of its own power and without any specific design or social intention, would eventually raise the incomes of the poor.

Hundreds if not thousands of academic papers have tried to test (A) and have not found any conclusive relation between inequality and growth—as Pope Francis said, the link "has never been confirmed by the facts."[39] Some find a positive relation, some a negative relation, depending on whether levels of inequality or changes in inequality are considered, and depending on the time frame,[40] some find no clear relation. Within poor countries, some find that more inequality is associated with more growth,[41] others find that it is associated with less growth: the opposite is true in rich countries, where more inequality is associated with less growth in some studies and with more growth in others.[42]

With respect to (B), there is abundant evidence of a high correlation between economic growth and the average incomes of the poorest fifth of society.

---

38. Cf. Sowell, *Basic Economics*, 516.

39. Francis, *Evangelii gaudium*, 54.

40. Cf. Berg and Ostry, "Inequality and Unsustainable Growth."

41. Barro, "Inequality and Growth in a Panel of Countries."

42. Brueckner and Lederman, *Effects of Income Inequality on Aggregate Output*.

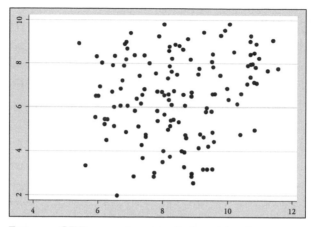

Figure 3. GDP per capita, 2014 (in logarithms)

Source: World Bank, *World Development Indicators*, 2016

While one can read this as evidence that economic "growth is good for the poor"[43] strong correlation does not establish causation. The evidence does not tell us whether sustained economic growth is a cause of, a result of, or simply correlated with improvements in income at the bottom of the distribution.[44]

Economic growth, however, is harder to sustain if it takes place in the context of income inequality. Berg and Ostry find that the degree of inequality is associated with the duration of an economic expansion[45]: a 10-percentile increase in inequality reduces the duration of a growth spell by 50 percent.[46] Economic growth that is based on inequality ends in crises,[47] which hurt the poor more.[48] This is empirical support for the pope's suggestion that top-down policies fail at producing both economic growth and social inclusion.

A huge literature has gone into trying to identify the policies (market-friendly or interventionist) that guarantee that the benefits of economic growth are shared with the poor. There simply seems to be no correlation between the

---

43. Dollar and Kraay, "Growth Still Is Good for the Poor."

44. Rodrik, "Growth versus Poverty Reduction."

45. Berg and Ostry, "Inequality and Unsustainable Growth."

46. Ibid.

47. Glaeser, *Does Economic Inequality Cause Crises?*

48. Halac and Schmukler, "Distributional Effects of Crises."

income share of the poor and the level of GDP per capita, even after controlling for a large number of plausible factors.

The most thorough analysis belongs to Dollar, Kleineberg, and Kraay,
who do not find that "market-friendly" variables (financial development, trade
openness, financial openness, inflation rate, government budget deficits, life
expectancy, population growth, civil liberties and political rights, political
stability and absence of violence) have much of an effect in predicting whether
economic growth will be shared by the poor.[49] Neither do most "redistribu-
tionist" variables (primary enrollment rates, public spending on health and
on education). Only the share of agriculture is found to be correlated with
poverty reduction:[50] "This reflects the reality that many of the poor in developing countries work in agriculture, so that faster growth in this sector is likely
to disproportionately benefit the poor."[51]

In short, there is no conclusive empirical, research-based evidence that a
growing disparity in income distribution eventually helps the poor, whether
in a market context or outside of it. In that sense, the trickle-down theory,
as Francis says, "has never been confirmed by the facts." Indeed, Michael
Novak argues,

> It takes a lot more than economic growth to make a system "equitable."
> It takes the rule of law, the protection of natural rights, and the Jewish/
> Christian concern for the widow, the orphan, the hungry, the sick,
> the imprisoned — in short, effective concern for all the vulnerable
> and needy.[52]

Conclusion

When people criticize paragraph 54 of *Evangelii gaudium*, they read it backwards. *Evangelii gaudium* was not written as economic analysis but as an apostolic exhortation: the main goal of the document is to remove excuses for

---

49. Dollar, Kleineberg, and Kraay, "Growth Still is Good for the Poor," 12–13.
50. See also Danielson, "When Do the Poor Benefit from Growth and Why?"
51. Dollar, Kleineberg, and Kraay, "Growth Still is Good for the Poor," 16.
52. Novak, "Agreeing with Pope Francis."

our indifference. That is, the pope is against "trickle down" explanations that misappropriate the free market as a cover in order to rationalize indifference towards the excluded and the dispossessed.

Insofar as societies are marked by oligarchy, that is, "rigged to help the privileged few at the expense of everyone else"[53] it is not enough to remove rules and regulations and let the oligarch have free rein. It is not the force of gravity, nor mere "economic growth," however attained, that yields inclusion.

Indeed, recommending free markets to a society marked by oligarchy is to offer them a poisonous combination. It is to the advantage of the already powerful that we focus exclusively on economic liberalization and assume that the other requirements of a free society will take care of themselves, as has been the experience of countries across the world, North, South, East, and West.

References

Acemoglu, Daron and James Robinson. *Why Nations Fail: The Origins of Power, Prosperity, and Poverty*. New York: Crown Business, 2012.

Barro, Robert J. "Inequality and Growth in a Panel of Countries." *Journal of Economic Growth* 5 no. 1 (2000): 5–32.

Bates, Robert H. "Comment." In *Political Economy of Policy Reform*, edited by John Williamson. Washington, D.C.: Institute for International Economics, 1994.

Berg, Andrew and Jonathan Ostry. "Inequality and Unsustainable Growth: Two Sides of the Same Coin?" *International Organisations Research Journal* 8, no. 4 (2013): 77–99.

Brueckner, Markus and Daniel Lederman. "Effects of Income Inequality on Aggregate Output." *World Bank Policy Discussion Paper 7317*, 2015.

Cowen, T. *Average Is Over: Powering America Beyond the Age of the Great Stagnation*. New York: Penguin, 2013.

Danielson, Anders. "When Do the Poor Benefit from Growth and Why?" *Tanzanian Economic Trends* 17, no. 2 (2004): 5–15.

Dollar, David, Tatjana Kleineberg, and Aart Kraay. "Growth Still Is Good for the Poor." *European Economic Review* 81 (January 2016): 68–85.

53. Koch, "Charles Koch."

Dollar, David, and Aart Kraay. "Growth is Good for the Poor." *Journal of Economic Growth* 7, no. 3 (2002): 195–225.

Francis. *Evangelii gaudium*. November 24, 2013. At http://w2.vatican.va/content /francesco/es/apost_exhortations/documents/papa-francesco_esortazione-ap _20131124_evangelii-gaudium.html

Glaeser, Edward L. "Does Economic Inequality Cause Crises?" *Economicx* (blog), *New York* Times, December 14, 2010.

Halac, Marina and Schmukler, Sergio. "Distributional Effects of Crises: The Financial Channel." *Economia* 5, no. 1 (2004): 1–67.

John Paul II. *Sollicitudo rei sociallis*. December 30, 1987. Available at http://w2.vatican .va/content/john-paul-ii/en/encyclicals/documents/hf_jp-ii_enc_30121987 _sollicitudo-rei-socialis.html

———. *Centesimus annus*. May 1, 1991. Available at http://w2.vatican.va/content /john-paul-ii/en/encyclicals/documents/hf_jp-ii_enc_01051991_centesimus -annus.html

Koch, Charles G. "Charles Koch: This Is the One Issue Where Bernie Sanders Is Right." *Washington Post*, February 18, 2016.

Leo XIII. *Rerum novarum*. May 15, 1891. Available at http://w2.vatican.va/content /leo-xiii/en/encyclicals/documents/hf_l-xiii_enc_15051891_rerum-novarum .html

Murray, Charles. *Coming Apart: The State of White America, 1960–2010*. New York: Crown Forum, 2012.

Novak, Michael. "Agreeing with Pope Francis." *National Review*. December 7, 2013.

———. *The Spirit of Democratic Capitalism*. Lanham, M.D.: Madison Books, 1982.

Rajan, Raghuram, and Luigi Zingales. *Saving Capitalism from the Capitalists*. New York: Crown Business, 2003.

Rodrik, Dani. "Growth versus Poverty Reduction: A Hollow Debate." *Finance & Development* 34, n. 4 (2000). Available at http://www.imf.org/external/pubs/ft /fandd/2000/12/rodrik.htm

Smith, Adam. *The Wealth of Nations: An Inquiry into the Nature and Causes*. Edited by Edwin Cannan. Chicago: University of Chicago Press, [1776] 1976.

Sowell, Thomas. *Basic Economics, Third Edition*. New York: Basic Books, 2007.

Wescott, Clay G. Review of *Oligarchy*. *Governance* 24, no. 4 (2011): 742–745.

Williamson, John. "What Washington Means by Policy Reform." In *Latin American Adjustment: How Much Has Happened?*, edited by John Williamson. Washington, DC: Institute for International Economics, 1990.

Williamson, John, editor. *Political Economy of Policy Reform*. Washington, DC: Institute for International Economics, 1994.

Winters, Jeffrey A. *Oligarchy*. New York: Cambridge University Press, 2011.

World Bank. *Doing Business: Measuring Business Regulations*. Accessed on October 4, 2016. Available at http://www.doingbusiness.org/

————. *World Development Indicators*. 2016. Accessed on October 4, 2016. Available at http://databank.worldbank.org/data/reports.aspx?source=world-development-indicators

Zaller, Anthony. "Silicon Valley Companies Sued Over Agreements Not to Hire Competitor's Employees." California Employment Law Report, October 26, 2012. Available at http://www.californiaemploymentlawreport.com/2012/10/silicon-valley-companies-sued-over-agreements-not-to-hire-competitors-employees/

4

Pope Francis, Capitalism, and Private Charitable Giving

Lawrence J. McQuillan and Hayeon Carol Park*

ON MARCH 13, 2013, Jorge Mario Bergoglio, S.J., archbishop of Buenos Aires, Argentina, became Pope Francis, the Roman Catholic Church's 266th bishop of Rome. From the start, the leitmotif of Francis's pontificate has been concern for the poor. The *Boston Globe* noted, "Francis' top priority has been to reach out to the world's poor and inspire Catholic leaders to go to slums and other peripheries to preach."[1] The *New York Times* reported, "Francis has placed the poor at the center of his papacy."[2] Speaking in Santa Cruz, Bolivia, in 2015, Pope Francis said, "Working for a just distribution of the fruits of the earth and human labor is not mere philanthropy. It is a moral obligation. For Christians, the responsibility is even greater: it is a commandment."[3]

Concern for the disadvantaged is reiterated in his book *The Name of God Is Mercy* (2016), his first book as pope: "We have received freely, we give freely. We are called to serve Christ the Crucified through every marginalized person. We touch the flesh of Christ in he who is outcast, hungry, thirsty, naked, imprisoned, ill, unemployed, persecuted, in search of refuge."[4] This statement follows closely his homily on Ash Wednesday of 2014: "Gratuitousness should be one of the characteristics of the Christian, who aware of having received

---

1. Winfield, "Pope Urges Catholics to Reject Idols of 'Money, Success, Power.'"
2. Yardley and Romero, "Pope's Focus on Poor Revives Scorned Theology."
3. Francis, Address at the Second World Meeting of Popular Movements, 3.1.
4. Francis, *The Name of God Is Mercy*, 98.

* This paper developed from our earlier commentary for *Forbes* titled "Pope Francis' Charity Goggles Ignore the Power of Capitalism" (McQuillan and Park 2015). We thank Jonathan Bean, William F. Shughart II, and the editor of this book for helpful comments on earlier drafts. Any errors or omissions are our responsibility.

everything from God gratuitously, that is, without any merit of his own, learns to give to others freely. Today gratuitousness is often not part of daily life where everything is bought and sold."[5]

To his considerable credit, Pope Francis has emphasized the moral responsibility to give to those less fortunate. But a careful review reveals that voluntary private giving is not the charitable "giving" the pope often speaks of. The pope instead emphasizes government redistribution and a larger role for international organizations in facilitating transfers. Unfortunately, the approach he advocates generally results in more human suffering, not less, thus undercutting his call to help the poor.

Pope Francis on Government Redistribution

Pope Francis calls for an expanded role for government redistribution in efforts to alleviate poverty, especially for more government-to-government transfers and more activism by international organizations.

Speaking at the United Nations (UN) in May 2014, Francis said, "A contribution to this equitable development will also be made both by international activity aimed at the integral human development of all the world's peoples and *by the legitimate redistribution of economic benefits by the State.*"[6] He views government redistribution as both legitimate and necessary to combat poverty; thus, his solution includes forcibly redistributing money and wealth from the rich to the poor: "I encourage financial experts and political leaders to ponder the words of one of the sages of antiquity [Doctor of the Church John Chrysostom, a fourth-century saint]: 'Not to share one's wealth with the poor is to steal from them and to take away their livelihood. It is not our own goods which we hold, but theirs.'"[7]

The pope puts much faith in the ability of international organizations such as the UN and its associated agencies to help solve major social problems. Speaking to the UN General Assembly in September 2015, he said, "The

---

5. Francis, Holy Mass, Blessing and Imposition of the Ashes.

6. Francis, Address of Pope Francis to the UN System Chief Executives Board for Coordination; emphasis added.

7. Francis, *Evangelii gaudium*, 57.

history of this organized community of states is one of important common achievements over a period of unusually fast-paced changes."[8]

The pope favors a more active role for international organizations to facilitate government redistribution and to regulate businesses: "The international financial agencies should care for the sustainable development of countries and should ensure that they are not subjected to oppressive lending systems which, far from promoting progress, subject people to mechanisms which generate greater poverty, exclusion, and dependence."[9]

Francis fails to recognize, however, an important difference between government redistribution and private charitable giving. Redistribution of income or wealth by government, whether domestically or internationally, is neither "giving" nor "charity" in the strict sense of these words. Government "giving"—redistribution through domestic welfare programs, foreign aid, or other programs—requires the government first to obtain the money from someone else, either through taxes or borrowing. Because borrowing must be eventually paid for with taxes, government "giving" always requires coercively taking some individual's or some group's income in the form of taxes or wealth, such as land, and giving it to some other individual or group—perhaps those deemed by government officials as more deserving or perhaps those who are merely members of the ruling coalition. The redistribution advocated by Francis appears to violate the commandment "You shall not steal" because government redistribution always and necessarily involves force or coercion.

Redefining charity as an entitlement of the poor ("It is not our own goods which we hold, but theirs") also encourages a war of one class against another and claims by the relative poor to hold "true" property ownership in other people's income (e.g., those who refuse to work living off the labor of those who do work).

In contrast, charitable giving within a capitalist economy is voluntary. Capitalism is first an expression of giving. An entrepreneur succeeds only by satisfying a customer's wants. Capitalism is a competition in giving. To survive and make a profit, the entrepreneur must create wealth, selling goods

8. Francis, Meeting with the Members of the General Assembly of the United Nations Organization, Address of the Holy Father.

9. Ibid.

and services that customers want and are willing to buy in mutually beneficial trades. Workers are rewarded based on their contributions, using their skills, to the happiness and well-being of others.

Charitable giving in a capitalist economy involves the willing transfer of resources acquired through voluntary trade to recipients chosen by the donor. The recipient must also voluntarily agree to accept the transfer. As Robert Whaples observes, true charity "is a mutual exchange between people with equal dignity."[10] Force or coercion is never used, and nobody has a property-right claim on the fruits of another's labor without voluntary agreement.

Whereas private giving is voluntary charity, government "giving"—that is, redistribution—is never a charitable act because it is always rooted in force. Only an act of free will to help those less fortunate is a true act of charity. If a charitable organization were to force people to donate to it, this would be an act of theft, not an act of kindness. And just because people donate to charities on their own does not mean the government should force people to "donate" an amount the government determines. Moreover, democratic state redistribution does not lend consent to such redistribution in comparison to nondemocratic redistribution. The position of a majority regarding charitable activities is not morally superior to the view of the individual, as Jesus stated clearly in Matthew 26:6–13, the Anointing at Bethany. This passage relates the story of a woman who anointed Jesus's feet with expensive perfume, prompting Jesus's disciples to remark that she could have instead given the money spent on the perfume to the poor. But Jesus defended the woman's voluntary charitable decision to help him rather than perform the alternative charitable action that was favored by the majority—the disciples.

It does little, if any, good to force people to "care" for others: it does not make them more compassionate citizens. Forced government transfers actually destroy genuine charity within society. They serve primarily to make people more accepting of the use of force to achieve ends they consider worthy and produce resentment and division among those forced to give to "charitable" endeavors they do not choose to support. Freedom of choice and the exercise of conscience are better suited to making people more compassionate citizens.

---

10. Whaples, Review of *The Philanthropic Revolution*, 611.

Ironically, by supporting government redistribution worldwide, Francis's suggestions result in removing free will from the equation and thus removing true charity or genuine compassion from the act of giving in favor of statist coercion.[11] The high taxes needed to fuel the redistributive state also undermine initiative and the incentives and institutions that drive wealth creation and end absolute poverty (which we discuss more fully later in this essay).

Francis never identifies real-world government programs that best achieve his vision of distributive justice. In this regard, he is guilty of the vice of vagueness, which is no substitute for knowledge and leaves the pope espousing nothing but what he sees as good intentions. Christians have long taught that faith alone is not sufficient for temporal matters such as economics—reason and knowledge are necessary. Indeed, Catholic theologians see faith and reason as complementary,[12] and the phrase *faith and reason* is often associated with Catholic discussions of science, economics, and other "worldly" disciplines.

While Francis calls for a more activist role for governments and international agencies in redistribution, he also makes unrelenting attacks on capitalism.

Pope Francis on Capitalism

Pope Francis frequently lambastes capitalism. In May 2015, he wrote that those who favor the invisible hand of markets suffer from the same mindset that leads to slavery, the sexual exploitation of children, and the abandonment of the elderly.[13] In 2016, standing just across the border from the United States in Ciudad Juárez, Mexico, Francis said that God will hold accountable the "slave drivers" who exploit workers. He alleged that capitalism leads to a "prevailing mentality [that] advocates for the greatest possible profits, immediately and at any cost."[14]

---

11. Mitchell, "Message for the Pope."

12. See, for example, the Franciscan University website Faith and Reason at http://www.faithandreason.com.

13. Francis, *Laudato si'*, 123.

14. Quoted in Pullella and Stargardter, "In Mexican Border City, Pope Criticizes Business 'Slave Drivers.'"

Francis argues that money has become an "idol," reducing people to "simple instruments of a social and economic system."[15] In July 2015, he famously called the "unfettered pursuit of money . . . the dung of the devil."[16] "Unbridled capitalism," he said in 2013, "has taught the logic of profit at any cost, of giving in order to receive, of exploitation without looking at the person."[17] Yet Francis has never said where "unbridled capitalism" actually operates. As noted later, indexes of economic freedom document a great degree of regulatory constraints placed on "capitalists" worldwide. And when governments leave markets alone, social norms—among businesspersons and the broader culture—impose considerable constraints on those who would care only about themselves. Businesspersons have generally learned that the ethic of "profit at any cost" is simply bad for business.

Francis encourages people to oppose the "new colonialism," which he describes as "the anonymous influence of mammon": corporations, loan agencies, free-trade treaties, government austerity measures, and large communications companies.[18]

In his hard-to-find book *Diálogos entre Juan Pablo II y Fidel Castro (Dialogues between John Paul II and Fidel Castro)*,[19] Pope Francis, then Jorge Bergoglio, archbishop of Buenos Aires, wrote a chapter on "the limits of capitalism." He argued that capitalism lacks morals, promotes selfish behavior, increases inequality, and fails to deliver "social justice." Experts consider the book one of the few publications laying out his political and social analysis. These statements are consistent with his involvement, though limited, in liberation theology, a movement that blossomed in Latin America in the 1960s and 1970s.

Liberation theology called for the Catholic Church to involve itself in the political and economic life of the poor by rejecting capitalism as immoral and incompatible with "social justice." It also rejected the idea that private-property rights are inviolable as "natural and inalienable" rights.[20] One of the

---

15. Quoted in Abela, "Pope Francis' Catechism for Economics."

16. Francis, Address at the Second World Meeting of Popular Movements, 1.

17. Quoted in Wooden, "Pope Francis Warns of the Dangers of 'Unbridled Capitalism.'"

18. Francis, Address at the Second World Meeting of Popular Movements, 3.2.

19. Bergoglio, *Diálogos entre Juan Pablo II y Fidel Castro*.

20. Dorner, *Latin American Land Reforms in Theory and Practice*, 20.

central tenets of liberation theology was land reform, specifically taking land from its owners and redistributing it to landless workers, tenants, peasants, and small-plot owners.[21]

Conservatives scorned liberation theology as overtly Marxist, and the Vatican, especially Pope John Paul II,[22] treated it with hostility. Jorge Bergoglio became the leader of the Jesuits in Argentina in 1973 in the middle of this fractious debate.

In 2007, Bergoglio led a meeting of Latin American bishops in Brazil, where they produced a document titled the *Aparecida*,[23] which advanced four key concepts: (1) a missionary drive; (2) the giving of priority to the "new faces of the poor"; (3) liberation theology; and (4) a populist religion.[24] During the initial months of his pontificate, Francis gave a copy of the *Aparecida* to every Latin American head of state he met, including Venezuelan president Nicolás Maduro, who now presides over the world's economic basket case.[25]

Just six months after becoming pontiff in 2013, Francis welcomed as a guest at the Vatican a founding father of liberation theology, Father Gustavo Gutiérrez, whom the Catholic Church's leadership once viewed with suspicion.[26] Gutiérrez is now a respected Vatican visitor, and his writings are praised in the official Vatican newspaper.[27] Cardinal Gerhard Muller, the Vatican's enforcer of doctrine, summed up the reversal under Francis, stating that liberation theology should "be included among the most important currents in twentieth century Catholic theology."[28]

In an interview by the Italian newspaper *La Stampa* in 2015, Francis was asked if Pope Paul VI's views that private property is not an absolute right remain valid. "Not only are they still valid, but the more time goes on, the

---

21. Ibid., 21.

22. Yardley and Romero, "Pope's Focus on Poor Revives Scorned Theology."

23. *General Conference of the Bishops of Latin America and the Caribbean.*

24. Allen, "A Journey to the Roots of Francis' Papacy."

25. Ibid.

26. Vallely, "Liberation Theology, Once Reviled by Church, Now Embraced by Pope."

27. Yardley and Romero, "Pope's Focus on Poor Revives Scorned Theology."

28. Quoted in Vallely, "Liberation Theology, Once Reviled by Church, Now Embraced by Pope."

more I find they have been proved by experience," he said.[29] Francis views forced government redistribution of income and wealth as acceptable and necessary to remedy inequality and to produce more "socially just" outcomes.

History demonstrates, however, that redistribution motivated by "social justice" ultimately leads to totalitarian government, as Nobel laureate economist Friedrich A. Hayek explained many years ago:

> [T]he more dependent the position of the individuals or groups is seen to become on the actions of government, the more they will insist that the governments aim at some recognizable scheme of distributive justice; and the more governments try to realize some preconceived pattern of desirable distribution, the more they must subject the position of the different individuals and groups to their control. So long as the belief in "social justice" governs political action, this process must progressively approach nearer and nearer to a totalitarian system.[30]

Although Francis sidesteps the injustices created by his preferred approach, historian Hilaire Belloc noted the problems inherent in that approach: "I might boldly confiscate and redistribute at a blow. But by what process should I choose the new owners? Even supposing that there was some machinery whereby the justice of the new distribution could be assured, how could I avoid the enormous and innumerable separate acts of injustice that would attach to general redistributions? To say 'none shall own' and to confiscate is one thing; to say 'all should own' and apportion ownership is another."[31]

Francis's primary criticism of market-based economies is his claim that they create injurious income inequality: "Inequality is the root of social ills."[32] Francis views capitalism as an ideology favoring the "absolute autonomy of the marketplace and financial speculation" to produce "a new tyranny" that results in the earnings of the rich "growing exponentially" while the poor

---

29. Quoted in Abela, "Pope Francis' Catechism for Economics."
30. Hayek, *The Mirage of Social Justice*, 68.
31. Quoted in Epstein, Block, and Woods, "Chesterton and Belloc: A Critique," 587–88.
32. Francis, *Evangelii gaudium*, 202.

suffer an income gap "separating the majority from the prosperity enjoyed by those happy few."[33]

"As long as the problems of the poor are not radically resolved by rejecting the absolute autonomy of markets and financial speculation and by attacking the structural causes of inequality, no solution will be found for the world's problems or, for that matter, to any problems," Francis wrote in *Evangelii gaudium*.[34] He has never said where the "absolute autonomy of markets" actually operates, though.

In an interview in 2015, he said, "It is true that in absolute terms the world's wealth has grown, but inequality and poverty have arisen."[35] But international statistics clearly show a profound decline in global poverty levels as market liberalization has spread in recent decades. From 1988 to 2011, the percentage of the world's population living in absolute poverty (with incomes less than $2 per day) fell from 38 percent to 16 percent.[36]

After a long upward trend, global income inequality has declined noticeably in recent years as liberalizing economic reforms around the world have lifted millions out of poverty and contributed to lessening intracountry income inequality in many nations as well. The global Gini value, a common measure of inequality, decreased from 72.2 in 1988 to 67 in 2011, driven largely by China and India.[37] Intracountry inequality has declined significantly in Brazil, South Africa, and Spain.[38]

Francis is thus ignoring some important lessons here regarding capitalism and charity.

Wealth must first be created before it can be given to others. Capitalism is the greatest wealth creator the world has ever seen, lifting billions of people out of abject poverty. The pope's antimarket fervor stands at some distance from the facts.

---

33. Ibid., 56.

34. Ibid., 202.

35. Quoted in "Pope Criticizes Globalization."

36. Milanovic, "We're Experiencing the Greatest Reshuffling of Income since the Industrial Revolution."

37. Milanovic, *Global Inequality*, 76, 121.

38. Ibid., 76, 81.

More than 500 million people in China lifted themselves out of crushing poverty after recent pro-market government reforms allowed unprecedented levels of new investment, new business startups, labor mobility, and trade.[39] China's government allowed economic freedoms to expand there more than in any other Asian country since 1980. As a result, hundreds of millions of people have escaped some of the worst poverty on earth. The same process has been at work in India, which benefited from the rejection of many antimarket philosophies that kept its people desperately poor.[40]

Francis has said that the benefits of the free market have "never been confirmed by the facts."[41] But the facts confirm that countries with freer economies have higher incomes and a better quality of life for the average person than countries with command-and-control economies dominated by politicians who dole out special privileges, sanctions, and redistributive transfers.[42] Compare South Korea to North Korea today or in the twentieth century West Germany to East Germany, Europe to the Soviet Union, Taiwan and Hong Kong to pre-reform China.

Contrast Francis's views with those expressed by Pope John Paul II, who experienced authoritarian socialism firsthand in Poland: "The *free market* is the most efficient instrument for utilizing resources and effectively responding to needs. . . . [Capitalism within the rule of law is] the model which ought to be proposed to the countries of the Third World, which are searching for the path to true economic and civil progress."[43]

About 900 million people live on less than $1.90 a day.[44] Their best hope for a better future is capitalism, which, when allowed to flourish, has lifted more people out of poverty throughout human history than any other system of economic organization. In countries with greater economic freedom, where entrepreneurship thrives and private property is secure, individuals accumulate more wealth and have more to give to others.

---

39. McQuillan, "Judge the Pope's Exhortation by Results, Not Rhetoric."
40. Das, *India Unbound.*
41. Francis, *Evangelii gaudium*, 54.
42. Gwartney, Lawson, and Hall, *Economic Freedom of the World.*
43. John Paul II, *Centesimus annus*, 34 and 42.
44. World Bank, "Poverty Overview."

In contrast, no country has ever achieved self-sustaining prosperity through government redistribution. History teaches that redistribution of money by politicians does not end poverty or create prosperity. It instead fosters dependency, cronyism, and government corruption. Most of the money is squandered, lining the pockets of the politically connected and powerful. People devote their time to capturing the transfers instead of enhancing their productive skills, thereby shrinking the total economic pie (as discussed later).

People are also less likely to give money or time to others when they are living hand to mouth. The greater abundance that capitalism affords makes people more willing to give and allows for increased charitable giving.

Freer economies also encourage a sense of individual compassion toward the disadvantaged rather than promoting the view that it is the government's responsibility to care for them. Historically, Americans did not wait for government or local noblemen to solve problems; they found solutions themselves. Capitalism reinforces the civic responsibilities that Francis promotes so well around the world.

Most large philanthropic organizations in the United States were founded on the wealth of one individual who amassed a personal fortune in a successful business.[45] Whether older organizations such as the Carnegie Foundation, the Ford Foundation, and the Rockefeller Foundation or newer organizations such as the Bill and Melinda Gates Foundation and the Chan Zuckerberg Initiative, these large philanthropic enterprises were created when millionaires and billionaires used the economic freedoms and private-property protections in the United States to build fortunes that they then used to help the disadvantaged.

Andrew Carnegie said famously, "The man who dies thus rich dies disgraced."[46] He would certainly have supported the "Giving Pledge" started

---

45. See Jeremy Beer's *The Philanthropic Revolution* for a discussion on historical differences and tensions between traditional charities and relatively modern philanthropies. The Roman Catholic Church has amassed a fortune as well. The church owns more than eighteen thousand works of art as well as gold, stocks, bonds, helicopters, land, and buildings, including St. Peter's Basilica and the Sistine Chapel. Some estimates peg the church's wealth at more than $300 billion (McQuillan, "Judge the Pope's Exhortation by Results").

46. Carnegie, *The Gospel of Wealth and Other Timely Essays*, 21.

by Bill Gates and Warren Buffett to encourage the world's super-rich to give away more than half of their wealth to philanthropic causes. Francis ignores the fact that capitalism's massive accumulation of personal wealth leads to greater assistance to those less fortunate, especially in the United States.

This assistance is not limited to the super-rich. According to the World Giving Index,[47] Americans rank second per capita worldwide in terms of donating money, volunteering time, and helping strangers. In 2014, U.S. private giving to charitable organizations amounted to $358 billion.[48] Although the composition varies year to year, generally about 15 percent of charitable giving in the United States comes from foundations and 5 percent from corporations. The vast majority comes from individuals, and most of it from small givers at an average amount of about $2,500 per household each year.[49] Individuals annually give nearly five times more than foundations combined.

Private giving produces a societal change that is different in approach from government transfers. The private nature of charity has long been viewed as one of its greatest virtues: it allows charity to stand outside the pressures of public opinion and to engage in projects that governments don't or won't undertake. Because of its often experimental and innovative nature, private charity adds variety and competition to civic life.

By ignoring these positive achievements of market liberalization—especially the decline in absolute, abject poverty—and continuing to push for more state-led redistribution, Francis is not only undermining capitalism but also indirectly reducing people's willingness and ability to help the poor voluntarily through local charitable activities.

Francis has long opposed capitalism—the "economy of exclusion and inequality," as he refers to it[50]—and has long opposed the sanctity of private-property rights, both in income and in wealth.[51] And as demonstrated in the

---

47. Charities Aid Foundation, *World Giving Index 2015*.

48. Charity Navigator, "Giving Statistics."

49. Zinsmeister, "Charitable Giving and the Fabric of America."

50. Francis, *Evangelii gaudium*, 53.

51. There has been a long struggle over economic ideology within the Catholic Church: the Spanish Scholastics (Jesuit "Adam Smiths") versus the medievalists (see Chafuen 2003, which describes the debate among learned Jesuits who advocated free-market economics based on Catholic theology and a rational understanding of human nature and who emphasized the important role private property plays in making people both wealthier and more

next section, his campaign to undercut capitalism and its core institutions of private property and economic freedom also undermines private charitable giving. With the undercutting of private charity, the case for government transfers as a "last resort" becomes easier to make, whether Francis intends it or not.

Popeometrics: Economic Freedom, Property Rights, and Private Charitable Giving

Pope Francis attacks with great fervor the institutions of capitalism. To better understand how these institutions enable and motivate individuals to engage in charitable giving, we use international data to analyze statistically the relationship between private charitable giving and (1) economic freedom and (2) private-property rights.

Data on individual charitable giving around the world come from the World Giving Index by Charities Aid Foundation.[52] Using surveys, the index measures the average percentage of people in each country who donate money, volunteer, or help a stranger in 145 countries representing about 96 percent of the world's population. The three questions asked were: (1) Have you helped a stranger or someone you didn't know who needed help? (2) Have you donated money to a charity? And (3) Have you volunteered your time to an organization?

Data on economic freedom come from the most recent *Economic Freedom of the World* report from the Fraser Institute, which measures the degree to which the policies and institutions of countries are supportive of economic freedom.[53] A summary score ranging from 0 (worst) to 10 (best) for each country's level of economic freedom was constructed for 157 countries by gathering country-specific data on forty-two distinct variables in five broad categories: (1) size of government (i.e., taxes and spending); (2) legal structure and security

---

humane); then the encyclical *Rerum novarum* by Pope Leo XIII (1891) and its follow-up from Pope Pius XI, *Quadragesimo anno* (1931); then the pro-market turn of other Catholics, such as Pope John Paul II and Michael Novak (1982), who traced the Catholic theology of economics and noted its limits; then the return to antimarket Catholicism under Pope Francis. Placed in context, Francis's views are and have been contested within the faith.

52. Charities Aid Foundation, *World Giving Index 2015*.

53. Gwartney, Lawson, and Hall, *Economic Freedom of the World*.

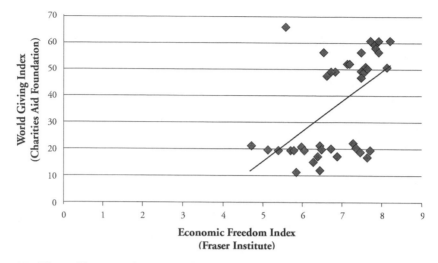

Note: The World Giving Index measures the average percentage of people in each country who donate money, volunteer, or help a stranger in 145 countries. The Economic Freedom Index measures the degree to which the policies and institutions of countries are supportive of economic freedom in 157 countries, with scores ranging from 0 (least supportive) to 10 (most supportive).

Figure 1 data compiled from Charities Aid Foundation, *World Giving Index 2015*, and Gwartney, Lawson, and Hall, *Economic Freedom of the World*.

Figure 1. Economic Freedom and Individual Giving

of property rights; (3) access to sound money; (4) freedom to trade internationally; and (5) regulation of credit, labor, and business.

Data on protections for private-property rights come from the most recent International Property Rights Index compiled by the Property Rights Alliance, which measures the degree to which private property is protected by law in 129 countries.[54] This index scores countries from 0 (least protection) to 10 (most protection) in three main components: the legal and political environment; physical-property rights; and intellectual-property rights. The first component features four subcomponents: judicial independence, rule of law, political stability, and control of corruption. The second component features three subcomponents: property rights, registering property, and ease of access to loans. The third component features three subcomponents: intellectual-property protection, patent protection, and the level of copyright piracy.

54. Levy-Carciente, *International Property Rights Index.*

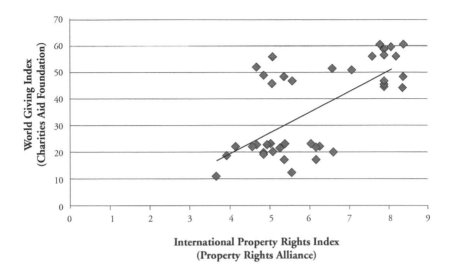

Note: The World Giving Index measures the average percentage of people in each country who donate money, volunteer, or help a stranger in 145 countries. The International Property Rights Index measures the degree to which private property is protected by law in 129 countries, with scores ranging from 0 (least protection) to 10 (most protection).

Figure 2 data compiled from Charities Aid Foundation, *World Giving Index* 2015, and Levy-Carciente, *International Property Rights Index*.

Figure 2. Property Rights and Individual Giving

As the results show, strong institutions of capitalism—economic freedom and private-property rights—increase the rate of private charitable giving. This result suggests that Francis, who favors the attenuation of economic freedom and property rights worldwide, endorses policies that, intentionally or not, undermine private charity.

Analysis of the full data set yields a strong positive relationship between economic freedom and individual giving. The economic-freedom coefficient is large and is statistically significant at the 99 percent confidence level—all by itself, variation in the economic-freedom score explains almost 20 percent of the variation in giving.[55] To remove some of the clutter, figure 1 demonstrates the relationship for the twenty most generous countries and the twenty least

55. Slope ¼ 6.4003; t statistic ¼ 5.56; R-squared ¼ 0.1933; F statistic ¼ 30.91; N ¼ 131 observations.

generous countries.[56] Individuals in countries with more economic freedom have a greater tendency to give to those less fortunate.

Even stronger was the positive relationship between private-property rights and individual giving. Analysis of the full data set reveals that the property-rights coefficient is large and statistically significant at the 99 percent confidence level—all by itself, variation in the property-rights score explains almost a quarter of the variation in giving.[57] Figure 2 demonstrates the relationship for the extreme data points: the twenty most-generous countries and the twenty least-generous countries.[58] Individuals in countries with stronger protections for personal property and wealth accumulation are more likely to give to others.

The ability to create wealth, to secure that wealth, and to transfer it easily to other people are key drivers of private charity. In contrast, government redistribution through taxes and transfer programs shrink total wealth in society. The more the government shifts income around, the less total income there is to redistribute.[59] A poorer society has fewer resources available to help the disadvantaged.

When politicians around the world undercut the institutions of capitalism by raising taxes or assaulting private-property rights, they attack the heart of private charity.

---

56. The twenty most-generous countries that also had an economic-freedom score were Myanmar, New Zealand, United States, Canada, Australia, United Kingdom, Ireland, Netherlands, Sri Lanka, Kenya, Malaysia, Bahrain, Malta, United Arab Emirates, Bhutan, Guatemala, Kyrgyzstan, Norway, Thailand, and Germany. The twenty least-generous countries that also had an economic-freedom score were Slovakia, Democratic Republic of the Congo, Morocco, Czech Republic, Ecuador, Russia, Vietnam, Angola, Armenia, Benin, Chad, Niger, Rwanda, Togo, Greece, Lithuania, Tunisia, Yemen, China, and Burundi.

57. Slope ¼ 4.0282; t statistic ¼ 6.13; R-squared ¼ 0.2493; F statistic ¼ 37.53; N ¼ 115 observations.

58. The twenty most-generous countries that also had a property-rights score were New Zealand, United States, Canada, Australia, United Kingdom, Netherlands, Ireland, Sri Lanka, Malaysia, Kenya, Malta, Norway, Guatemala, Thailand, Germany, Jamaica, Austria, Indonesia, Hong Kong, and Sweden. The twenty least-generous countries that also had a property-rights score were Jordan, Bulgaria, Peru, El Salvador, Egypt, Slovakia, Hungary, Mali, Paraguay, Morocco, Czech Republic, Ecuador, Russia, Vietnam, Benin, Chad, Lithuania, Greece, China, and Burundi.

59. Okun, *Equality and Efficiency*; Smith, "The Cost of Redistributing Wealth"; Hendren, "The Policy Elasticity."

Supporting Literature

Numerous studies confirm the positive relationship between economic freedom and private charitable giving. Researchers have found that higher taxes—that is, less economic freedom—result in less private giving. Greater economic freedom has produced surges in private philanthropy.

Nobel laureate economist Milton Friedman described the close connection between charitable giving and political and economic freedom. He argued that market capitalism and philanthropy go hand in hand and that it was no accident that the nineteenth century, the age of individual cooperation and limited government, "was the period of the greatest private eleemosynary activity in the history of the United States":

> The period of unrestrained, rugged individualism was a period when the modern type of nonprofit community hospital was first established and developed. It was the period of the Carnegie Libraries and their spread through the philanthropy of Andrew Carnegie. It was the period when so many colleges were founded throughout the country. . . . There was no income tax, no deductibility of contributions, so what people spent on charity came out of their pocket and not, as now, largely out of taxes they would otherwise pay. And yet, in every aspect of private charitable activity, it was a boom period.[60]

Friedman argued that philanthropy is a voluntary decision by individuals or by groups of individuals freely coming together to assist others. He articulated the vital connections between economic freedom, a flourishing charitable sector, and a free civil society. The freedoms enjoyed by Americans allowed them to decide how much money to give and to what purposes—the freedom to sustain cherished institutions or to create new ones.

Friedman claimed that the government welfare system, in contrast, "has destroyed private charitable arrangements that are far more effective, far more compassionate, far more person-to-person in helping people who are really, for no fault of their own, in a disadvantaged situation."[61] Government welfare

---

60. Friedman, *Bright Promises, Dismal Performance*, 64–65.

61. Friedman, "Milton Friedman Describes the Welfare State's Effect on Private Charitable Activity."

programs and the taxes imposed to fuel these transfers substitute for and crowd out private charitable activities.

Peter G. Warr provides theoretical support for Friedman's position. Modeling an economy without tax deductions for charitable giving, Warr looked into the effects of progressively raising a lump-sum tax on each donor by one dollar and found that taxing donors induces each to reduce their voluntary charitable donations by exactly the amount of the tax so as to reestablish equilibrium at the margin: "When the response of donors is taken into account these measures result in no net redistribution at all; far from being additional to voluntary redistribution, these taxes merely substitute public [i.e., government] fiscal redistribution for private charity, dollar for dollar."[62]

More recently, in 2015, a study titled *The Effect of State Taxes on Charitable Giving* used econometric analysis to determine the nature and strength of the relationship between state taxes and charitable giving in the United States, apart from the charitable-giving deduction. The researchers concluded: "When all state taxes are considered, a 1 percentage point increase in the total tax burden is associated with a 1.16 percent drop in charitable giving per dollar of state income."[63]

These studies support our earlier finding that economic freedom helps drive private charitable giving. Freer economies supply greater abundance, leaving individuals with more money to give to the charities of their choice. Freer economies also foster a sense of individual moral responsibility toward the poor, resulting in true giving as opposed to forced redistribution by governments.

A larger role for governments, as advocated by Pope Francis, generally crowds out and replaces effective private charity with ineffective and inefficient government redistribution while smothering the individual moral responsibility to help the poor. The next section discusses research that demonstrates overwhelmingly that private charitable giving is effective giving, whereas government transfers are largely ineffective and often counterproductive.

---

62. Warr, "Pareto Optimal Redistribution and Private Charity," 132.
63. Freeland, Wilterdink, and Williams, *The Effect of State Taxes on Charitable Giving*, 1.

The Effectiveness of Voluntary Giving Versus Forced Government Transfers

The long-term effect of any implementation of Pope Francis's recommendations will be to substitute forced government transfers for voluntary private charity, whether Francis intends that effect or not. Research strongly suggests that this substitution results in less effective assistance for the poor and the suffering.

A large body of scholarly research reveals the pitfalls of government redistribution, government-to-government aid, and assistance programs operated by international organizations such as the UN. Nobel laureate economist Angus Deaton studied the behavior of poorer households around the world at a microeconomic level and concluded: "If poverty is not a result of lack of resources or opportunities, but of poor institutions, poor government, and toxic politics, giving money to poor countries—particularly giving money to the *governments* of poor countries—is likely to perpetuate and prolong poverty, not eliminate it."[64]

Deaton and others have cited dozens of examples in which aid has propped up despotic regimes, which merely compounds misery, including in Biafra, Ethiopia, Rwanda, Somalia, and Zaire and on the border of Cambodia and Thailand. Citing work by researcher Alex de Waal, Deaton writes: "Aid can only reach the victims of war by paying off the warlords, and sometimes extending the war."[65]

Deaton instead argues for direct giving and against government foreign aid: "What about bypassing governments and giving aid directly to the poor? Certainly, the immediate effects are likely to be better, especially in countries where little government-to-government aid actually reaches the poor. . . . One thing that we *can* do is to agitate for our own governments to stop doing those things that make it harder for poor countries to stop being poor. Reducing aid is one."[66]

---

64. Deaton, *The Great Escape*, 273–74.

65. Quoted in Swanson, "Why Trying to Help Poor Countries Might Actually Hurt Them."

66. Deaton, "Weak States, Poor Countries."

In some cases, however, foreign governments limit or ban direct private aid to their citizens, including aid from the Catholic Church, whereby they strengthen government channels. In May 2016, Vatican Radio reported: "Venezuela's bishops urged the government of President Maduro to allow the Church to bring in much-needed supplies such as food and medicine. They warned that never before had the country suffered from such an 'extreme lack of goods and basic food and health products' combined with 'an upsurge in murderous and inhuman crime, the unreliable rationing of electricity and water, and deep corruption in all levels of the government and society.'"[67]

The idea of wealthier countries giving government-to-government aid to poorer countries blossomed in the late 1960s as conditions abroad first reached mass audiences on television. Data have suggested, however, that the aid community's claims often were not borne out. Many studies have found no relationship between foreign aid and growth. Peter Boone's frequently cited study "Politics and the Effectiveness of Foreign Aid" (1996) concluded that aid has had no impact on investment and by extension on growth. Boone found that foreign aid does not benefit the poor as measured by improvements in human development indicators; it instead increases the size of government.

Moreover, William Easterly demonstrates convincingly that even as foreign aid into Africa soared during the 1980s and 1990s, African economies performed *worse*.[68] Easterly thus writes in his book *The White Man's Burden,* "Remember, aid cannot achieve the end of poverty. Only homegrown development based on the dynamism of individuals and firms in free markets can do that."[69]

Dambisa Moyo argues in her book *Dead Aid* that during the past fifty years more than $1 trillion in development aid was transferred from wealthy countries to African governments, yet across the continent the recipient countries are worse off. More people in Africa are poor today than in 1990. Misguided development policy is largely to blame. Moyo argues that overreliance on aid has trapped developing nations in a circle of aid dependency, corruption, market distortions, and further poverty, leaving them with nothing but the "need" for more aid.

---

67. "Pope Francis Writes Letter."
68. Easterly, "Can Foreign Aid Buy Growth?"
69. Easterly, *The White Man's Burden,* 368.

Peter Bauer was an early prominent and outspoken critic of foreign aid.[70,71] Bauer objected to the term *foreign aid,* arguing that such "aid" was really intergovernmental subsidies.[72] He argued that the word *aid* implied that the foreign governmental transfers must be helping, when in fact they harmed recipient countries. The money subsidized governments, making them stronger, but the problem in many of these underdeveloped countries was that governments were already too strong and dictatorial, choking off entrepreneurship.

According to Steven Radelet, the most popular criticisms of foreign governmental aid are that aid has enlarged government bureaucracies, perpetuated bad governments, and enriched the elite in poor countries. Despite his overall optimism about foreign aid, Radelet acknowledges that one of the most valid criticisms of aid is that it keeps bad governments in power. Wealthy countries provided large transfers to some of the world's worst dictators, especially during the Cold War, such as Mobutu Sese Seko of Zaire, François ("Papa Doc") Duvalier of Haiti, and Ferdinand Marcos of the Philippines.[73]

In addition to foreign aid, the public sector is less effective than private charity in dealing with natural disasters and domestic poverty. Sixty to eighty cents of each Medicaid dollar provides no benefit to recipients.[74] The inefficiency of government programs explains the estimate by the U.S. Bureau of the Census that total welfare spending is four times the amount that would be needed to lift all Americans currently living in poverty above the poverty line by directly giving them cash.[75]

This result is unsurprising to public-choice scholars. Large government programs that are insulated from competition and financial loss, such as public schools and the U.S. Postal Service, approximate a monopoly, which inevitably leads to inefficiency. The biggest supporters of welfare programs, who lobby for expansion of the programs, are typically the beneficiaries themselves, along

---

70. See Bauer, *Dissent on Development* and *Equality, the Third World, and Economic Delusion.*

71. On Bauer, see Vasquez, "Peter Bauer," and Shleifer, "Peter Bauer and the Failure of Foreign Aid."

72. Friedman and Sowell, "Reflections on Peter Bauer's Contributions to Development Economics," 444.

73. Radelet, *The Great Surge.*

74. Finkelstein, Hendren, and Luttmer, *The Value of Medicaid.*

75. Ferrara, "'Welfare State.'"

with budget-maximizing bureaucrats.[76] The U.S. welfare system has cost $15 trillion since the War on Poverty began in 1964, yet the official poverty rate has declined by less than 4 percentage points.[77] This system is best described as poverty maintenance, not poverty reduction.[78,79]

In contrast, private charities and philanthropic organizations face the reality of hard budget constraints; thus, they must assess accurately who will benefit from aid, what type of assistance best fits each person, and how well activities advance the mission of promoting the recipient's long-term self-sufficiency. This individualized process helps to effectively channel organizations' limited resources and to measure results. Budget-maximizing bureaucrats, in contrast, want ever-expanding caseloads.

James Rolph Edwards found that private charities are three to four times more efficient than government agencies. Analyzing data from Charity Navigator, he found that 70 percent of private charities spend at least seventy-five cents of each dollar on the disadvantaged; 90 percent spend at least sixty-five cents per dollar. In contrast, government agencies typically spend only thirty cents on the poor per welfare dollar.[80]

Regarding natural disasters, a study of Hurricane Katrina relief by William F. Shughart II examined the lethargy of the public sector's response. He argued that the private sector, which has the distribution networks already in place with the organizational structure and equipment required for a smooth operation, has a comparative advantage in easing the suffering of disaster victims. The response to Hurricane Katrina provided strong evidence that the public sector is institutionally incapable of anticipating and responding to catastrophe in a timely manner.[81] More recently in Africa, "a third of Sierra Leone's Ebola budget [is] unaccounted for" and is now thought to have been stolen by government officials.[82]

---

76. Henderson, "The Policy Elasticity."
77. Tanner, *The American Welfare State.*
78. Coyne, *Doing Bad by Doing Good.*
79. In a 2011 working paper, Bruce D. Meyer and James X. Sullivan argue that official U.S. poverty statistics underestimate the actual material well-being of the poor and middle class in America.
80. Edwards, "The Costs of Public Income Redistribution and Private Charity."
81. Shughart, "Katrinanomics."
82. O'Carroll, "A Third of Sierra Leone's Ebola Budget."

Much of the ineffectiveness of government programs to alleviate poverty and ease suffering, both domestically and internationally, can be traced to the "knowledge problem," articulated by Friedrich Hayek in 1945. Hayek pointed out that sensibly allocating scarce resources requires collating knowledge dispersed among many people and that no individual or group of experts is capable of acquiring all that knowledge. In that sense, the market is essential precisely because it allows people to benefit from widely dispersed knowledge. "To act on the belief that we possess the knowledge and the power which enable us to shape the processes of society entirely to our liking, knowledge which in fact we do *not* possess, is likely to make us do much harm," Hayek pointed out again years later.[83]

The knowledge problem provides a framework to understand why private giving is relatively more effective than government programs. Private charity is superior in its ability to be individualized or "personalist": successful charity programs require face-to-face assessments and individual accountability, often tied to spiritual principles, and they capitalize on the advantage of the information available when they take time to know individual recipients and to track outcomes.

In contrast, centrally administered forced government handouts focus on the crowd, typically offer a one-size-fits-all approach that is uniform, imprecise, impersonal, and dehumanizing,[84] and foster a "culture of dependency."[85] In 1935, U.S. president Franklin Roosevelt foreshadowed the dependency problem: "Continued dependence upon relief induces a spiritual and moral disintegration fundamentally destructive to the national fiber. To dole out relief in this way is to administer a narcotic, a subtle destroyer of the human spirit."[86]

Hayek pointed out that the decision regarding whose needs we as individuals make our concern is an essential part of freedom and of the moral aspects of a free society. Therefore, general altruism is meaningless—nobody can care effectively for other people without knowing concrete facts about the specific individuals who need help and without having personal attachment to them or to their plight. Hayek argued that it is one of the fundamental

---

83. Hayek, "The Pretence of Knowledge," 276.
84. Funiciello, *The Tyranny of Kindness.*
85. Murray, *Losing Ground*; Harvey and Conyers, *The Human Cost of Welfare.*
86. Quoted in Payne, "What FDR Knew about Welfare."

rights and duties of a free man to decide what and whose needs appear to him most important.[87]

Ironically, the approach advocated by Pope Francis, in contrast, usurps the rightful moral judgments and personal responsibilities of free people. Doug Bandow observes that, "at its most basic level, real charity doesn't mean giving away someone else's money. As Marvin Olasky has pointed out, compassion once meant to 'suffer with.' Over time it came to mean writing a check. Now it seems to be equated with making someone else write a check."[88] Jesus said people should follow the example of the Good Samaritan, who did not make someone else pay money to a government program, but instead spent his own time and money to help a man in distress.

Many studies have demonstrated that private giving is more effective at helping the poor to achieve long-term self-sufficiency than government redistribution programs, which are inefficient, largely ineffective, and often counterproductive.[89] Based on these findings and our econometric results, Francis is generally wrong to seek a larger role for government in the economy and in charity. The approach he advocates is yet another step toward what the Catholic Church has historically warned against: dismantling civil society and shredding its moral connective tissue.

Conclusion

Since becoming pope in 2013, Francis has called for greater efforts worldwide to reduce poverty, emphasizing government redistribution over voluntary private giving. He defines philanthropy as "working for a just distribution of the fruits of the earth and human labor," and to this end he has called on governments and international organizations to expand the "redistribution of economic benefits by the State." In a nod to liberation theology, the pope

---

87. Hayek, *The Constitution of Liberty.*

88. Bandow, "National Service—or Government Service?," 34.

89. Other examples of counterproductive government programs include unemployment insurance, the minimum wage, food stamps, housing programs, and the crowding out of donations to public institutions of higher learning by state government expenditures (Becker and Lindsay, "Does the Government Free Ride?").

supports government redistribution of income and wealth, sidestepping thorny issues over the use of force in redistribution and what policy tools are preferred.

A parallel narrative by Francis is that capitalism lacks morals, promotes selfish behavior, increases inequality, and does not deliver "social justice." He has criticized "unbridled capitalism" and the "unfettered pursuit of money," yet he has never said where these things actually operate.

Beyond the rhetoric opposing capitalism are recommendations to attenuate private-property rights and economic freedom in order to use the state to redistribute income and wealth to people deemed more worthy of both. Francis is off the mark when he attacks capitalism and promotes a larger role for government in the economy and in charity. His condemnation of capitalism in fact undercuts his call to help the poor.

There is ample evidence that capitalism and its core institutions—private-property rights and economic freedom—are key drivers of private charitable giving. This link is important because private charity is the most effective form of charity for uplifting the poor, whereas government redistribution is inefficient, largely ineffective, and often counterproductive.

Under capitalism, the ability to create wealth, to secure that wealth, and to easily and freely transfer it to other people are vital to the success of private charity. The econometric analyses presented here and elsewhere confirm these results. Economic freedom and private property help drive unbridled individual giving and effective private charity. Freer economies supply greater abundance, leaving individuals with more money to give to the charities of their choice. Freer economies also foster a sense of individual moral responsibility toward the less fortunate, resulting in true giving that comes from compassion as opposed to forced redistribution by governments.

The approach favored by Francis substitutes forced government redistribution for voluntary private giving, whether that is what Francis intends or not. The more the government intervenes in the economy, however, the more voluntary charity declines. Additional taxes, welfare programs, and redistribution shrink the private sector and, along with it, private giving. A poorer society has fewer resources available to help the disadvantaged and leaves the poor with fewer tools to care for themselves. The road to hell and to poverty is paved with good intentions.

As government programs crowd out and replace private giving, they remove the act of free choice and thus sever the link between moral responsibility, genuine compassion, and true giving. By undercutting voluntary charity, the case for government transfers as a "last resort" becomes easier to make, whether Francis intends this or not.

Pope Francis chooses to denigrate capitalism, but his approach leads to declining economies, government corruption, and prolonged human misery. He should instead recognize capitalism as one of the greatest blessings and channel his fervor into unleashing capitalism worldwide to boost effective giving and to encourage governments around the world to expand economic freedom and strengthen private-property rights. These outcomes will help to spur the type of voluntary charity that alleviates human suffering and improves the well-being of those less fortunate around the world.

References

Abela, Andrew V. "Pope Francis' Catechism for Economics." *National Catholic Register*, February 6, 2015.

Allen, John L., Jr. "A Journey to the Roots of Francis' Papacy." *National Catholic Reporter*, July 24, 2013.

Bandow, Doug. "National Service—or Government Service?" *Policy Review* 79 (September–October 1996): 33–36.

Bauer, Peter T. *Dissent on Development: Studies and Debates in Development Economics*. Cambridge, MA: Harvard University Press, 1972.

———. *Equality, the Third World, and Economic Delusion*. Cambridge, MA: Harvard University Press, 1981.

Becker, Elizabeth, and Cotton M. Lindsay. "Does the Government Free Ride?" *Journal of Law and Economics* 37 (April 1994): 277–96.

Beer, Jeremy. *The Philanthropic Revolution: An Alternative History of American Charity*. Philadelphia: University of Pennsylvania Press, 2015.

Bergoglio, Jorge Mario. *Diálogos entre Juan Pablo II y Fidel Castro*. Buenos Aires: Editorial de Ciencia y Cultura, 1998.

Boone, Peter. "Politics and the Effectiveness of Foreign Aid." *European Economic Review* 40 (February 1996): 289–329.

Carnegie, Andrew. *The Gospel of Wealth and Other Timely Essays*. New York: Century, [1889] 1901.

Chafuen, Alejandro A. *Faith and Liberty: The Economic Thought of the Late Scholastics.* Lanham, MD: Lexington Books, 2003.

Charities Aid Foundation. *World Giving Index 2015.* West Malling, UK: Charities Aid Foundation, 2015.

Charity Navigator. "Giving Statistics." 2015. At http://www.charitynavigator.org /index.cfm?bay=content.view&cpid=42.

Coyne, Christopher J. *Doing Bad by Doing Good: Why Humanitarian Action Fails.* Stanford, CA: Stanford University Press, 2013.

Das, Gurcharan. *India Unbound: A Personal Account of a Social and Economic Revolution from Independence to the Global Information Age.* New York: Knopf, 2000.

Deaton, Angus. *The Great Escape: Health, Wealth, and the Origins of Inequality.* Princeton, NJ: Princeton University Press, 2013.

————. "Weak States, Poor Countries." *Project Syndicate,* October 12, 2015.

Dorner, Peter. *Latin American Land Reforms in Theory and Practice: A Retrospective Analysis.* Madison: University of Wisconsin Press, 1992.

Easterly, William. "Can Foreign Aid Buy Growth?" *Journal of Economic Perspectives* 17 (Summer 2003): 23–48.

————. *The White Man's Burden: Why the West's Efforts to Aid the Rest Have Done so Much Ill and so Little Good.* Oxford: Oxford University Press, 2006.

Edwards, James Rolph. "The Costs of Public Income Redistribution and Private Charity." *Journal of Libertarian Studies* 21 (Summer 2007): 3–20.

Epstein, Marcus, Walter Block, and Thomas E. Woods Jr. "Chesterton and Belloc: A Critique." *The Independent Review* 11, no. 4 (Spring 2007): 579–94.

Ferrara, Peter. "'Welfare State' Doesn't Adequately Describe How Much America's Poor Control Your Wallet." *Forbes,* June 23, 2013.

Finkelstein, Amy, Nathaniel Hendren, and Erzo F. P. Luttmer. *The Value of Medicaid: Interpreting Results from the Oregon Health Insurance Experiment.* National Bureau of Economic Research (NBER) Working Paper no. 21308. Cambridge, MA: NBER, 2015.

Francis. Address of Pope Francis to the UN System Chief Executives Board for Coordination. Rome, Consistory Hall, May 9, 2014. At https://w2.vatican.va/content /francesco/en/speeches/2014/may/documents/papa-francesco_20140509 _consiglio-nazioni-unite.html.

————. Address at the Second World Meeting of Popular Movements. Expo Feria Exhibition Center, Santa Cruz de la Sierra, Bolivia, July 9, 2015. At http://w2 .vatican.va/ content/francesco/en/speeches/2015/july/documents/papa-francesco _20150709_bolivia- movimenti-popolari.html.

————. *Evangelii gaudium* (authorized English translation). Vatican City: Libreria Editrice Vaticana, November 24, 2013. At http://w2.vatican.va/content/francesco /en/ apost_exhortations/documents/papa-francesco_esortazione-ap_20131124 _evangelii- gaudium.html.

————. Holy Mass, Blessing and Imposition of the Ashes. Homily of Pope Francis, Basilica of Santa Sabina, March 5, 2014. At http://w2.vatican.va/content/francesco /en/homilies/ 2014/documents/papa-francesco_20140305_omelia-ceneri.html.

————. *Laudato si'* (authorized English translation). May 24, 2015. Vatican City: Libreria Editrice Vaticana. At http://w2.vatican.va/content/francesco/en/encyclicals /documents/papa-francesco_20150524_enciclica-laudato-si.html.

————. Meeting with the Members of the General Assembly of the United Nations Organization, Address of the Holy Father. United Nations Headquarters, New York, September 25, 2015. At http://w2.vatican.va/content/francesco/en /speeches/2015/september/documents/papa-francesco_20150925_onu-visita.html.

————. *The Name of God Is Mercy.* New York: Random House, 2016.

Freeland, William, Ben Wilterdink, and Jonathan Williams. *The Effect of State Taxes on Charitable Giving.* Arlington, VA: American Legislative Exchange Council, 2015.

Friedman, Milton. "Milton Friedman Describes the Welfare State's Effect on Private Charitable Activity." *Free to Choose,* part 4: "From Cradle to Grave." PBS, 1980.

————. *Bright Promises, Dismal Performance: An Economist's Protest.* New York: Harcourt Brace Jovanovich, 1983.

Friedman, Milton, and Thomas Sowell. "Reflections on Peter Bauer's Contributions to Development Economics." *Cato Journal* 25 (Fall 2005): 441–47.

Funiciello, Theresa. *The Tyranny of Kindness: Dismantling the Welfare System to End Poverty in America.* New York: Atlantic Monthly Press, 1993.

General Conference of the Bishops of Latin America and the Caribbean—Aparecida, Concluding Document. Aparecida, Brazil, May 13–31, 2007. At http://www.aecrc .org/documents/ Aparecida-Concluding%20Document.pdf.

Gwartney, James, Robert Lawson, and Joshua Hall. *Economic Freedom of the World: 2015 Annual Report.* Vancouver: Fraser Institute, 2015.

Harvey, Phil, and Lisa Conyers. *The Human Cost of Welfare: How the System Hurts the People It's Supposed to Help.* Santa Barbara, CA: Praeger, 2016.

Hayek, Friedrich A. "The Use of Knowledge in Society." *American Economic Review* 35, no. 4 (September 1945): 519–30.

————. *The Constitution of Liberty.* Chicago: University of Chicago Press, 1960.

————. *The Mirage of Social Justice.* Vol. 2 of *Law, Legislation, and Liberty.* Chicago: University of Chicago Press, 1976.

————. "The Pretence of Knowledge." Prize lecture, Sveriges Riksbank Prize in Economic Sciences in Memory of Alfred Nobel, December 11, 1974. In *The Essence of Hayek,* edited by Chiaki Nishiyama and Kurt R. Leube, 266–77. Stanford, CA: Hoover Institution Press, 1984.

Henderson, David R. "Public Choice and Two of Its Founders: An Appreciation." In *Public Choice, Past and Present: The Legacy of James M. Buchanan and Gordon Tullock,* edited by Dwight R. Lee, 157–67. New York: Springer, 2013.

Hendren, Nathaniel. "The Policy Elasticity." *Tax Policy and the Economy* 30, no. 1 (2016): 51–89.

John Paul II. *Centesimus annus* (authorized English translation). Vatican City: Libreria Editrice Vaticana, May 1, 1991. At http://w2.vatican.va/content/john-paul-ii/en/encyclicals/ documents/hf_jp-ii_enc_01051991_centesimus-annus.html.

Leo XIII. *Rerum novarum* (authorized English translation). Vatican City: Libreria Editrice Vaticana, May 15, 1891. At http://w2.vatican.va/content/leo-xiii/en/encyclicals/ documents/hf_l-xiii_enc_15051891_rerum-novarum.html.

Levy-Carciente, Sary. *International Property Rights Index.* Washington, DC: Property Rights Alliance, 2015.

McQuillan, Lawrence J. "Judge the Pope's Exhortation by Results, Not Rhetoric." *The Beacon* (blog), Independent Institute, January 8, 2014.

McQuillan, Lawrence J., and Hayeon Carol Park. "Pope Francis' Charity Goggles Ignore the Power of Capitalism." *Forbes,* December 22, 2015.

Meyer, Bruce D., and James X. Sullivan. *The Material Well-Being of the Poor and the Middle Class since 1980.* American Enterprise Institute (AEI) Working Paper no. 2011-04. Washington, DC: AEI, 2011.

Milanovic, Branko. "We're Experiencing the Greatest Reshuffling of Income since the Industrial Revolution." *World Post,* July 22, 2015.

————. *Global Inequality. A New Approach for the Age of Globalization.* Cambridge, MA: Belknap Press of Harvard University Press, 2016.

Mitchell, Daniel J. "Message for the Pope: Caring for Poor Isn't Communist, but Advancing Statism Misguided." *CNSNews.com,* November 6, 2014.

Moyo, Dambisa. *Dead Aid: Why Aid Is Not Working and How There Is a Better Way for Africa.* New York: Farrar, Straus, and Giroux, 2009.

Murray, Charles. *Losing Ground: American Social Policy, 1950–1980.* New York: Basic Books, 1984.

Novak, Michael. *The Spirit of Democratic Capitalism*. New York: Simon and Schuster, 1982.

O'Carroll, Lisa. "A Third of Sierra Leone's Ebola Budget Unaccounted for, Says Report." *Guardian*, February 16, 2015.

Okun, Arthur M. *Equality and Efficiency: The Big Tradeoff*. Washington, DC: Brookings Institution, 1975.

Payne, James L. "What FDR Knew about Welfare." *Wall Street Journal*, May 19, 2016.

Pius XI. *Quadragesimo anno* (authorized English translation). Vatican City: Libreria Editrice Vaticana, May 15, 1931. At http://w2.vatican.va/content/pius-xi/en/encyclicals/ documents/hf_p-xi_enc_19310515_quadragesimo-anno.html.

"Pope Criticizes Globalization, Denies He Is Marxist." *Telesurtv.net*, January 11, 2015.

"Pope Francis Writes Letter to Venezuelan President Maduro." Vatican Radio, May 2, 2016.

Pullella, Philip, and Gabriel Stargardter. "In Mexican Border City, Pope Criticizes Business 'Slave Drivers.'" *Reuters*, February 17, 2016.

Radelet, Steven. *The Great Surge: The Ascent of the Developing World*. New York: Simon and Schuster, 2015.

Shleifer, Andrei. "Peter Bauer and the Failure of Foreign Aid." *Cato Journal* 29 (2009): 379–90.

Shughart, William F., II. "Katrinanomics: The Politics and Economics of Disaster Relief." *Public Choice* 127 (April 2006): 31–53.

Smith, Noah. "The Cost of Redistributing Wealth." *Bloomberg View*, November 25, 2015.

Swanson, Ana. "Why Trying to Help Poor Countries Might Actually Hurt Them." *Wonkblog, Washington Post*, October 13, 2015.

Tanner, Michael. *The American Welfare State: How We Spend Nearly $1 Trillion a Year Fighting Poverty—and Fail*. Cato Policy Analysis no. 694 (April 11, 2012). Washington, DC: Cato Institute.

Vallely, Paul. "Liberation Theology, Once Reviled by Church, Now Embraced by Pope." *Al Jazeera America*, September 22, 2015.

Vasquez, Ian. "Peter Bauer: Blazing the Trail of Development." *Econ Journal Watch* 4 (May 2007): 197–212.

Warr, Peter G. "Pareto Optimal Redistribution and Private Charity." *Journal of Public Economics* 19 (1982): 131–38.

Whaples, Robert. Review of *The Philanthropic Revolution: An Alternative History of American Charity* by Jeremy Beer. *The Independent Review* 20, no. 4 (Spring 2016): 609–12.

Winfield, Nicole. "Pope Urges Catholics to Reject Idols of 'Money, Success, Power.'" *Boston Globe*, July 25, 2013.

Wooden, Cindy. "Pope Francis Warns of the Dangers of 'Unbridled Capitalism.'" *Catholic Herald*, May 22, 2013.

World Bank. "Poverty Overview." April 13, 2016. At http://www.worldbank.org /en/topic/poverty/overview.

Yardley, Jim, and Simon Romero. "Pope's Focus on Poor Revives Scorned Theology." *New York Times*, May 23, 2015.

Zinsmeister, Karl. "Charitable Giving and the Fabric of America." *Imprimis* 45, no. 1 (January 2016). Hillsdale, MI: Hillsdale College. At https://imprimis.hillsdale .edu/wp-content/uploads/2016/02/Imprimis-January-2016.pdf.

5

Pope Francis on the Environmental Crisis

A. M. C. Waterman

IN THE EARLY months of his papacy, Francis promulgated the apostolic exhortation *Evangelii gaudium* (The joy of the Gospel), which declared the evangelical basis of his commitment to environmental protection: "An authentic faith . . . always involves a deep desire to change the world, to transmit values, to leave this earth somehow better than we found it. We love this magnificent planet on which God has put us . . . The earth is our common home and all of us are brothers and sisters."[1]

The encyclical *Laudato si'* ("Praise be to thee"), which appeared in May 2015, is an extended exposition of that theme.[2] With the possible exception of John Paul II's encyclical *Centesimus annus* in 1991, *Laudato si'* has attracted more attention, both favorable and unfavorable, than any papal utterance since *Humanae vitae* by Paul VI in 1968.

The evident degradation of the human environment appears to many, including some of the best informed, to be a matter of life and death: if not for ourselves, then for our children and grandchildren. Reliable diagnoses of causes and well-informed consideration of cures are essential for public policy. The matter has attracted a wide range of responses, in many of which it is hard to disentangle objective analysis from sectional interest and ideological bias. Whether the Christian religion can throw any light on such questions about the environment is important for millions worldwide. Pope Francis makes a very strong claim that it can.

---

1. Francis, *Evangelii gaudium*, 182.
2. Francis, *Laudato si'*, 3.

It is therefore my purpose in this article to examine that claim critically. In the first section, I attempt a summary. In the second, I attend to the intellectual context. In the last, I consider some of the more contentious issues the encyclical raises: in economics, in biological science, and in theology.

What Does the Encyclical Say?

Laudato si, mi Signore, per sora nostra matre Terra,
la quale ne sustenta et gouerna,
et produce diuersi fructi con coloriti fior et herba.
                    —Francis of Assisi, "Cantico del sole," c. 1224

Laudato si' is "addressed to every person living on this planet."[3] It is inspired by St. Francis of Assisi, whom John Paul II in 1979 declared to be "the patron saint of all who study and work in the area of ecology."[4] The seventh stanza of that saint's perennially popular "Cantico del sole" celebrates "Our Sister, Mother Earth who feeds us and rules us" and is quoted at the outset of *Laudato si'*.[5] The theme of the encyclical is "care for our common home." It echoes Paul VI, John Paul II, and Benedict XVI's judgment in perceiving the ecological crisis to be a consequence of the "irresponsible behaviour" of human beings.[6] It has six chapters.

Taking Stock

The first of these chapters, "What Is Happening to Our Common Home," deals with pollution and climate change,[7] the availability of water,[8] loss of biodiversity,[9] decline in the quality of human life and the breakdown of society,[10]

---

3. Francis, *Laudato si'*, 3.
4. John Paul II, Bulla: *Inter sanctos*, 10 (my translation).
5. Francis, *Laudato si'*, 1.
6. Ibid., 6.
7. Ibid., 20–25.
8. Ibid., 27–31.
9. Ibid., 32–42.
10. Ibid., 43–47.

global inequality,[11] "weak responses" to these challenges,[12] and a variety of options.[13] It seems probable that this chapter has been the one most carefully read—perhaps, indeed, the only chapter most people have read. At any rate, its matter appears to have attracted the most attention.

Pollution of the atmosphere, soil, and water undermines the health of millions. Accumulation of nonbiodegradable, toxic, and radioactive industrial waste is beginning to make our common home look like "an immense pile of filth."[14] Much of this pollution is a consequence of our "throwaway culture." Therefore, "technology, linked to business interests" is not "the only way of solving these problems" and may indeed make matters worse.[15] We must limit our use of nonrenewable resources and recycle those we do use.

Continuing use of fossil fuels causes carbonic, sulfurous, and nitric pollution—the first of which is directly linked to global warming and its train of ecological evils—which, by increasing the acidification of the oceans, "compromise the marine food chain."[16] Rich nations' increasing demand for water and increasing amounts of chemical pollution threaten the availability of potable water for millions, with far-reaching effects on nutrition, health, food production, and poverty.

Industrial and agricultural expansion have encroached on forests and woodlands, bringing loss of species diversification, and—in the case of tropical rain forests (the "lungs of our planet"[17])—diminishing their capacity to absorb carbon dioxide. It has also produced "the disproportionate and unruly growth of many cities," with consequent "decline in the quality of human life" and even "the breakdown of society."[18] And because industrialization has been controlled by advanced capitalist nations in the Northern Hemisphere, many of its social costs have been externalized upon the economically subject South, thus increasing global inequality.[19]

---

11. Ibid., 48–52.

12. Ibid., 53–59.

13. Ibid., 60–61.

14. Ibid., 21.

15. Ibid., 22, 20.

16. Ibid., 20, 23, 24.

17. Ibid., 90.

18. Ibid., 44.

19. Ibid., 48–52.

Most of these claims are widely known and generally—if not universally —accepted, yet official response has been weak, says Francis. We have come to expect only "superficial rhetoric, sporadic acts of philanthropy and perfunctory expressions of concern for the environment."[20]

The second chapter of *Laudato si'*, on the "Gospel of creation," abruptly changes the subject. "Why should this document, addressed to all people of goodwill, include a chapter dealing with the convictions of believers?"[21]: because there is "light offered by faith,"[22] much of which may be found in "the wisdom of the biblical accounts";[23] because it is salutary to be reminded of "the mystery of the universe";[24] because of "the message of each creature in the harmony of creation";[25] because there is "a universal communion" of all living beings;[26] because there is a "common destination of goods,"[27] for "God created the world for everyone";[28] and because "before the gaze of Jesus"[29] "the very flowers of the field and the birds which his human eyes contemplated are now imbued with his radiant presence."[30] This chapter rests on the assumption that "science and religion, with their distinctive approaches to understanding reality, can enter into . . . dialogue fruitful for both."[31]

The most substantial section of this chapter[32] examines "what the great biblical narratives say about the relationship of human beings with the world."[33] It rebuts (effectively, in my opinion) the charge sometimes brought against biblical religion: that the "dominion" granted to humankind (Gen. 1:28) "has encouraged the unbridled exploitation of nature."[34] Rather, Francis argues,

---

20. Francis, *Laudato si'*, 54.
21. Ibid., 62.
22. Ibid., 62–63.
23. Ibid., 65–75.
24. Ibid., 76–83.
25. Ibid., 84–88.
26. Ibid., 89–92.
27. Ibid., 93–95.
28. Ibid., 93.
29. Ibid., 96–100.
30. Ibid., 100.
31. Ibid., 62.
32. Ibid., 65–75.
33. Ibid., 65.
34. Ibid., 67.

it is human sin that has disrupted our "three fundamental . . . relationships: with God, with our neighbour and with the earth itself."[35]

We must distinguish "nature" from "creation."[36] The universe did not come about by "chance" but by a "decision" of God.[37] Though we may study and understand "nature," God's "creation" is inherently mysterious. Therefore, it is "faith" that "allows us to interpret the meaning and the mysterious beauty" of the "unfolding" of "creation."[38]

Chapter 3 addresses "[t]he human roots of the ecological crisis." It is based on the assumption—stated at the beginning of the encyclical—that the crisis is caused not by ineluctable natural constraints but by "the violence present in our hearts, wounded by sin."[39] Following his predecessor's critique of technology (in *Caritas in veritate*[40]), Francis identifies as a manifestation of this "violence" the so-called technocratic paradigm, which "exalts the concept of a subject who, using logical and rational procedures, progressively approaches and gains control over an external object."[41] "Technological products are not neutral"; they condition lifestyles and shape social possibilities "dictated by the interests of certain powerful social groups."[42] "Genuine ethical horizons" are obliterated, and "life gradually becomes a surrender to situations created by technology, itself viewed as the principal key to the meaning of existence."[43] Therefore, we need "a distinctive way of looking at things"—policies, education, lifestyle, spirituality—that may "generate resistance to the assault of the technocratic paradigm."[44] Francis calls for "a bold cultural revolution."[45] What the pope calls "modernity" evinces "an excessive anthropocentrism."[46] The "human being declares independence from reality" and "behaves with

35. Ibid., 66.
36. Ibid., 76.
37. Ibid., 77.
38. Ibid., 79.
39. Ibid., 2.
40. Benedict XVI, *Caritas in veritate*, 69–72.
41. Francis, *Laudato si'*, 106.
42. Ibid., 107.
43. Ibid., 110.
44. Ibid., 111.
45. Ibid., 114.
46. Ibid., 116.

absolute dominion."[47] "Man sets himself up as God and thus ends up provoking a rebellion on the part of nature."[48] Therefore, "the ecological crisis" is a sign of "the ethical, cultural and spiritual crisis of modernity,"[49] for anthropocentrism produces "a relativism which sees everything as irrelevant unless it serves one's own immediate interests."[50] "Objective truth and universally valid principles are no longer upheld."[51]

The rest of chapter 3 descends to particularity. There is a "need to protect employment,"[52] for "we were created with a vocation to work."[53] And we must be aware of "new biological technologies"[54] and understand their possibilities for both good and ill.

The fourth chapter introduces what appears to be a new concept: that of "integral ecology."[55] It begins with the usual definition of "ecology": a scientific study of the relations of organisms to one another and to their surroundings.[56] But because "everything is interconnected," this scientific study "necessarily entails reflection and debate about the conditions required for the life and survival of [human] society."[57] It is a short step from this view to the bold assertion, quoted from *Caritas in veritate,*[58] that "every violation of solidarity and civic friendship harms the environment."[59] For example, "drug use in affluent societies creates a continual and growing demand for products imported from poorer regions, where behaviour is corrupted, lives are destroyed, and the environment continues to deteriorate."[60] Though the term *integral ecology* is never defined, it soon becomes apparent that it is not a detached and disinterested study but a program for advancing certain ends that are not themselves the

---

47. Francis, *Laudato si'*, 117.
48. Ibid.; see also John Paul II, *Centesimus annus*, 37.
49. Francis, *Laudato si'*, 119.
50. Ibid., 122.
51. Ibid., 123.
52. Ibid., 124–29.
53. Ibid., 128.
54. Ibid., 130–36.
55. Ibid., 137.
56. Ibid., 138.
57. Ibid.
58. Benedict XVI, *Caritas in veritate*, 51.
59. Francis, *Laudato si'*, n. 116.
60. Ibid., 142.

result of scientific inquiry and that instead proceed from ethical and aesthetic imperatives that seem to be taken for granted. Because, for example, "there is a need" to "preserve the original identity" of cities being rebuilt, "ecology . . . involves protecting the cultural treasures of humanity in the broadest sense."[61]

There is thus a "cultural ecology."[62] There is also an "ecology of daily life"[63] aimed at "efforts to bring about an integral improvement in the quality of human life."[64] For "if communities are created," the very poorest victims of "densely populated residential areas" may "feel held within a network of solidarity and belonging. In this way, any place can turn from being a hell on earth into a setting of a dignified life."[65]

"Human ecology is inseparable from the notion of the common good, a central and underlying principle of social ethics."[66] And it requires "justice between the generations."[67]

What Must We Do?

The first four chapters of *Laudato si'* are intended "to take stock of our present situation." In chapter 5,[68] Francis lays out some "lines of approach and action" in light of "the profoundly human causes of environmental degradation"[69] and issues a call for "dialogue": "in the international community";[70] "for new national and local policies";[71] on "transparency in decision-making";[72] on "politics and economy" in relation to "human fulfilment";[73] and on "religions" in relation to "science."[74]

---

61. Ibid., 143.
62. Ibid., 143–46.
63. Ibid., 147–55.
64. Ibid., 147.
65. Ibid., 148.
66. Ibid., 156, 156–58.
67. Ibid., 158–62.
68. Ibid., 163–201.
69. Ibid., 163.
70. Ibid., 164–75.
71. Ibid., 176–81.
72. Ibid., 182–88.
73. Ibid., 189–98.
74. Ibid., 199–201.

Because the world is "interdependent," solutions to "environmental problems" must be proposed from a "global perspective"; hence, "a global consensus is essential."[75] The United Nations Stockholm Declaration of 1972 was echoed twenty years later at the Earth Summit in Rio de Janeiro. There have been conventions on hazardous wastes, on trade in endangered species, and on protection of the ozone layer.[76] But "international negotiations cannot make significant progress" when countries "place their national interest above the global common good"—as illustrated by the ineffectual outcome of the United Nations conference on sustainable development in Rio de Janeiro in 2012, which the pope denounces as a "failure of conscience and responsibility."[77]

National and local policy is often supported "by consumerist sectors of the population" and driven by "electoral interests."[78] "The mindset of short-term gain and results which dominates present-day politics and economics" inhibits politicians from supporting comprehensive environmental policies.[79] Even when these policies are in place, corruption may "conceal the actual environmental impact of a given project";[80] hence, there is continual need of "dialogue and transparency."[81]

The common good requires "politics and economics to enter into a frank dialogue in the service of life."[82] The "absolute power of the financial system" is counterproductive and requires us to rethink "the outdated criteria which continue to rule the world."[83] The pope rejects "a magical conception of the market"[84] and in the next paragraph—almost in passing—offers what is perhaps the most radical suggestion of the entire encyclical but never develops it further: "a decrease in the pace of production and consumption can at times give rise to another form of progress and development."[85]

---

75. Francis, *Laudato si'*, 164.
76. Ibid., 167–68.
77. Ibid., 169.
78. Ibid., 178.
79. Ibid., 181.
80. Ibid., 182.
81. Ibid., 182–88.
82. Ibid., 189.
83. Ibid.
84. Ibid., 190.
85. Ibid., 191.

"It cannot be maintained that empirical science provides a complete explanation of life . . . and the whole of reality."[86] Hence, there is need for dialogue among "religions" (note the plural) and "the various sciences" for the sake of "protecting nature, defending the poor, and building networks of respect and fraternity."[87]

"Many things have to change course, but it is we human beings above all who need to change."[88] Thus, the final chapter of *Laudato si'*, on "ecological education and spirituality," proposes a "new lifestyle";[89] encourages education "for the covenant between humanity and the environment";[90] calls for "ecological conversion";[91] notes the "joy and peace"[92] we may feel when "free of the obsession with consumption";[93] promotes "civic and political love"[94] because "care for nature . . . includes the capacity for living together and communion";[95] speaks of "sacramental signs and the celebration of rest";[96] proclaims "the Trinity and the relationship between creatures";[97] celebrates Mary, the "Queen of all Creation";[98] and takes us "*beyond* the sun,"[99] where "at the end, we will find ourselves face to face with the infinite beauty of God."[100]

The encyclical ends with two prayers: the first for "all who believe in a God who is the all-powerful Creator"; the second for Christians who seek "for inspiration to take up the commitment to creation set before us by the Gospel of Jesus."[101]

---

86. Ibid., 199.
87. Ibid., 201.
88. Ibid., 202.
89. Ibid., 203–8.
90. Ibid., 209–15.
91. Ibid., 216–21.
92. Ibid., 222–27.
93. Ibid., 222.
94. Ibid., 228–32.
95. Ibid., 228.
96. Ibid., 233–37.
97. Ibid., 238–40.
98. Ibid., 241–42.
99. Ibid., 243–45, my italics; cf. "Cantico del sole."
100. Ibid., 243.
101. Ibid., 246.

The Intellectual Context of *Laudato Si'*

To a far greater extent than in any previous social encyclical, *Laudato si'* acknowledges the authority of independent, secular scientific research. But like all of the social encyclicals after Leo XIII's *Rerum novarum* (1891), it locates itself in the tradition of its predecessors and explicitly declares that it "is now added to the body of the Church's social teaching."[102] And far more than any of its predecessors, it makes use of nonofficial sources.

The Scientific Background

The Ecological Society of America welcomed *Laudato si'* as "an eloquent plea for responsible Earth stewardship."

> The pope is clearly informed by the science underpinning today's environmental challenges. The encyclical deals directly with climate change, its potential effects on humanity and disproportionate consequences for the poor, and the need for intergenerational equity. The document is remarkable for its breadth, as it also addresses pollution, overuse of natural resources, landscape change, sense of place, and the loss of biodiversity. The pope recognizes that slow rates of change can mask the seriousness of environmental problems and the urgency to act. Pope Francis also acknowledges the importance of all taxa and all levels of biodiversity in sustaining our global commons.[103]

Though there has been much criticism of this encyclical, relatively little of that criticism has been directed at its scientific assumptions: that climate change has produced a drastic and increasing degradation of the conditions of life for humans and for many other species; that it is caused by human economic activity; and that it is causally related to other obvious environmental evils such as atmospheric and oceanic pollution.

---

102. Francis, *Laudato si'*, 15.

103. Ecological Society of America, "Ecological Society of America Responds to Pope Francis' Encyclical."

What criticism there has been seems to have occurred chiefly in the United States. A number of privately funded bodies, such as the libertarian Heartland Institute of Chicago and the Center for the Study of Carbon Dioxide and Global Change, accept the fact that global warming is occurring but promote research intended to challenge the official doctrine—as maintained by the United Nations Intergovernmental Panel on Climate Change (IPCC)—that it is caused by human greenhouse gas emissions. Although 31,487 American scientists (9,029 of whom have doctorates, but chiefly in engineering) signed the 2009 Oregon Petition, "urging the United States government to reject the global warming Kyoto Protocol of 1997 and similar policies," the effect on the world scientific community of such minority reports appears to have been negligible. For "the 'scientific voice' is no longer the voice of the sage individual, or a small group of sages, but the collective voice of essentially the entire community of relevant experts. The growth of the institutionalised assessment [as required by the IPCC]. . . permits scientists to speak with a collective voice."[104]

Oddly enough, the other chief objections to *Laudato si'* on this score appear to have come from Roman Catholics who wish to distance themselves from unwelcome features of their pope's message. The Australian cardinal George Pell "informed the *Financial Times* that the Church has no particular expertise in science. . . . [T]he Church has got no mandate from the Lord to pronounce on scientific matters. We believe in the autonomy of science."[105] In the United States, a Roman Catholic candidate for the Republican presidential nomination in 2016, Rick Santorum, judged that "we probably are better off leaving science to the scientists."[106] It is obvious that these assessments, whether deliberate or not, are misrepresentations of the encyclical. There is no attempt in *Laudato si'* to "pronounce on scientific matters." There are, on the contrary, many signs that Francis and his drafting committee sought and received expert scientific advice.

104. Oreskes, Jamieson, and Oppenheimer, "What Role for Scientists?," 639.

105. Quoted in Scammel, "Cardinal George Pell Takes a Swing at Pope Francis' Environmental Encyclical."

106. Quoted in vanden Heuvel, "Pope Francis vs. Wall Street."

Chief among the expert resources available to the papacy is the Pontifical Academy of Sciences, founded by Pius XI in 1936 and consisting of eighty eminent scientists from many countries who are elected without regard to religion. Its mission is "to promote the progress of the mathematical, physical and natural sciences and the study of epistemological problems relating thereto."[107] Since 1936, forty-six of its members have received Nobel prizes. Its activities include conferences, workshops, and publications. A workshop in May 2014, titled "Sustainable Humanity, Sustainable Nature, Our Responsibility"[108]—jointly held with the Pontifical Academy of Social Sciences—received thirty-eight communications by leading authorities, not all of whom were academicians.

The principal author of one of the papers presented at this workshop[109] was Hans Joachim Schellnhuber of the Potsdam Institute for Climate Impact Research (which he founded) and the Santa Fe Institute for Complex Systems Research. Schellnhuber—an atheist, a mathematician, and a theoretical physicist—is a world expert on the macroecological effects of climate change. In a recent essay, he considers the "common ground" that now exists between the scientific community and the papacy. "'Laudato si" does not provide technical guidance. . . . However Pope Francis highlights the ethical dimension of the climate problem and provides fundamental principles to be applied for solutions."[110] Schellnhuber, "who is said to have helped draft the encyclical,"[111] was appointed to the Pontifical Academy of Sciences in June 2015.

Maureen Mullarkey, writing for *First Things*, "America's most influential journal of religion and public life" (as it styles itself on its website), regarded Schellnhuber's appointment as "incomprehensible." "We can only make sense of it if we ask ourselves an unwelcome question: Is the Academy risking—if not engaged in—guerilla war against the pro-life movement?"[112] Whether one applauds or derides such sentiments (also found in other Christian, in

---

107. Pontifical Academy of the Sciences, Statutes of the Academy, art. 2.

108. See the proceedings in Dasgupta, Ramanathan, and Sánchez Sorondo, *Sustainable Humanity, Sustainable Nature, Our Responsibility*.

109. Schellnhuber and Martin, "Climate-System Tipping Points and Extreme Weather Events."

110. Schellnhuber, "Common Ground," 7.

111. Niles, "Breaking: Schellnhuber Appointed to Pontifical Academy of Science."

112. Mullarkey, "Notes on the Vatican Climate."

particular Roman Catholic, reactions to *Laudato si'* in the United States), they do seem to imply a perception that modern, secular science, with its utter disregard of religious dogma, is now an element in the intellectual context of papal social doctrine to an extent that would have been unimaginable until quite recently.

In this openness to science, perhaps, Francis has sought to realize the ideal of his immediate predecessor, the intellectual Benedict XVI: "Open to the truth, *from whichever branch of knowledge it comes,* the Church's social doctrine receives it, [and] assembles into a unity the fragments in which it is often found."[113]

Papal Social Doctrine

"The Church's social doctrine" was inaugurated in 1891 with the Leo XIII's encyclical *Rerum novarum.* When Pius XI celebrated the fortieth anniversary of that celebrated document with his own "social encyclical" in 1931, *Quadragesimo anno,* he started a tradition that has continued to the present. John XXIII's *Mater et magistra* marked the seventieth anniversary of *Rerum novarum* in 1961; Paul VI's *Octogesima adveniens* the eightieth in 1971; John Paul II's *Laborem exercens* the ninetieth in 1981; and John Paul II's *Centesimus annus* the hundredth in 1991. To these we must add John XXIII's 1963 encyclical *Pacem in terris*; *Populorum progressio* in 1967 by Paul VI; John Paul II's 1987 encyclical *Sollicitudo rei socialis,* which marks the twentieth anniversary of *Populorum progressio*; *Caritas in veritate* in 2009 by Benedict XVI; and now *Laudato si'.* It is customary to supplement that list of strictly papal utterances with a few episcopal or synodal documents, beginning with those of the Second Vatican Council, in order to complete the primary sources of "Catholic social teaching."[114] For obvious reasons, this tradition forms the most important part of the intellectual context within which each new member of the series is conceived.

Two themes dominated *Rerum novarum*: first, "the misery and wretchedness pressing so unjustly on the majority of the working class";[115] second, the

---

113. Benedict XVI, *Caritas in veritate,* 9, my italics.

114. Curran, *Catholic Social Teaching,* 7.

115. Leo XIII, *Rerum novarum,* 3.

rejection of "the main tenet of socialism, community of goods."[116] The former were seen as a consequence of industrialization. The latter was provoked by the activity of "crafty agitators" but more fundamentally by the rapacity of secularizing European governments eager to seize the church's ancient patrimony.[117] Leo rejected class conflict and exhorted "masters and wealthy owners" to be "mindful of their duty."[118]

Although Leo blamed "the greed of unchecked competition"[119] for the misery and wretchedness of the workers, it was Pius XI who in *Quadragesimo anno* (1931) attacked "the so-called Manchesterian Liberals" and thus engendered the distrust of the unregulated market economy that characterized papal social doctrine until very lately and that Francis is seen to have revived.

> The right ordering of economic life cannot be left to a free competition of forces. For from this source, as from a poisoned spring, have originated and spread all the errors of individualist economic teaching. Destroying... the social and moral character of economic life, it held that economic life must be considered and treated as altogether free from and independent of public authority, because in the market, i.e., in the free struggle of competitors, it would have a principle of self direction which governs it much more perfectly than would the intervention of any created intellect.[120]

It would seem from this passage and cognate passages in *Quadragesimo anno*[121] that Pius explicitly denied the possibility of a "spontaneous order"[122] that arises when the unintended consequences of private, self-regarding actions by individuals are socially benign. For the "individualist economic teaching" of Adam Smith was based in the insight that "the sovereign must not be

---

116. Leo XIII, *Rerum novarum*, 15.

117. Waterman, "Property Rights in John Locke and in Christian Social Teaching," "The Intellectual Context of *Rerum novarum*."

118. Leo XIII, *Rerum novarum*, 62.

119. Ibid., 2.

120. Pius XI, *Quadragesimo anno*, 88.

121. E.g., 14, 27, 54, 69, 109, 132 of *Quandragesimo anno*.

122. Hayek, *Studies in Philosophy, Politics, and Economics*, 85.

charged with a duty . . . *for the proper performance of which no human wisdom or knowledge could ever be sufficient*; the duty of superintending the industry of private people, and of directing it towards the employments most suitable to the interest of the society."[123]

Where the information required to comprehend the working of a complex modern economy (e.g. eighteenth-century Britain) is beyond the power of any individual human mind to grasp, society can only remain viable if there is, in fact, "a free competition of forces"—constrained only by commutative justice among individuals and the rule of law.

Pius failed to grasp this because he was committed to a pre-Enlightenment organicist social theory according to which society is conceived as a *body* that, by analogy with the human body, must be controlled by its *head*.[124] And like many early-modern social theorists,[125] he conceived that *body politic* in quasi-ecclesiological terms: "it will be possible to say in a certain sense even of this body what the Apostle says of the mystical body of Christ: 'The whole body (being closely joined and knit together through every joint of the system according to the functioning in due measure of each single part) derives its increase to the building up of itself in love.'"[126]

It is evident that "liberalism" of any kind, being founded on an individualistic conception of human life, must appear inimical to such a vision of society, as Pius's repeated animadversions made clear.[127]

The "poisoned spring" of Smithian doctrine and of the "Manchesterian Liberals" who developed and in some ways vulgarized it was part of the mainstream of intellectual life in Britain and France in the eighteenth and nineteenth centuries. But for reasons I have outlined elsewhere,[128] the Church of Rome excommunicated itself from that mainstream from about the middle of the

---

123. Smith, *Wealth of Nations*, 687, my italics.

124. Pius XI, *Quadragesimo anno*, 69, 75, 79, 83.

125. E.g., Starkey, *A Dialogue between Pole and Lupsett*.

126. Pius XI, *Quadragesimo anno*, 90.

127. Ibid., 10, 14, 25, 27, 30, 122.

128. Waterman, "The Intellectual Context of *Rerum novarum*"; Waterman, "Market Social Order and Christian Organicism in *Centesimus annus*"; Waterman, *Political Economy and Christian Theology since the Enlightenment*, chap. 2.

eighteenth century until the accession of Leo XIII in 1878. And although Leo's long pontificate did much to restore rigor and coherence to the intellectual life of his church, his adoption of Thomism as its official philosophy meant that the church would maintain a distance from mainstream thinking that wasn't bridged until after the Second Vatican Council (1962–65).

Official hostility to "liberalism" therefore persisted in the social encyclicals down to the 1970s. "Unrestricted competition in the liberal sense" is "clearly contrary to Christian teaching."[129] "Unbridled liberalism paves the way for a certain type of tyranny."[130] The Christian cannot "adhere to the *liberal ideology* which believes it exalts individual freedom by withdrawing it from every limitation."[131] Corresponding to their scepticism about the efficacy of competitive markets, the popes were until recently far more willing than "Manchesterian Liberals" to trust the state—that is, "the public authority."[132] For, according to Pius XI, "man's productive effort cannot yield its fruits unless a truly social and organic body exists, unless a social and juridical order watches over the exercise of work."[133] However, by the mid-1980s, the economic inefficiency and moral evil of Soviet communism had undermined faith in the state. John Paul II condemned communism's destruction of "creative initiative" and consequent "passivity, dependence and submission to the bureaucratic apparatus."[134] More importantly, he was led by his experience of socialism to introduce a radically new element into the church's social doctrine. The antimarket rhetoric of Leo XI and his successors was suddenly set aside: "the *free market* is the most efficient instrument for utilizing resources and effectively responding to needs,"[135] because of which "the Church acknowledges the legitimate *role of profit*."[136] John Paul's successor cautiously recognized "the proper economic function of the market,"[137] and the new doctrine has been

---

129. John XXIII, *Mater et magistra*, 23.

130. John XXIII, *Pacem in terris*, 26.

131. Paul VI, *Octogesima adveniens*, 26.

132. E.g., Pius XI, *Quadragesimo anno*, 88; John XXIII, *Mater et magistra*, 54 and *Pacem in terries*, 136; Paul VI, *Populorum progressio*, 33.

133. Pius XI, *Quadragesimo anno*, 69.

134. John Paul II, *Sollicitudo rei socialis*, 15; see also John Paul II, *Centesimus annus*, 25.

135. John Paul II, *Centesimus annus*, 34.

136. Ibid., 35.

137. Benedict XVI, *Caritas in veritate*, 35.

codified in the official *Compendium*,[138] compiled in 2004 by the Pontifical Council for Justice and Peace.

How much of this tradition has Francis handed on? Though he makes no mention of Leo XIII or Pius XI, their distrust of the market economy has resurfaced in *Laudato si'*,[139] as many have remarked. Paul VI gets five citations and John XXIII one. But Francis cites John Paul II thirty-seven times and Benedict XVI thirty times. No fewer than fifteen of the latter references are to *Caritas in veritate,* and the whole of *Laudato si'* is little more than a vast elaboration of *Caritas*'s paragraph 51. That paragraph in turn depends on three key ideas from *Centesimus annus* by John Paul II,[140] who appears to have originated the term *human ecology* as used by Francis. Though one crucially important element of John Paul's thinking—"the proper economic function of the market"—is missing, by far the most influential element in the intellectual context of *Laudato si'* is the scholarly and philosophical thinking of Francis's two immediate predecessors.

Nonofficial Sources

Not everyone has this perception of *Laudato si'*. According to R. R. Reno, "Francis expresses strikingly anti-scientific, anti-technological, and anti-progressive sentiments. In fact, this is perhaps the most anti-modern encyclical since the Syllabus of Errors in 1864." Reno contrasts this putative attitude with the recognition by John Paul II and Benedict XVI of "modernity's positive achievements." He sees in *Laudato si'* a fear and distrust of technology, which in its view seeks "a lordship over all" and "tends to absorb everything into its ironclad logic," as Reno explains. There may thus be, says Reno, "an internal contradiction" between the pope's endorsement of "the consensus view about global warming" and his view that "'the scientific and experimental method' *itself*" is "part of the problem."[141]

---

138. Pontifical Council for Justice and Peace, *Compendium of the Social Doctrine of the Church*, 347–50.

139. E.g., Francis, *Laudato si'*, 56, 123, 203.

140. John Paul II, *Centesimus annus*, notes 123, 124, 125.

141. Reno, "The Return of Catholic Anti-modernism."

Benedict certainly expressed a profound appreciation of technology,[142] but Francis echoes that appreciation in *Laudato si'*.[143] His seemingly more pessimistic view in paragraphs 106–10 appears to have been influenced by the German philosopher of religion Romano Guardini (1885–1968), whose works Jorge Mario Bergoglio (a.k.a. Francis) studied in the 1980s with a view to a doctoral thesis. To a much greater extent than his predecessors, Francis has been willing to cite nonofficial sources in his encyclical—including Aristotle, Dante, Teilhard de Chardin, and Paul Ricoeur, among others—and there are eight citations of Guardini, all to *The End of the Modern World*.[144] Guardini's thought is the third important component of the intellectual context of *Laudato si'*.

Guardini's *Das Ende der Neuzeit*, originally translated into English in 1957 as *The End of the Modern World*, was also a powerful influence on Benedict XVI, much of whose writing "has been, at least implicitly, a long meditation on the work of Guardini."[145] Chapter 3, "The Dissolution of the Modern World and the World Which Is to Come," is the source of all the citations of Guardini in *Laudato si'*. Power can create evil as well as good and has become demonic.[146] Note Guardini's assertion that his hypothesis "*has nothing in common with that desire which would surrender the valid achievements of modern man*."[147] "The world outlook now being born . . . refuse[s] to venerate nature. . . . [M]an motivated by technology broke into the field of history and took possession. . . . The technological mind sees nature . . . as raw material to be hammered into useful shape."[148] The "gadgets and technics [*sic*]" forced upon "Mass man" by "patterns of machine production and of abstract planning" he "accepts quite simply; they are the forms of life itself."[149] But "the process of conformity" that "has done so much violence to man" also has a "positive meaning." For "when all other substantial values have disintegrated comrade-

---

142. E.g., Benedict XVI, *Caritas in veritate*, 69.

143. Francis, *Laudato si'*, 102, 103.

144. Guardini *Das Ende der Neuzeit*, *The End of the Modern World*.

145. Shannon, "Romano Guardini: Father of the New Evangelization."

146. Guardini, *The End of the Modern World*, 82–83.

147. Ibid., 51, my italics.

148. Ibid., 55.

149. Ibid., 60.

ship remains . . . a sign of what is to come. . . . comradeship could help regain the values of the 'Person': benevolence, understanding and justice."[150]

Guardini's analysis of the dehumanizing effects of technology and the destructive consequences of its instrumental conception of nature lies behind chapter 3 of the encyclical *Laudato si'*, "The Human Roots of the Ecological Crisis," especially paragraphs 102–113 and 115–119, in which six of the references to Guardini occur. The other two references are in chapter 6, "Ecological Education and Spirituality," paragraphs 203 and 219. These paragraphs evince not so much a fear and distrust of technology as a well-informed understanding of technology's human and environmental costs. And they are fully consistent with Benedict's critique of technology in *Caritas in veritate*.[151]

The United Nations Rio Declaration on the Environment and Development of 1992 is cited three times in *Laudato si'*, and the Earth Charter of 2000 is cited once. But, aside from Guardini, the most cited nonofficial source is the Greek Orthodox patriarch Bartholomew I of Constantinople (1940–), with five citations.[152] Bartholomew, known as "the Green Patriarch" for his widely influential advocacy of environmental causes, has insisted that "to commit a crime against the natural world is a sin against ourselves and a sin against God"[153] and "has drawn attention to the ethical and spiritual roots of environmental problems, which require that we look for solutions not only in technology but in a change of humanity."[154] It is evident that Francis finds the patriarch's theological view of the environmental crisis congenial and in harmony with his own.

Discussion

The message of *Laudato si'* is so important and so ecumenical that it deserves the most careful and critical attention. Much of it is profoundly true and compelling. But in some places it seems either wrong or wrong-headed and in

150. Ibid., 66.
151. Benedict XVI, *Caritas in veritate*, 68–74.
152. Francis, *Laudato si'*, 7–9.
153. Ibid., 8.
154. Ibid., 9.

some others questionable or unnecessarily controversial. Pope Francis invites dialogue (chapter 5). We "people of goodwill"[155] to whom the encyclical is addressed can do our bit by helping to clear away some of the clutter. I address three of the more contentious sets of issues: in economics, in biological science, and in theology.

The Market Economy

Many commentators have observed that *Laudato si'* is "economically flawed"[156] and have noted the pope's "well-established distrust of free-market capitalism"[157] and his attack on what he calls "a magical conception of the market."[158] As I explained earlier, papal social doctrine was consistently hostile to "Manchesterian liberalism" until 1991. In that year, in the aftermath of the collapse of Soviet communism, John Paul II acknowledged in *Centesimus annus* that "on the level of individual nations and of international relations, the *free market* is the most efficient instrument for utilizing resources and effectively responding to needs." Thus, "the Church acknowledges the legitimate *role of profit* as an indication that a business is functioning well. When a firm makes a profit, this means that productive factors have been properly employed and corresponding human needs have been duly satisfied."[159]

Immediately following these passages, John Paul adumbrated most of what was to become the content of *Laudato si'*: "consumerism," "the ecological question" and "senseless destruction of the natural environment," a Guardini-like critique of technology, and John Paul's new concept of "human ecology."[160] Therefore, although John Paul guarded and qualified acceptance of "the proper economic function" of the market,[161] and Benedict even more so,[162] it is evident that neither believed that his attention to environmental

---

155. Francis, *Laudato si'*, 62.

156. Gregg, "*Laudato si'*: Well-Intentioned, Economically Flawed."

157. Gardner, "An Activist Pope Puts His Faith in Science."

158. Vanden Heuvel, "Pope Francis vs. Wall Street."

159. John Paul II, *Centesimus annus*, 34, 35.

160. Ibid., 36, 37, 38.

161. E.g., *Centesimus annus*, 42.

162. Benedict XVI, *Caritas in veritate*, 35.

questions required him to revive the automatic hostility to markets evinced by Pius XI. In this important respect, *Laudato si'* would seem to be a turning back of the clock. It claims to be an addition to "the Church's social teaching,"[163] yet it appears to ignore or even deny that this teaching now recognizes the "proper economic function of the market."

Sometimes this denial is more apparent than real in *Laudato si'*. The assertion, for example, that "the environment is defenceless before the interests of a deified market"[164] has attracted much unfavorable notice. Yet some of the pope's highly colored adjectives are explicable and not in themselves unreasonable. No economist entertains "a magical conception of the market."[165] Some noneconomists may indeed lapse into idolatry of a "deified market."

On careful examination, therefore, some of the pope's strictures turn out to contain valid criticisms, which are undermined or weakened by hyperbolic language. For example, "Caring for ecosystems demands far-sightedness, since no one looking for quick and easy profit is truly interested in their preservation. But the cost of the damage caused by such selfish lack of concern is much greater than the economic benefits to be obtained."[166] Here we need only delete "caused by such selfish lack of concern." In another example, few readers would deny that "saving banks at any cost, making the public pay the price,"[167] is bad public policy. But many would question what follows in the same sentence: that to do so only "reaffirms the absolute power of a financial system, a power which has no future"[168]—although they might then go on to agree, once again, that such action to save banks at the public's expense may "only give rise to new crises after a slow, costly and only apparent recovery."[169] In all such passages, and there are many, Francis is his own worst enemy, offering easy excuses to those who wish to evade or reject his message.

Many economists are willing, therefore, to go along with Francis at least to the extent of conceding that the market economy, both nationally and

---

163. Francis, *Laudato si'*, 15.

164. Ibid., 56.

165. Ibid., 190.

166. Ibid., 36.

167. Ibid., 189.

168. Ibid.

169. Ibid.

internationally, may not be in the best health—at any rate as judged by the standards of neoclassical theory.

According to that theory, a fully employed economy in which there is perfect information and in which there are perfectly competitive spot and futures markets for each good and service (and indeed in which there are markets for all contingencies in all future periods) will yield rates of production and consumption—when in general equilibrium—that are optimal in Pareto's sense: no one individual can be made better off save at the expense of others. Some have regarded this theory as a rationalization of Adam Smith's "invisible hand." It must be noted that individuals' relative position in equilibrium depends on the initial assignment of endowments.

It is obvious that some of these conditions are not met and perhaps can never be met. There is not a complete set of markets, and those markets that do exist are often far from perfectly competitive. Vigorous price competition, cutting profits to the bone for the benefit of customers, is all too often hard to find. Monopoly, or collusion between a few giants, is now typical in many sectors. Hence, these producers may levy a private and unofficial sales tax on their customers, which is inefficient and may be perceived as unjust. When there is high unemployment, which has often been common in developed economies in recent decades, prices may no longer signal relative scarcities; hence, production may no longer match relative needs. Idle productive resources, moreover, are both a waste and a cause of human misery. It is evident, too, that information is often far from perfect and that public goods and other causes of market failure abound. Last, because even under ideal conditions individual incomes are determined by initial endowments that depend simply on luck, any great disparity in incomes—such as exists at present, especially in the United States and Britain[170]—may lead some to call in question the ethical basis of capitalism.

In addition to these departures from theoretical optimality, there is the fact, increasingly observed by economists, that an unprecedented relative expansion of the financial sector in recent decades has produced a "misalignment of private and social incentives,"[171] which perhaps is a cause of what

---

170. Wilkinson and Pickett, *The Spirit Level.*
171. Collier, "Wrong for the Poor," 3.

Laudato si' refers to as that "mindset of short-term gain and results which dominates present-day . . . economics."[172]

However, it is one thing to agree that the market economy of the present day falls short of its own standards of performance as these standards are formalized in economic theory, but quite another to conceive any more satisfactory alternative.

In many instances, no doubt, government regulation of markets may prevent or correct some of the worst failures of private enterprise. Yet government itself may sometimes be part of the problem. In every country where government's desire to regulate exceeds its power to control its functionaries, corruption will flourish. And in stable and wealthy democracies where government depends on electoral success, strong incentives exist for rich and powerful individuals and corporations as well as for powerful labor and professional unions to engage in rent seeking by trading political support for exclusive favors. As in Britain before Margaret Thatcher's reforms, for example, big business and big unions may unite with government in a conspiracy to rob the public.

Yet the capitalist (mixed) economy, despite its many infirmities, has since 1945 provided far more productive employment and generated far more wealth for more people and in more countries than ever before in human history. Pope Francis's antimarket bias thus sometimes looks like willful blindness.

Most seriously for its argument, *Laudato si'* simply misses the point of the "deified market." This is apparent, among other places, in the "the issue of water":[173] "Even as the quality of available water is constantly diminishing, in some places there is a growing tendency, despite its scarcity, to privatize this resource, turning it into a commodity subject to the laws of the market. Yet *access to safe drinkable water is a basic and universal human right, since it is essential to human survival.* . . . [W]ater continues to be wasted, not only in the developed world but also in developing countries which possess it in abundance."[174]

Economists know that it is not "despite its scarcity" but precisely *because of that scarcity* that water should be "subject to the laws of the market," for until people have to pay a price for water's use that reflects its relative scarcity, they

---

172. Francis, *Laudato si'*, 181.

173. Ibid., second section of chap. 1, para. 27–31.

174. Ibid., 30.

will continue to waste it. If there are some who cannot afford that price, the remedy lies not in quantitative control by bureaucrats but in legislated transfers of income from the rich to the poor. Though water cannot possibly be a "human right" (because there can be no right to that which may be unfeasible), the "human survival" that depends on water is better served by the peaceable rationing of the market than by any conceivable alternative. And because it is not so much "waste" as paucity of infrastructure that creates water shortages in sub-Saharan Africa, Southeast Asia, and Latin America, the profit possibilities offered by the market would create powerful incentives to invest in that infrastructure.[175]

Even Pius XI recognized in *Quadragesimo anno* that "the laws of economics . . . determine the limits of what productive human effort cannot, and of what it can attain in the economic field and by what means."[176] In 1994, John Paul II established the Pontifical Academy of the Social Sciences on lines similar to the Pontifical Academy of Sciences. It collaborated with the latter in a joint workshop on sustainability in 2014. The Pontifical Academy of the Social Sciences includes seven eminent economists, among them Joseph Stiglitz and Partha Dasgupta. Kenneth Arrow is an honorary member. (The late Gary Becker was a member of the Pontifical Academy of *Sciences*—which claims him as one of its own Nobel laureates.) It would appear, however, that the influence of economists on *Laudato si'* has been far less than that of natural scientists—possibly because fellow academicians from some other disciplines,[177] especially sociology, are uneasy with the methodological individualism at the core of economic theory.

Ecology

Economics is the scientific study of the human response to scarcity. It is thus a special case of ecology, which includes the scientific study of the response of

---

175. Segerfeldt, "Private Water Saves Lives."

176. Pius XI, *Quadragesimo anno*, 42.

177. The disciplines of the twenty-four ordinary academicians in the Pontifical Academy of Sciences include: demography (1), economics and development studies (7), history and religious studies (2), philosophy and political philosophy (5), political science and international relations (5), and sociology (4).

all living organisms to scarcity. Biological scarcity arises from natural fecundity in a finite world. "Necessity, that imperious all pervading law of nature, restrains [all species] within the prescribed bounds. The race of plants and the race of animals shrink under this great restrictive law."[178] Charles Darwin got the key ecological concept of "the struggle for existence" from Robert Malthus and used it to develop his theory of natural selection.[179] What John Stuart Mill called "the spontaneous order of nature"[180] occurs when each coexisting species in a particular habitat has reached its maximum population as set by physical geography and by the competition (or availability) of all other species. It may be regarded as a gigantic analogue of general competitive equilibrium in neoclassical economic theory—and, like the latter, it can seldom if ever be observed because of continual flux in its exogenous determinants.

The never-ending "struggle for existence" means a nature "red in tooth and claw." For though symbiosis, mutualism, commensalism, and peaceful coexistence are widespread, both interspecific predation and intraspecific predation are so common as to appear usual and to justify Tennyson's dismal characterization of "Nature" in his poem "In Memoriam, A. H. H." (canto 56). The weak are parasitic on the strong. The strong prey on the weak. Even humans will kill and eat weaker humans if there is no other food.

This is not quite the picture of nature we get in *Laudato si'*. St. Francis of Assisi "communed with all creation, even preaching to the flowers. . . . [T]o him each and every creature was a sister united to him by bonds of affection."[181] The pope warns us that "if we no longer speak the language of fraternity and beauty in our relationship with the world, our language *will be* that of masters, consumers, ruthless exploiters, unable to set limits on their immediate needs."[182] Here, too, however, Pope Francis jeopardizes his meaning by overstatement. A change of "will be" to "may become" converts this assertion into a valid and important proposition.

Like William Paley, whose work *Natural Theology* (1802) underpinned religious belief in Britain and America until Darwin, "St Francis . . . invites us to

---

178. Malthus, *An Essay on the Principle of Population*, 15.

179. Darwin, *The Autobiography of Charles Darwin*, 120.

180. Mill, *Nature*, 381.

181. Francis, *Laudato si'*, 11.

182. Ibid., 11; my italics.

see Nature as a magnificent book" in which we can glimpse the "infinite beauty and goodness of God," says Francis.[183] However, when we no longer perceive the adaptation of species as God's benevolent "design" but rather as blind and purposeless, the Book of Nature tells us a different story.[184] The pope rescues his namesake by correctly noting that "the harmony between the Creator, humanity and creation as a whole" was disrupted at the Fall (Gen. 3:17–19) and by reporting St. Bonaventure's belief "that through universal reconciliation with every creature, St Francis in some way returned to the state of original innocence."[185] So the "struggle for existence" and organic evolution that results from it are not denied.[186] Yet Aristotle is later quoted in support of "design": "Nature is nothing other than a certain kind of art, namely God's art."[187]

It may be that the pre-Malthusian view of nature that still lingers in *Laudato si'* lies behind the pronatalism[188] that Francis shares with all of his predecessors.[189] Like them, he believes that "demographic growth is fully compatible with an integral and shared development. To blame population growth instead of extreme and selective consumerism on the part of some, is one way of refusing to face the issues."[190] But once again Francis overstates his case. It seems probable that what John Paul II identified as "consumerism"[191] is indeed an important part of the problem today. But even had "consumerism" never existed, increased population consequent upon industrialization in the past two centuries is the fundamental cause of the environmental degradation we perceive today. World population, which was only very gradually increasing up to 1700, grew from one billion in 1800 to seven billion in 2011—all because industrialization produces more goods. And what "the Church's social doctrine" has yet to accept and internalize is the biblical insight that "when goods increase, they are increased that eat them" (Eccles. 5:11). More human beings,

---

183. Francis, *Laudato si'*, 12.

184. Darwin, *The Autobiography of Charles Darwin*, 87.

185. Francis, *Laudato si'*, 66.

186. Ibid., 18, 81.

187. Quoted in ibid., 80.

188. Ibid., 180.

189. E.g., Pius XI, *Casti connubii*, 11, 54, 95; John XXIII, *Mater et magistra*, 185–94; Paul VI, *Humanae vitae*, 2; John Paul II, *Sollicitudo rei socialis*, 25.

190. Francis, *Laudato si'*, 50.

191. John Paul II, *Sollicitudo rei socialis*, 28.

however scrupulously they might eschew "consumerism," place more strain on the environment. It is important to note that this strain is not primarily a matter of resource scarcity.

When John XXIII declared that "the resources which God in His goodness and wisdom has implanted in Nature are well-nigh inexhaustible,"[192] he unwittingly resurrected the futile attempt by Marx and Engels[193] to answer Malthus through faith in "the progress of science and technology."[194] In this, he ran counter to the findings of those ecologists who believe that population has already exceeded the earth's sustainable carrying capacity.[195] Yet economists note that technical progress (i.e., "science and technology") and Smithian increasing returns to scale have so far outweighed Malthusian diminishing returns. Julian Simon, for example, would appear to agree with John XXIII,[196] and he won a famous wager with Paul Ehrlich over a mutually agreed measure of resource scarcity from 1980 to 1990.[197] Perhaps economists tend in general to be more skeptical about carrying capacity and more optimistic about resource elasticity than ecologists and other natural scientists. In economists' models, available resource inputs into production are usually increasing functions of price, whereas in engineers' and natural scientists' models they are taken as data.

Yet even if the ecologists are wrong, and productive resources are as elastic as John XXIII and the most optimistic of the economists believe, environmental degradation will worsen as the human population increases. More humans produce more greenhouse gases, and the earth's capacity to absorb these gases without disastrous consequences is limited.[198] This capacity does not appear to be an ordinary resource constraint capable of being identified and made elastic with respect to price. Though the only demographer in the Pontifical Academy might dissent,[199] it therefore seems unlikely that, as Francis puts it

---

192. John XXIII, *Mater et magistra*, 189.

193. Perelman, "Marx, Malthus, and the Organic Composition of Capital," 465–70.

194. John XXIII, *Mater et magistra*, 189.

195. E.g., Daily and Ehrlich, "Population, Sustainability, and the Earth's Carrying Capacity"; Burger et al., "The Macroecology of Sustainability."

196. Simon, *The Ultimate Resource.*

197. "Simon–Ehrlich Wager."

198. Burger et al., "The Macroecology of Sustainability."

199. Dumont, "Population et nature: Antagonisme ou concordance?"

in *Laudato si'*, "demographic growth is fully compatible with an integral and shared development."[200]

Virtue, Self-Interest, and Original Sin

Even if population were not a problem, there can be no serious doubt that the environmental evils described in chapter 1 of *Laudato si'* are caused by human agency, as the pope tells us. And only we humans can rescue ourselves from disaster—if it is not already too late. Not only do we all have to learn sustainable ways of living as individuals, but, what is going to be much more difficult, governments of sovereign states also have to become willing to enact and enforce laws and regulations that will inevitably injure the short-term interests of many of their subjects, including some of the most powerful. "The Church does not propose economic systems or programs,"[201] but she does claim to be "an expert in humanity."[202] It is for this reason, I think, that Pope Francis believes that the Christian religion can throw light on these matters.

There are many references in *Laudato si'* to individuals' and groups' *duty* with respect to environmental protection,[203] all of them relevant. "The existence of laws and regulations is insufficient in the long run to curb bad conduct, even when effective means of enforcement are present. If the laws are to bring about significant, long-lasting effects, the majority of the members of society must be adequately motivated to accept them, and personally transformed to respond."[204]

Perfectly true as this proposition is, it raises an important question: *How can individuals be "adequately motivated"*? Like Patriarch Bartholomew, the pope believes that we need "a change in humanity."[205] "Only by cultivating sound virtues," Francis tells us, "will people be able to make a selfless ecological commitment. . . . Education in environmental responsibility can encourage ways of acting which directly and significantly affect the world around us."[206]

---

200. Francis, *Laudato si'*, 50.
201. John Paul II, *Sollicitudo rei socialis*, 41.
202. Paul VI, *Populorum progressio*, 13.
203. Francis, *Laudato si'*, 41, 64, 67, 70, 78, 79, 129, 167, 178, 211.
204. Ibid., 211.
205. Ibid., 9.
206. Ibid., 211.

I wish to suggest that though virtue is indeed *necessary,* it is not *sufficient* to bring about the profound change in "lifestyle" that the pope very properly calls for.[207] A "change in humanity" is very desirable. But even if such a change is possible, in principle it may take too long. Few of us will achieve the heroic virtue of St. Francis of Assisi because doing the right thing is often too costly. Consider a middle-level bureaucrat in Nigeria, with authority to enforce some environmental measure contrary to the interest of a powerful private corporation. He is wretchedly underpaid and has an ailing wife and four children to support. The corporation offers him a bribe. If he acts with integrity, his dependents will bear most of the cost. What he needs is a powerful incentive to refuse the bribe: in this case an adequate salary from his government. Then should we instead appeal to the better nature of the corporation's managers? No. Not because they are "obsessed with maximizing profits"[208] but because they, too, are sinful human beings like the rest of us, who may not have the moral courage to incur serious costs for themselves and their loved ones if they act lawfully and justly. In all such cases, and they are well-nigh universal, we must also appeal to each agent's *self-interest.*

Exclusive reliance on incentives might be self-defeating, of course. If individuals are expected to act well only when sufficiently rewarded, deliberately bad behavior might be rational, and corruption will become institutionalized. Even if this were not the case, the difficulty of achieving that degree of cooperation and collaboration at the national and international levels required to remedy environmental degradation would be exacerbated by the defection of free riders. Virtue is always necessary. But self-interest is the stuff of practical politics.

A famous archbishop of Canterbury declared in 1942 that "the art of government is . . . the art of so ordering life that self-interest prompts what justice demands."[209] Why should this be? John Paul II tells us in *Centesimus annus,*

> [M]an, who was created for freedom, bears within himself the wound of original sin, which constantly draws him towards evil and puts him in need of redemption. Not only is *this doctrine an integral part of Christian revelation;* it also has great hermeneutical value insofar as it helps

207. Ibid., 23, 59, 111, 164, 193, 203–8, 222.
208. Ibid., 190.
209. Temple, *Christianity and Social Order,* 65.

one to understand human reality. Man tends towards good, but he is also capable of evil. He can transcend his immediate interest and still remain bound to it. The social order will be all the more stable, the more it takes this fact into account and does not place in opposition personal interest and the interests of society as a whole, but rather seeks ways to bring them into fruitful harmony. In fact, where self-interest is violently suppressed, it is replaced by a burdensome system of bureaucratic control which dries up the wellsprings of initiative and creativity.[210]

The market economy, even in its present state, is a powerful instrument for bringing "personal interest" and "the interest of society as a whole" into "fruitful harmony." Jansenists of the late seventeenth century were the first to see this confluence clearly,[211] and their insight was fully developed in the classical political economy of the English School.[212]

Jansenist theology was deeply Augustinian. St. Augustine, who seems to have coined the term *original sin*, taught that God inflicted the state and its institutions on humanity as a *punishment* for sin, but under His mercy they may become *remedies* for sin by harnessing the self-regarding acts of sinful men and women to produce unintended consequences that are socially benign.[213] When *Centesimus annus* was promulgated, it was hailed in the United States as "a ringing endorsement of the market economy,"[214] but its true significance was missed by all. It was in fact a belated recognition in papal social doctrine of Augustinian theodicy. The institutions of human society, such as the market economy, are conceived in sin and must always be imperfect. Yet under Divine Providence they may become a remedy for "the wound of original sin" by recruiting self-interest to the common good.

Laudato si' completely ignores this essential element in "the Church's social doctrine." Francis tells us instead that we must "learn to reject self-interested pragmatism,"[215] for "our freedom fades when it is handed over to the blind forces of the unconscious, of immediate needs, of self-interest, and of

210. John Paul II, *Centesimus annus*, 25.
211. Faccarello, *The Foundations of Laissez-faire*, 22–29.
212. Waterman, "The English School of Political Economy," 2014.
213. Deane, *The Political and Social Ideas of St. Augustine*, chaps. 3 and 4, passim.
214. Neuhaus, Review Essay, S8–S9.
215. Francis, *Laudato si'*, 215.

violence."[216] True as this statement may be in general, its rejection of self-interest undermines his very proper desire that we should be "adequately motivated" to cultivate the ecological virtues. And by turning a blind eye to "the proper economic function" of the market, as in his seeming rejection of "carbon credits,"[217] for example, he shoots himself in the foot, for virtue alone is not enough. We need all the incentives we can muster to induce individuals, corporations, and governments to behave in an ecologically responsible manner.

Conclusion

What can we conclude? *Laudato si'* is a vitally important contribution to public discourse on the environmental crisis. Its account of the evils now facing us and its warning of the disaster that impends are truly prophetic in the biblical sense. Its Christian understanding of God's creation and of our proper place in it (chapters 2 and 6) provides a normative framework—perhaps the only adequate normative framework—for environmental stewardship. And its recognition that virtue is necessary if laws and regulations are to be effectual is unquestionably right. But the force of its message is weakened in two ways: first, by its inability to recognize that population is crucial; second, by its failure to appreciate that in public policy human sin makes it necessary to supplement virtue by an appeal to self-interest—and that the market economy can be a very good way of achieving this.

References

Benedict XVI. *Caritas in veritate* (authorized English translation). Vatican City: Libreria Editrice Vaticana, June 29, 2009. At http://w2.vatican.va/content/benedict -xvi/en/encyclicals/ documents/hf_ben-xvi_enc_20090629_caritas-in-veritate .html.

Burger, Joseph R., Craig D. Allen, James H. Brown, William R. Burnside, Ana D. Davidson, Trevor S. Fristoe, Marcus J. Hamilton, et al. "The Macroecology of Sustainability." *PLOS Biology* 10, no. 6 (2012): 1–6.

---

216. Ibid., 105.
217. Ibid., 171.

Collier, Paul. "Wrong for the Poor." *Times Literary Supplement* (London), September 25, 2015.

Curran, C. E. *Catholic Social Teaching, 1891–Present: A Historical, Theological, and Ethical Analysis*. Washington, DC: Georgetown University Press, 2002.

Daily, G. C., and P. R. Ehrlich. "Population, Sustainability, and the Earth's Carrying Capacity." *BioScience* 42, no. 10 (1992): 761–71.

Darwin, Charles. *The Autobiography of Charles Darwin*. Edited by Norah Barlow. London: Collins, 1958.

Dasgupta, Partha, Veerabhadran Ramanathan, and Marcelo Sánchez Sorondo, eds. *Sustainable Humanity, Sustainable Nature, Our Responsibility: Proceedings of the Joint Workshop, 2–6 May 2014*. Extra Series 41. Vatican City: Pontifical Academy of Sciences, 2015.

Deane, Herbert A. *The Political and Social Ideas of St. Augustine*. New York: Columbia University Press, 1963.

Dumont, Gérard-François. "Population et nature: Antagonisme ou concordance?" In Pontifical Academy of Sciences, *Sustainable Humanity, Sustainable Nature, Our Responsibility: Proceedings of the Joint Workshop 2–6 May 2014*, Extra Series 41, edited by Partha Dasgupta, Veerabhadran Ramanathan, and Marcelo Sánchez Sorondo, 79–124. Vatican City: Pontifical Academy of Sciences, 2015.

Ecological Society of America. "Ecological Society of America Responds to Pope Francis' Encyclical, *Laudato Si: On Care for Our Common Home*." Press release, June 29, 2015.

Faccarello, Gilbert. *The Foundations of Laissez-faire: The Economics of Pierre de Boisguilbert*. London: Routledge, 1999.

Francis. *Evangelii gaudium* (authorized English translation). Vatican City: Libreria Editrice Vaticana, 2013. At http://w2.vatican.va/content/francesco/en/apost_exhortations/documents/ papa-francesco_esortazione-ap_20131124_evangelii-gaudium.html.

————. *Laudato si'* (authorized English translation). Vatican City: Libreria Editrice Vaticana, May 24, 2015. At http://w2.vatican.va/content/francesco/en/encyclicals/documents/ papa-francesco_20150524_enciclica-laudato-si.html.

Gardner, David. "An Activist Pope Puts His Faith in Science." *Financial Times,* June 19, 2015.

Gregg, Samuel. "*Laudato si'*: Well-Intentioned, Economically Flawed." *American Spectator,* June 19, 2015. At http://spectator.org/63160_laudato-si-well-intentioned-economically-flawed/.

Guardini, Romano. *Das Ende der Neuzeit*. Basel: Hess, 1950.

―――. *The End of the Modern World*. Wilmington, Del.: ISI Books, 1998.

Hayek, F. A. *Studies in Philosophy, Politics, and Economics*. New York: Simon & Schuster, 1967.

John XXIII. *Mater et magistra* (authorized English translation). Vatican City: Libreria Editrice Vaticana, May 15, 1961. At http://w2.vatican.va/content/john-xxiii/en/encyclicals/documents/hf_j-xxiii_enc_15051961_mater.html.

―――. *Pacem in terris* (authorized English translation). Vatican City: Libreria Editrice Vaticana, April 11, 1963. At http://w2.vatican.va/content/john-xxiii/en/encyclicals/documents/hf_j-xxiii_enc_11041963_pacem.html.

John Paul II. Bulla: *Inter sanctos* (in Latin). November 29, 1979. At http://w2.vatican.va/content/john-paul-ii/la/apost_letters/1979/documents/hf_jp-ii_apl_19791129_inter- sanctos.html.

―――. *Laborem exercens* (authorized English translation). Vatican City: Libreria Editrice Vaticana, September 14, 1981. At http://w2.vatican.va/content/john-paul-ii/en/encyclicals/ documents/hf_jp-ii_enc_14091981_laborem-exercens.html.

―――. *Sollicitudo rei socialis* (authorized English translation). Vatican City: Libreria Editrice Vaticana, December 30, 1987. At http://w2.vatican.va/content/john-paul-ii/en/encyclicals/documents/hf_jp-ii_enc_30121987_sollicitudo-rei-socialis.html.

―――. *Centesimus annus* (authorized English translation). Vatican City: Libreria Editrice Vaticana, May 1, 1991. At http://w2.vatican.va/content/john-paul-ii/en/encyclicals/ documents/hf_jp-ii_enc_01051991_centesimus-annus.html.

Leo XIII. *Rerum novarum* (authorized English translation). Vatican City: Libreria Editrice Vaticana, May 15, 1891. At http://w2.vatican.va/content/leo-xiii/en/encyclicals/documents/ hf_l-xiii_enc_15051891_rerum-novarum.html.

Malthus, T. Robert. *An Essay on the Principle of Population* . . . . London: Johnson, 1798.

Mill, John Stuart. *Nature*. In *Three Essays on Religion*, vol. 10 of *Collected Works of John Stuart Mill*. Toronto: University of Toronto Press, [1874] 1969.

Mullarkey, Maureen. "Notes on the Vatican Climate." *First Things,* July 14, 2015.

Neuhaus, Richard John. Review Essay. *National Review* 43, no. 11 (Special Supplement, 1991): S8–S9.

Niles, Christina. "Breaking: Schellnhuber Appointed to Pontifical Academy of Science." *Church Militant*, June 17, 2015.

"Oregon Petition." n.d. Wikipedia.

Oreskes, Naomi, Dale Jamieson, and Michael Oppenheimer. "What Role for Scientists?" In Pontifical Academy of Sciences, *Sustainable Humanity, Sustainable Nature, Our Responsibility: Proceedings of the Joint Workshop, 2–4 May 2014*, Extra Series 41, edited by Partha Dasgupta, Veerabhadran Ramanathan, and Marcelo Sánchez Sorondo, 617–49. Vatican City: Pontifical Academy of Sciences, 2015.

Paley, William. *Natural Theology*. London: n.p., 1802.

Paul VI. *Populorum progressio* (authorized English translation). Vatican City: Libreria Editrice Vaticana, March 26, 1967. At http://w2.vatican.va/content/paul-vi/en /encyclicals/documents/ hf_p-vi_enc_26031967_populorum.html.

———. *Humanae vitae* (authorized English translation). Vatican City: Libreria Editrice Vaticana, July 25, 1968. At http://w2.vatican.va/content/paul-vi/en /encyclicals/ documents/hf_p-vi_enc_25071968_humanae-vitae.html.

———. *Octogesima adveniens* (authorized English translation). Vatican City: Libreria Editrice Vaticana, May 14, 1971. At http://w2.vatican.va/content/paul-vi/en /apost_letters/documents/hf_p-vi_apl_19710514_octogesima-adveniens.html.

Perelman, Michael. "Marx, Malthus, and the Organic Composition of Capital." *History of Political Economy* 17, no. 3 (1985): 461–90.

Pius XI. *Casti connubii* (authorized English translation). Vatican City: Libreria Editrice Vaticana, December 31, 1930. At https://w2.vatican.va/content/pius-xi/en /encyclicals/ documents/hf_p-xi_enc_19301231_casti-connubii.html.

———. *Quadragesimo anno* (authorized English translation). Vatican City: Libreria Editrice Vaticana, May 15, 1931. At http://w2.vatican.va/content/pius-xi/en /encyclicals/ documents/hf_p-xi_enc_19310515_quadragesimo-anno.html.

Pontifical Academy of Sciences. Statutes of the Academy. n.d. At http://www.pas .va/content/accademia/en/about/statutes.html.

Pontifical Council for Justice and Peace. *Compendium of the Social Doctrine of the Church*. Vatican City: Libreria Editrice Vaticana, 2004. At http://www.vatican .va/roman_curia/pontifical_councils/justpeace/documents/rc_pc_justpeace _doc_20060526_compendio-dott- soc_en.html.

Reno, R. R. "The Return of Catholic Anti-modernism." *First Things*, June 18, 2015.

Scammel, Rosie. "Cardinal George Pell Takes a Swing at Pope Francis' Environmental Encyclical." *Crux*, July 17, 2015.

Schellnhuber, Hans Joachim. "Common Ground: The Papal Encyclical, Science, and the Protection of Planet Earth." Potsdam Institute for Climate Impact Research, 2015. At https://www.pik-potsdam.de/images/common-ground.

Schellnhuber, Hans Joachim, and Maria A. Martin. "Climate-System Tipping Points and Extreme Weather Events." In *Sustainable Humanity, Sustainable Nature, Our*

Responsibility: Proceedings of the Joint Workshop, 2–4 May 2014, Extra Series 41, edited by Partha Dasgupta, Veerabhadran Ramanathan, and Marcelo Sánchez Sorondo, 151–70. Vatican City: Pontifical Academy of Sciences, 2015.

Segerfeldt, Fredrik. "Private Water Saves Lives." *Financial Times,* August 25, 2005.

Shannon, Christopher. "Romano Guardini: Father of the New Evangelization." *Crisis,* February 17, 2014.

"Simon–Ehrlich Wager." n.d. Wikipedia.

Simon, Julian. *The Ultimate Resource.* Princeton, N.J.: Princeton University Press, 1981.

Smith, Adam. *An Inquiry into the Nature and Causes of the Wealth of Nations.* 2 vols. Oxford: Oxford University Press, [1776] 1976.

Starkey, Thomas. *A Dialogue between Pole and Lupset.* Edited by T. F. Mayer. London: Royal Historical Society, [1538] 1989.

Temple, William. *Christianity and Social Order.* London: Society for Promoting Christian Knowledge, [1942] 1976.

Vanden Heuvel, Katrina. "Pope Francis vs. Wall Street." *Washington Post,* June 23, 2015.

Waterman, A. M. C. "Property Rights in John Locke and in Christian Social Teaching." *Review of Social Economy* 40, no. 2 (1982): 97–115.

———. "The Intellectual Context of *Rerum novarum.*" *Review of Social Economy* 49, no. 4 (1991): 465–82.

———. "Market Social Order and Christian Organicism in *Centesimus annus.*" *Journal of Markets and Morality* 2, no. 2 (Fall 1999): 220–33.

———. *Political Economy and Christian Theology since the Enlightenment: Essays in Intellectual History.* Studies in Modern History. Basingstoke, U.K.: Palgrave Macmillan, 2004.

———. "The English School of Political Economy." In *The New Palgrave Dictionary of Economics*, 2nd ed., edited by Steven N. Durlauf and Lawrence E. Blume. London: Palgrave Macmillan, 2008. At http.//www.dictionaryofeconomics.com /article?id=pde2008_P000355. doi:10.1057/9780230226203.0480.

———. "Theology and the Rise of Political Economy in Britain in the Eighteenth and Nineteenth Centuries." In *The Oxford Handbook of Christianity and Economics,* edited by Paul Oslington, 94–112. Oxford: Oxford University Press, 2014.

Wilkinson, Richard, and Kate Pickett. *The Spirit Level: Why Greater Equality Makes Societies Stronger.* London: Allen Lane, 2009.

6

Property Rights and Conservation

The Missing Theme of Laudato si'

Philip Booth

THE DEFENSE OF private property has generally been a key principle of Catholic social teaching. In some senses, this defense reached its zenith in *Rerum novarum* published in 1891. Often described as the "workers' encyclical," this papal letter by Leo XIII also had a vigorous defense of private property grounded in natural law. In later Catholic teaching, the importance of the institution of private property has often been stressed, but it has also been qualified. Furthermore, in writing about environmental issues, not only has the importance of private property rarely been put forward as a solution to environmental problems, but it has also been hinted that private-property rights may be one of the causes of environmental problems and that limits must therefore be put on private property to prevent environmental degradation.

This line of reasoning is interesting because in modern economics it is generally thought that better definition and enforcement of property rights are an important *solution* to environmental problems.[1] Thus, despite the Catholic Church's belief in the importance of private-property rights in general, the church seems to regard them as problematic in the very context that many modern economists see them as helpful.

This paper examines the importance of private property in Catholic teaching. It then considers the qualifications that the church has made in relation

---

1. Ronald Coase's "The Problem of Social Cost" is often thought to be an important early-modern contribution to this literature, though it is worth noting that Coase's main point was a more specific one than the simple idea that property rights are important for environmental protection.

to private-property rights and their role in environmental protection. Finally, it presents some of the economic work that shows how the institution of private property is crucial for the protection of environmental resources and amenities. The paper concludes by making the case that the recent papal encyclical *Laudato si'* would have been a more rounded document if it had considered the importance of private property for the protection of the environment. In the paper—explicitly so in the later sections—private property is broadly defined to include community control of property, too. This is something that Pope Francis is likely to be sympathetic with but that the encyclical does not explore systematically.

Private Property and the Early Church Teaching

Hermann Chroust and Robert Affeldt trace the church's attitude to private property from its earliest days. They argue that early Christians were initially hostile to private property, to large degree because they believed that the Second Coming was imminent and therefore that Christians should not focus on earthly things.[2] As time went on, this apocalyptic view of the world changed, and Christian societies became more integrated with wider society. The result of this integration was greater acceptance of private property. However, in most cases the argument was still made that private property should be put to social—in particular charitable—use.[3]

Despite this greater acceptance of private property, in the fourth and fifth centuries St. Athanasius and St. Basil were still very critical. The latter, for example, suggested that individuals who owned property had usurped what should be common to all.[4] St. Ambrose of Milan and St. Jerome also argued that before the Fall all property was held in common. Taking a similar view, St. John Chrysostom said in his eleventh homily on the Acts of the Apostles

---

2. Rodger Charles notes, however, that by reasserting the Ten Commandments, Christ affirmed the morality of private property (*Christian Social Witness and Teaching*, 40).

3. Chroust and Affeldt, "The Problem of Private Property According to St. Thomas Aquinas."

4. Ibid., 166.

that all people should sell their possessions and deliver the receipts to the community[5] and that private property was a product of the Fall.[6]

In his magisterial work on Catholic social teaching, Rodger Charles suggests, however, that the ownership of private property was widespread and that, taking the early church as a whole, the general view was favorable toward private property as long as those with riches were generous to those without.[7] Thus, although views may have been divided and important figures in the church spoke out against private property (and, in particular, against riches), there was clearly some acceptance of private property in practice, even in the early church.

Beginning in the medieval period, the concept of private property became much more widely accepted among Christian thinkers, especially if it was put to good social use—an issue I return to later. As Chroust and Affeldt put it,

> The ecclesiastic conception of property rights was cogently expressed by William of Auxerre, who says that the motive which induces one to acquire property is the element that determines the good or badness of the act. If a man accumulates property from the mere desire of possession, he commits a mortal sin. If, however, he does so from the practical realization that the weakness and greed of human nature demand distinct and pronounced property rights, the abolishment of which would lead to a war of all against all—then he does a good act.[8]

Furthermore, it can be reasonably argued that although private property was not necessary before the Fall, the reality of the Fall requires adaptations in sociopolitical-legal systems. Chroust and Affeldt continue: "Hence it might

---

5. "For at any rate this is evident, even from the facts which took place then, that by selling their possessions they did not come to be in need, but made them rich that were in need. However, let us now depict this state of things in words, and let all sell their possessions, and bring them into the common stock" ("Homily 11 on the Acts of the Apostles", Acts IV.23, at newadvent.org.)

6. As we shall see, though, the fact that private property was a product of the Fall does not mean that it is not an important and acceptable institution in a fallen world.

7. Charles, *Christian Social Witness and Teaching*, esp. 42–43, 92–94.

8. Chroust and Affeldt, "The Problem of Private Property According to St. Thomas Aquinas," 176.

be said that despite the radically idealistic exhortations of the Apologists and the Church fathers, a practico-social attitude of toleration toward private property and individual wealth finally prevailed and became accepted in the social teachings of the Church."[9]

Indeed, this was an important aspect of the teaching of St. Thomas Aquinas. He developed and clarified thinking on the right to property and expressed it in a form that has, in essence, remained the mainstay of the Catholic Church's teaching ever since. According to Chroust and Affeldt, Aquinas argues that the natural law can be used to justify the position that all property should be held in common, but this does not mean that natural law prevents persons from having possessions of their own.[10] Indeed, according to Aquinas, reason and experience suggest that private property is a product of the intelligent coexistence of human persons. This was especially true in the developing urban societies. As Aquinas states in *Summa theologica* 2.2, "Community of goods is ascribed to the natural law, not that the natural law dictates that all things should be possessed in common and that nothing should be possessed as one's own: but because the division of possessions is not according to the natural law, but rather arose from human agreement which belongs to positive law, as stated above. Hence the ownership of possessions is not contrary to the natural law, but an addition thereto devised by human reason."[11]

Aquinas and others believed that private property should be encouraged because it served important social purposes. According to Aquinas, private property has at least three important social functions.[12] First, it encourages people to work harder because they are working for what they might own— otherwise, people would shirk. Second, it ensures that affairs are conducted in a more orderly manner—people would understand what they are responsible for rather than everything being everybody's responsibility. And third, private property ensures peace if it is divided and its ownership understood.

---

9. Chroust and Affeldt, "The Problem of Private Property According to St. Thomas Aquinas," 176.

10. Ibid., 180.

11. Aquinas, *Summa theologica*, 1969.

12. See Charles, *Christian Social Witness and Teaching*, 207.

The late Scholastics continued to articulate the case for private property.[13] Indeed, Domingo de Soto (1494–1560) was explicit in defending it. He states: "[I]n a corrupted [i.e., fallen] state of nature, if men lived in common they would not live in peace, nor would the fields be fruitfully cultivated."[14] Here we see a relationship drawn between cultivation and caring for property and private ownership of property. As we shall see, this is something that is important in the context of the preservation of the environment.

Andre Alves and Jose Moreira elaborate on this point, noting that the position of the late Scholastics can be described in the following way: "the prime goal of material goods created by God is to allow the flourishing of human life. . . . [The late Scholastics] then followed (and significantly developed) the Thomist line of associating the justification for private property with its importance for the common good."[15] In this framework, it was generally recognized that private property led to incentives for the better use of resources.

It was argued that although private property is essential for the functioning of society, it must serve society and not be an end in itself. Thus, the extinguishing of private property through the extreme forms of socialism is not acceptable and is contrary to reason, but the existence of private property does not give human persons an untrammeled freedom not to use property for a social purpose, and the state may also own property for the good of society. The social purposes of private property can, though, be defined widely. For example, a social purpose may include housing one's family, running a business, and so on. But wantonly destroying property would not be a social purpose, and this distinction is of relevance to debates about private ownership and the environment.

It is worth noting that there is some debate in Catholic teaching as to whether private property is a natural right or a prudent device adopted because of its social benefits. I discuss this issue briefly later. Alves and Moreira argue that the late Scholastics, like Aquinas, held the belief that "the justification

---

13. For an excellent English-language introduction to the thinking of the late Scholastics, see Alves and Moreira, *The Salamanca School.*

14. Quoted in Alves and Moreira, *The Salamanca School,* 67.

15. Ibid.

for property was regarded as deriving from the promotion of the common good (and not as an absolute natural right)."[16] When it comes to the issue of the protection of the environment, it is private property's social role that is important and that will form the basis of the subsequent discussion.

Private Property and *Rerum novarum*

In 1891, Pope Leo XIII published what can be regarded as the Catholic Church's first modern social encyclical. In that document, *Rerum novarum*, there was a trenchant defense of private property. It followed many briefer and less analytical statements from the previous pontiff about the importance of property. For example, Pope Pius IX regularly mentioned the importance of private property in the context of attacks on the institution from socialism and communism.

Pope Leo came close to stating—and certainly implied—that property rights are a natural right. Such a justification would be stronger than the quasi-utilitarian argument based on the promotion of the common good in the context of the Fall generally used by theologians prior to *Rerum novarum*. Pope Leo stated, for example,

> It is surely undeniable that, when a man engages in remunerative labor, the impelling reason and motive of his work is to obtain property, and thereafter to hold it as his very own. If one man hires out to another his strength or skill, he does so for the purpose of receiving in return what is necessary for the satisfaction of his needs; he therefore expressly intends to acquire a right full and real, not only to the remuneration, but also to the disposal of such remuneration, just as he pleases. Thus, if he lives sparingly, saves money, and, for greater security, invests his savings in land, the land, in such case, is only his wages under another form; and, consequently, a working man's little estate thus purchased should be as completely at his full disposal as are the wages he receives for his labor.[17]

---

16. Quoted in Alves and Moreira, *The Salamanca School*, 44.

17. Leo XIII, *Rerum novarum*, 5.

The argument that property is a man's wages in another form is important because there has always been a very strong biblical and Catholic Church injunction against depriving a person of his justly earned wages. If justly acquired property simply amounts to wages in another form, the entitlement to property is much stronger than if such entitlement is justified on the prudential grounds of promoting the common good. Indeed, *Rerum novarum* went on to say, invoking natural rights again, "For, every man has by nature the right to possess property as his own."[18] However, it should be noted that just because all have the right to possess property, it does not mean that all property should be privately owned.

Continuing the theme of natural rights, but also linking private property, natural rights, and the human person's relationship with the environment, Pope Leo wrote:

> Here, again, we have further proof that private ownership is in accordance with the law of nature. Truly, that which is required for the preservation of life, and for life's well-being, is produced in great abundance from the soil, but not until man has brought it into cultivation and expended upon it his solicitude and skill. Now, when man thus turns the activity of his mind and the strength of his body toward procuring the fruits of nature, by such act he makes his own that portion of nature's field which he cultivates—that portion on which he leaves, as it were, the impress of his personality; and it cannot but be just that he should possess that portion as his very own, and have a right to hold it without any one being justified in violating that right.[19]

In paragraph 15, Pope Leo went further and described private-property rights as "inviolable."

A hint of the relevance of private property for the environment comes in paragraph 47: "Men always work harder and more readily when they work on that which belongs to them; nay, they learn to love the very soil that yields in response to the labor of their hands, not only food to eat, but an abundance

---

18. Ibid., 6.
19. Ibid., 8.

of good things for themselves and those that are dear to them." The suggestion is that they may love and better look after what is owned by them.

Thus, in *Rerum novarum* we have a strong defense of private property and possibly a widening of its justification. Catholic teaching in later social encyclicals have used arguments, certainly in terms of their emphasis, that are more similar to those of Thomas Aquinas and the late Scholastics than to those in *Rerum novarum*.

Private Property and Catholic Social Teaching in the Modern Era

John Paul II took up the theme of private property in *Centesimus annus* (1991), an encyclical written to celebrate the one-hundredth anniversary of *Rerum novarum*. Referring back to *Rerum novarum*, John Paul II restated the importance of that encyclical for modern times. Then he made an important qualification when it comes to the subject of private property. He stressed that private ownership must be subordinated to the social function of property and to the principle of the universal destination of goods. In this sense, *Centesimus annus* reiterated the teaching of the early church that if private ownership does not fulfill a social function in a particular context, then it should be questioned. Or, as the same writer put it four years earlier in *Sollicitudo rei socialis* (1987), referring also to the documents of Vatican II, "Private property, in fact, is under a 'social mortgage,' which means that it has an intrinsically social function."[20]

Indeed, in *Centesimus annus* John Paul specifically raised what he described as the "ecological question" in relation to private property.[21] He suggested that "[i]t is the task of the State to provide for the defense and preservation of common goods such as the natural and human environments, which cannot be safeguarded simply by market forces."[22] In doing so, he called into question the ability of private ownership to protect the environment. This is a key statement in Catholic thinking that has been at the root of criticism of private property in the context of protecting the environment.

---

20. John Paul II, *Sollicitudo rei socialis*, 42.
21. Ibid., 37.
22. Ibid., 40.

In *Laudato si'* (2015), Pope Francis repeats this argument without developing the reasoning further. This is something that could be regarded as an omission in a document that is wholly about ecological issues and was published nearly twenty-five years after *Centesimus annus*. In the intervening time, a huge amount of academic work had been undertaken on the relationship between the environment and property rights. Between the publication of *Centesimus annus* and *Laudato si'*, the Nobel Prize in Economics was awarded twice—in 1991 to Ronald Coase and in 2009 to Elinor Ostrom—at least in part for work relating to property rights, social costs, and the environment. Given the importance of the subject and the importance of private property in the church's teaching, *Laudato si'* would have made a bigger contribution to the church's social teaching if it considered property rights more fully.

The question of private property is raised in chapter 2, section 6, paragraphs 93–95, of *Laudato si'*. Pope Francis says that the Christian tradition has never recognized property rights as absolute or inviolable[23] and that they must be subordinated to a social purpose. This is merely reiterating previous teaching, though perhaps with a more negative emphasis. Then Pope Francis says, "The natural environment is a collective good, the patrimony of all humanity and the responsibility of everyone. If we make something our own, it is only to administer it for the good of all."[24]

This statement implicitly raises two very important questions, though the document simply moves on to another section and leaves them unaddressed. The first question is whether private-property rights are the best way to deal with the protection of the natural environment despite the implicit skepticism of recent Catholic social teaching in this area. The argument offered by Aquinas, the late Scholastics, and Catholic social teaching more generally is that private ownership helps deliver the social mortgage—in general, if not always. Might that be the case with the environment, too? Second, there is the question of whether there are particular forms of property rights that do not necessarily involve individualized ownership and thus might be especially effective in protecting environmental goods.

---

23. As it happens, Pope Leo XIII did specifically use the word inviolable, but it does not tend to appear in Catholic teaching elsewhere.

24. Francis, *Laudato si'*, 95.

Property Rights and Environmental Protection

The "Tragedy of the Commons"

In understanding the importance of property rights for environmental protection, it is instructive first to consider the problems caused by the absence of private property. The much-cited work on this question is Garrett Hardin's essay "The Tragedy of the Commons" (1968).

Hardin referred back to a pamphlet written in 1833 by William Forster Lloyd that described a situation whereby common land was open to grazing by all. The land would be overgrazed because a person would get the benefit of putting additional cattle on the land without the cost that arises from overgrazing, which would be shared by all users. This is even clearer with fish stocks. A trawler taking extra tuna from the ocean will benefit from doing so, but the—perhaps hugely greater—cost of taking the extra tuna in terms of lower levels of breeding will be shared among all trawler owners. The latter group includes not just those who own trawlers today but also those who will own them in the distant future.

As it happens, Hardin's article, which is regularly cited in relation to environmental protection and the importance of property rights, was really about another topic entirely. It proposed compulsory population control, and in this and other ways it is completely at odds with Catholic social teaching.[25] Hardin was also not specifically proposing private ownership as a way of dealing with the tragedy of the commons; he was simply using the example of the environmental commons as an entrée into his argument for controlling what he described as "human breeding." However, it is the lesson of the tragedy of the commons that is perhaps most widely repeated.

---

25. It is interesting that Hardin's essay seems to have become the "go to" reference on the environmental commons, especially by supporters of private property. However, Hardin did not originate the idea of the commons, which had come at least 130 years earlier, and his essay was on a subject that would be problematical not just to Catholics but to any supporters of a free economy: Hardin discussed coercive control of what he described as "human breeding" ("freedom to breed will bring ruin to all" [1968, 1248]) and the rejection of the Universal Declaration of Human Rights.

Government Control or Private Ownership?

The point of the tragedy of the commons is that it is the nonexistence of either property rights or the regulation of the use of an environmental resource that is said to be disastrous for environmental outcomes. This point cannot be reasonably disputed. However, the commons problem can be solved several ways: by state ownership, regulation, and control; by community ownership of one form or another; or by private ownership. It would appear that recent Catholic teaching has suggested, in the rather brief treatment of the issue, that some form of government control is necessary. However, if government control is not the only approach to protecting the environment, given other aspects of Catholic social teaching on property rights, it would seem that the church should favor private ownership—or at least welcome the possibility of private ownership. Certainly, the church should prudently consider the alternatives.

Private Property and the Environment

There is, indeed, much evidence that private property can play an important part in protecting the environment, just as it has an important social function in other contexts. Indeed, the absence of private property is often disastrous for environmental outcomes.

A stark example of how the lack of private-property rights can have an impact on the environment is given by the dramatic difference between forest cover on the two sides of the border between Haiti and the Dominican Republic. There is a distinct difference between the ecology of the two areas. As the United Nations puts it, "Environmental degradation in the worst affected parts of the Haitian border zone is almost completely irreversible, due to a near total loss of vegetation cover and productive topsoil across wide areas."[26] The Haitian side of the border is subject to almost complete loss of environmental resources. The same United Nations document reports that Haiti has 4 percent forest cover in contrast to 41 percent in the Dominican

---

26. United Nations Environment Program, "Haiti–Dominican Republic Environmental Challenges in the Border Zone," 6.

Republic.[27] Private ownership and the institutions that surround it provide the incentives for sustainability. Under private ownership, the value of a piece of land at any time will reflect the present value of all that can be yielded from the land in the indefinite future. The costs of damaging land in private ownership are huge because those costs can relate to all possible lost future production and not just to lost production over a year or two. Furthermore, land will not be nurtured and people will not invest in the land if they believe that it is going to be polluted or plundered by others. Private-property rights will often (though not always) need to be protected by good governance, good courts systems, and so on that can be provided by governments (see Catechism 2449, quoting from John Paul II's *Centesimus annus*). However, the absence of private-property rights properly enforced—not their presence—can be the problem when it comes to environmental protection. As Sebastien Marchand puts it, "[I]nstitutions such as property rights influence the importance of opportunity costs generated by deforestation. Therefore creating appropriate institutions allows for the reduction of uncertainty in exchange and results in reduced transaction and production costs of long-term activities such as sustainable forestry. The poor quality of institutions in developing countries may thus constitute a major impediment for forest conservation."[28]

In effect, the Haitian side of the border is a huge, ungoverned, and unowned commons. Haiti has been for much of the recent past a failed state (ranked eleventh in the *Foreign Policy* Fragile States Index[29]) and has a terrible record of corruption (175 out of 182 in the Transparency International Corruption Perception Index[30]). In relation to Haiti, the 2016 Heritage Index of Economic Freedom states that "clear titles to property are virtually nonexistent."[31] By no means is the Dominican Republic perfect, but it ranks about halfway up the latter index when it comes to the protection of property rights.

---

27. United Nations Environment Program, "Haiti–Dominican Republic Environmental Challenges in the Border Zone," 20, table 1.

28. Marchand, "The Colonial Origins of Deforestation," 323.

29. Fund for Peace, "Fragile States Index."

30. United Nations Environment Program, "Haiti–Dominican Republic Environmental Challenges in the Border Zone," 19, table 1.

31. "Haiti," Heritage Foundation.

Haiti and the Dominican Republic are a particularly interesting contrast because of their proximity to each other. However, there is abundant evidence that the lessons from this example can be generalized. For example, Claudio Araujo and his colleagues argue that "insecure property rights in land drive deforestation in the Brazilian Amazon."[32] The authors demonstrate a causal relationship that arises through several channels. Their results are strong and lead to the conclusion that an exogenous escalation in property-rights insecurity brings a significant increase in the rate of deforestation.

Interestingly, another paper that draws the same conclusions relates the problem of the lack of secure property rights to past imperial activity. David Novoa concludes, "[S]tronger property rights encourage less deforestation controlling for a number of variables."[33] He also argues that former British colonies have significantly better deforestation records (i.e., less deforestation) than former Spanish colonies. He believes that this result may have arisen because different colonial regimes had a different impact on the long-term security of property rights. Novoa argues that British regimes established local ownership of the forest so that local people (pioneers) had direct control over forest resources. "Thus, the British Colonial system provided incentives for joint maximization of the net present value of timber and nontimber forest products. In addition, the system promoted the internalization of external benefits that did not accrue to the owner of the land such as conservation of the soil or prevention of floods. Therefore, forest land use value tended to be comparatively higher than [in] a system of ill-defined property rights, consequently encouraging less deforestation."[34] In contrast, in Spanish colonies "[t]imber and most valuable nontimber forest products were property of the Spanish Crown by royal decree. . . . Therefore, the Spanish Colonial system intended to extract the main forest resources without building any kind of institutional framework for joint maximization of the total value of the forested land. . . . After colonial independence, government took over the ownership of the resources, however the control was in [the] hands of a powerful elite who was giving land concessions to the military."[35]

---

32. Araujo et al., "Property Rights and Deforestation in the Brazilian Amazon," 2467.
33. Novoa, *Deforestation and Property Rights*, 1.
34. Ibid., 3.
35. Ibid.

To make matters worse, because trees are often government-owned re-sources on private land, there is no incentive for the private owners of the land to manage them, and the owners take every opportunity possible to clear the forest so that the land can be used for private productive purposes. In this situation, the trees are utterly without value to the owners and cannot be managed sustainably.

This problem of a lack of well-defined and enforced property rights lead-ing to environmental degradation is repeated in relation to a wide range of environmental resources in many different circumstances.[36] It is exactly the sort of problem that ought to have been of interest to Catholic theologians and philosophers who gave these issues serious thought.

With respect to the statement in *Laudato si'* that "[t]he natural environ-ment is a collective good, the patrimony of all humanity and the responsibility of everyone. If we make something our own, it is only to administer it for the good of all,"[37] the general position held by Aquinas, the late Scholastics, and the early social encyclicals would be that by allowing people to make something their own, that something is more likely to be administered for the good of all. This principle is so crucial in relation to environmental goods and so widely discussed among economists examining environmental problems that it should have been an important subject of discussion in *Laudato si'*.

Wider Issues

Many other aspects of the relationship between property rights and the envi-ronment are important and, though not necessarily appropriate for discussion within an encyclical, might form a research agenda for Catholic scholars going forward. For example, where there are well-defined owners of an environ-mental resource in a regime characterized by good governance and juridical systems, it is less likely that individuals or corporations will damage property they do not own. In a regime of well-protected private-property rights, dam-age to one's neighbor's property will lead to prosecution or a requirement for

---

36. There are many other examples of the role of property rights in conservation, some of which can be found at the Property and Environment Research Center website, http://www .perc.org/.

37. Francis, *Laudato si'*, 95.

compensation. This will not be the case where environmental resources are effectively unowned, as indicated by the rain forest examples given earlier.

There are broader ways, too, in which a regime of strong private rights in the context of good governance can help protect the environment. First, a country with good governance, effective rule of law, and enforcement of private property in general is more likely to be able to protect effectively those environmental goods where limits do need to be put on commercial exploitation for the purposes of environmental protection. A state that performs well the task of enforcing property rights is more likely to be able to regulate the use of private property if that is deemed necessary because such regulation requires uncorrupt and efficient legal systems, law enforcement, and administration.

The absence of these aspects of good governance is probably the biggest threat to those environmental resources that cannot be commercially exploited and that are regulated to promote conservation.[38] For example, it has been estimated that "almost half (49 percent) of total tropical deforestation between 2000 and 2012 was due to illegal conversion for commercial agriculture."[39] Further analysis of Brazil by Sam Lawson suggests that such illegal forest destruction included deforestation in areas where those involved did not have land title as well as the flouting of regulations designed to limit deforestation.[40] This example also illustrates the difficulty of resorting to government control of property in the name of environmental protection when private ownership is deemed to have failed. If the legal systems for the protection and regulation of private property are not effective, it is highly unlikely that the state will be able to manage resources effectively and escape serious problems caused by corruption and other features of bad governance.

It is also worth noting that economies broadly based on the principles of economic freedom and private property are more likely to prosper. And as countries become more prosperous, they tend not only to adopt technologies that are less resource intensive per unit of gross domestic product (GDP) but

---

38. I am making no judgement as to whether such regulation is either a good thing or necessary. The point is that those who believe that it is a good thing or necessary would see their objectives better achieved in a political context where these aspects of good governance are present.

39. Lawson, "Consumer Goods and Deforestation," 2.

40. Ibid., 27.

also to value environmental goods more. When a community has a choice between eating and deforestation, eating wins. In more technical terms, a clean
environment is an income elastic good.[41] One example of this effect relates to
the emission of pollutants. In the United States, emissions, as measured by
an index of six major air pollutants, have fallen by 65 percent per head since
1980.[42] Indeed, no nation with an annual GDP per capita of more than $4,600
per annum had net forest loss in the period 2000 to 2005.[43] Though there is
still net deforestation taking place in the world as a whole, the annual rate has
more than halved—the rate was 0.08 percent between 2010 and 2015, fallen
from 0.18 percent in the early 1990s.[44,45]

Quasi–Property Rights

There may be practical reasons why it is difficult to develop property rights
in environmental resources in the classical sense of an individual, group, or
corporate organization having the right of exclusion in relation to the use
of property. Problems can sometimes be dealt with through more informal
property structures (as discussed later). However, in some cases, some of the
benefits of property rights can be obtained by using structures that mimic
the features of private property.

For example, quasi–property rights such as tradable quotas have been
successful in marine preservation. It is not the purpose of social encyclicals

---

41. The phenomenon of environmental outcomes first deteriorating and then improving
with income is described by what is often called an "environmental Kuznets curve." This idea
posits that as incomes rise from absolute poverty levels, environmental damage is likely to
increase, but after some higher-income level environmental damage will decrease. The idea
does not necessarily apply to all environmental goods. For example, there isn't a clear a priori
reason why it should apply where one country is imposing external costs on another country
(such as in the case of carbon emissions). However, here we are talking about environmental
resources that can be related to property, such as fisheries and forests.

42. U.S. Environmental Protection Agency, "National Air Quality: Status and Trends
of Key Air Pollutants."

43. See Kauppi et al., "Returning Forests Analyzed with the Forest Identity."

44. United Nations Food and Agriculture Organization, "World Deforestation Slows
Down as More Forests Are Better Managed."

45. Allowing for the effect of compounding, a 0.08 percent rate of deforestation would
lead to a loss of one-third of forest cover in about five hundred years.

to answer all problems pertaining to political economy. However, there is a clear a priori case for suggesting that the institution of private property—directly and indirectly—plays an important role in environmental protection and that there might be a role for the state in encouraging the development of quasi–property rights that are then traded in a formal framework.[46]

One field where such a tradable-property-rights approach has been used is fisheries. Christopher Costello and his colleagues suggest that various rights-based approaches to fishery management can have a substantial and rapid beneficial effect on fish stocks. Such systems can also reduce conflict by aligning the interests of trawler owners and those who set the fishing quotas. For example, if trawler owners are given a percentage share of the allowable catch in perpetuity, they have an incentive to maximize the long-term sustainability of the fishery in order to maximize the value of their tradable quota. Under many other systems, the trawler owners simply have an incentive to extract as many fish from the sea as soon as possible.[47] Hannes Gissurarson, writing about the Icelandic system of fishing quotas, which effectively divides up property rights in the total fishing catch to trawler owners in perpetuity, argues: "In Iceland, owners of fishing vessels now fully support a cautious setting of TACs [total allowable catches] in different species. They have become ardent conservationists. . . . [T]he private interests of individual fishermen coincide with the public interest."[48]

Neither Government nor Market: Elinor Ostrom

Elinor Ostrom won her Nobel Prize in economics in 2009 for demonstrating "how common property can be successfully managed by user associations and that economic analysis can shed light on most forms of social organization."[49] Given that Ostrom's work focuses on natural resources, that

---

46. *Laudato si'* does mention tradable quotas in the field of carbon emissions and strongly rejects them. If the drafters had looked more closely at such mechanisms, they might have noted the mechanisms' success in conserving resources and in ensuring that environmental resources are put to their most efficient uses.

47. Costello et al., "Global Fishery Prospects under Contrasting Management Regimes."

48. Gissurarson, *The Icelandic Fisheries*, 70.

49. "Elinor Ostrom—Facts."

the prize committee said that "[h]er research had great impact amongst political scientists and economists,"[50] and especially that there are many similarities between her way of thinking and some important strands of Catholic social teaching, it is perhaps surprising that some of her ideas are not reflected in *Laudato si'.*[51]

Despite the importance of private-property rights in dealing with environmental problems, not all such problems can be solved by the individualization of property rights.[52] Property rights can be much more complex—even when privately held—than the simple freehold ownership that is often common in Western societies,[53] and the regulation and enforcement of such property rights can take many forms.

Ostrom's thesis is simple. Communities can from the bottom up develop methods of controlling the consumption of environmental resources—fish and forests in particular—methods that are remarkably stable and effective. They can develop their own systems of enforcement, and the main role of government is to support those systems and not to take them over.

Perhaps the starting point for thinking about Ostrom's work in the context of Catholic social teaching is the principle of subsidiarity. This principle was defined by Pius XI in *Quadragesimo anno* in 1931.[54] That encyclical stated, "[I]t is an injustice and at the same time a grave evil and disturbance of right order to assign to a greater and higher association what lesser and subordinate organizations can do."[55] The principle of subsidiarity does not suggest that

---

50. "Elinor Ostrom—Facts."

51. Nathan Schneider "How Pope Francis Is Reviving Radical Catholic Economics" quotes Stefano Zamagni (who was close to the process that led to the development of Pope Benedict XVI's social encyclical *Caritas in veritate* [2009]) as reporting that Ostrom's work is on the "reading list" of the Pontifical Academy of Social Sciences.

52. I do not have space to explain why this might not be the case. However, tradition, weak institutions, and the nature of particular environmental problems might be reasons.

53. Even in Western societies, of course, more complex ownership arrangements can develop, and they often develop specifically to deal with problems of externalities relating to local aspects of the environment—for example, restrictive covenants on housing estates or restrictions on the use of shopswithin shopping centers. However, these arrangements tend to be laid down in formal legal agreements, which is not the case with many of the arrangements Ostrom discusses.

54. Though the word subsidiarity is not used in that encyclical.

55. Pius XI, *Quadragesimo anno*, 79.

there is no role for higher organizations (such as the state), but it does propose that their role should be limited. Specifically, it proposes that the state should aid other organizations in society in their function of promoting the common good. The principle of subsidiarity is important for many reasons, not least because the socialization that comes from people cooperating together itself promotes the virtues. This process can be undermined by unnecessary top-down intervention by the government, which instead should support rather than take initiative from the family and institutions of society.[56]

Ostrom defines a particular type of resource as a "common-pool resource."[57] Such a resource is reducible in consumption in the same way that a purely private good is reducible, and, as such, a common-pool resource is rivalrous in consumption (that is, if one person consumes the resource, it is not available for another person). However, as with what economists describe as a pure public good, it is difficult to exclude people from consuming a common-pool resource.[58]

Ostrom cites forests, fisheries, and the benefits of a clean atmosphere as common-pool resources. These are precisely the environmental resources about which Catholic social teaching has shown great concern and that are discussed in *Laudato si'*.

Ostrom found that certain design features of systems are important for the sustainability of a natural resource.[59] Some of these features are especially relevant to Catholic social teaching.

- *There should be clear and locally understood boundaries between legitimate users and nonusers.* This feature clearly implies some kind of private-property rights (at least rights of exclusion) even if those rights are not individualized.

---

56. See *Catechism of the Catholic Church*, paragraphs 1882 and 1883.

57. Ostrom and Ostrom, "Public Goods and Public Choices."

58. Ostrom's addition of the common-pool resource to the range of forms of goods leads to four categories in the economist's lexicon: a common-pool resource is reducible but not excludable; a club good (see Buchanan, "An Economic Theory of Clubs") is excludable but not reducible in consumption; a public good is both not reducible in consumption and non-excludable; finally, a private good is both excludable and reducible.

59. Discussed in Ostrom, "Beyond Markets and States," 422.

- There should be congruence with local social and environmental conditions. This feature is strongly in accord with the principle of subsidiarity.
- *The rights of local users to make their own rules are recognized by the government.* Again, this feature is a manifestation of the principle of subsidiarity. The role of the government is to facilitate users in developing and enforcing the rules rather than to take over that function from the people.
- When a common-pool resource is closely connected to a larger social-ecological system, governance activities are organized in multiple nested layers. Ostrom calls this feature "polycentricity." In many senses, this idea might be closer to the Calvinist principle of "sphere sovereignty," but it is another expression of the principle of subsidiarity whereby, as Pius XI wrote,

> Just as it is gravely wrong to take from individuals what they can accomplish by their own initiative and industry and give it to the community, so also it is an injustice and at the same time a grave evil and disturbance of right order to assign to a greater and higher association what lesser and subordinate organizations can do. For every social activity ought of its very nature to furnish help to the members of the body social, and never destroy and absorb them. . . . Thereby the State will more freely, powerfully, and effectively do all those things that belong to it alone because it alone can do them. . . . Therefore, those in power should be sure that the more perfectly a graduated order is kept among the various associations, in observance of the principle of "subsidiary function," the stronger social authority and effectiveness will be [and] the happier and more prosperous the condition of the State.[60]

In other words, if we think of the main role of the state in Ostrom's framework as being to aid the community in managing the resource, this role is a very clear aspect of the principle of subsidiarity.

---

60. Pius XI, *Quadragesimo anno*, 78–80.

Ostrom gives examples of how such stratified systems work.[61] She points out that textbook solutions to overfishing normally propose individual transferable quotas. These quotas might work in some circumstances (see the earlier discussion). But in other circumstances enforcement can be difficult. In the community-managed systems proposed by Ostrom, methods of exclusion from the resource are developed within the community itself. These methods might include limitations on the time boats can fish or limitations on the equipment they can use. These mechanisms are developed by the community itself so that "ownership" of the resource is, in effect, a qualified and shared right to fish, but monitoring and enforcement might be undertaken at a different level.[62] Also, information about the sustainability of the resource might be provided by a different body to help the community make decisions about the use of the resource. Higher levels of government can also provide mechanisms for dispute resolution (for example, through court systems).

Wai-Fung Lam describes how such polycentric systems might work in practice in the case of water use. He found that irrigation systems governed by the farmers themselves perform significantly better in terms of both agricultural productivity and environmental outcomes. In the farmer-governed systems, farmers communicate with one another at annual meetings and informally on a regular basis, develop their own agreements, establish the positions of monitors, and sanction those who do not conform to their own rules. He found that although farmer-governed systems do vary in performance, few perform as poorly as government systems. The farmers have a common interest in promoting conservation of water resources and are arguably in the best position to manage the water resource. If the water were an unowned and unmanaged resource, it would be overused. If it were managed by the government, there would be no strong incentive for the government to manage it sustainably, or the government may simply lack the capacity to manage it even if it has the will to do so.[63]

---

61. Ostrom, *The Future of the Commons*, 80–81.

62. However, methods of enforcement can often be quite informal—for instance, the general membership may shun a member of the community who has transgressed.

63. Lam, *Governing Irrigation Systems in Nepal*.

As has been noted, the support within Catholic social teaching for the principle of private property has generally been based on prudence. Given our human nature, private property is the best way to ensure economic harmony and prosperity. Researchers have provided much evidence to suggest that the form of community control proposed by Ostrom is successful at maintaining environmental resources in a range of situations—especially in poor countries. One example she provides is that of forests, which are especially important in both the promotion of biodiversity and as carbon sinks. They should therefore have been especially interesting to those involved in drafting *Laudato si'*.

Ostrom cites a great deal of evidence that local monitoring of forests tends to lead to better outcomes. Furthermore, the centralization of the control of forests within government can lead to the deforestation of stable forests. Ostrom concludes: "[I]t is not the general type of forest governance that is crucial in explaining forest conditions; rather, it is how a particular governance arrangement fits the local ecology, how specific rules are developed and adapted over time, and whether users consider the system to be legitimate and equitable."[64] This, again, is an important expression of the principle of subsidiarity: the key principle is not the absence of or presence of government but the fact that the government is operating in a way that supports the community's initiative rather than supplanting it.

Ostrom is clear that the social context in which environmental resources are managed must run with the grain of self-interest. As such, a system will be more successful where individuals know that their actions are likely to make a difference to the outcome, from which they will benefit along with the wider community. Certainly, there is nothing in Catholic social teaching against social institutions running with the grain of benign forms of self-interest, and, indeed, Ostrom here seems to echo *Centesimus annus*, which states: "The social order will be all the more stable, the more it takes this fact into account and does not place in opposition personal interest and the interests of society as a whole, but rather seeks ways to bring them into fruitful harmony. In fact, where self-interest is violently suppressed, it is replaced by

---

64. Ostrom, "Beyond Markets and States," 429.

a burdensome system of bureaucratic control which dries up the wellsprings of initiative and creativity."[65]

Ostrom ends her Nobel lecture by saying: "Extensive empirical research leads me to argue that instead [of designing institutions that force individuals to achieve better outcomes], a core goal of public policy should be to facilitate the development of institutions that bring out the best in humans."[66] In many ways, this summary of Elinor Ostrom's thinking accords with the principle of subsidiarity and with the thinking of Thomas Aquinas. Not only should action take place at the lowest level possible, but action by higher levels of government should also *support* rather than displace action by lower levels in society. Pope Benedict XVI expressed this point especially well in *Deus caritas est*: "We do not need a State which regulates and controls everything, but a State which, in accordance with the principle of subsidiarity, generously acknowledges and supports initiatives arising from the different social forces and combines spontaneity with closeness to those in need."[67] Pope Benedict was specifically referring to action in the field of welfare here, but the principle applies with equal weight to community action to develop structures to preserve natural resources.

Conclusion

The Catholic Church has generally promoted the principle of private property. Private property has sometimes been regarded as a natural right, and the church's attacks on socialism's undermining of property in the nineteenth century were particularly strong. At the very least, the church has regarded private property as socially useful in a fallen world, though recent social encyclicals have suggested that it might be reasonable to put constraints on private ownership to promote environmental aims.

Pope Francis's recent encyclical on environmental matters, *Laudato si'*, repeats such qualifications of the church's support for private property. However,

---

65. John Paul II, *Centesimus annus*, 25.
66. Ostrom, "Beyond Markets and States," 435–36.
67. Benedict XVI, *Deus caritas est*, 28.

between the publication of *Sollicitudo rei socialis* in 1987, which *Laudato si'* quotes on private property and the environment, and the publication of *Laudato si'* itself in 2015, a huge amount of work has demonstrated the importance of private property for the environment.

Private property can promote environmental conservation in a number of direct and indirect ways. The environmental record of countries without a good record of protecting the institution of private property is lamentable, and this relationship applies across a wide range of ecologies.

It may sometimes be the case that some kind of government regulation is important for environmental conservation. However, even this is easier to achieve in a country that has good governance combined with well-defined and well-protected property rights.

Pope Francis could have used *Laudato si'* to update and develop the church's teaching on private property and, in particular, to explain that the institution in various forms can be important for environmental conservation.

The work of Nobel laureate Elinor Ostrom is especially pertinent. In many respects, it rests on similar premises to Catholic social teaching. Essentially empirical, her work shows indirectly that the basic pillars of Catholic social teaching lead to effective results in practice and empower communities in a way consistent with a Catholic view of integral human development. *Laudato si'* would have been greatly enriched by including Ostrom's ideas. The absence of these ideas and the lack of a considered and positive discussion of the role that private property plays in the protection of our natural ecology are regrettable omissions. The church has missed an opportunity to enable its faithful to contribute in a positive way to a debate with long-term consequences for the environment and for social policy. Because of its long tradition of concern for the environment and for poor communities and its interest in the right to private property, the church should contribute to that debate in the future.

References

Alves, Andre, and Jose Moreira. *The Salamanca School*. London: Continuum, 2010.

Aquinas, Thomas. *Summa theologica*. [1265–74]. At http://www.basilica.org/pages /ebooks/ St.%20Thomas%20Aquinas-Summa%20Theologica.pdf.

Araujo, Claudio, Catherine Araujo Bonjean, Jean-Louis Combes, Motel Pascal Combes, Eustaquio J. Reis. "Property Rights and Deforestation in the Brazilian Amazon." *Ecological Economics* 68, nos. 8–9 (June 2009): 2461–68.

Benedict XVI. *Deus caritas est* (authorized English translation). Vatican City: Libreria Editrice Vaticana, December 25, 2005. At http://w2.vatican.va/content /benedict-xvi/en/encyclicals/documents/hf_ben-xvi_enc_20051225_deus -caritas-est.html.

———. *Caritas in veritate* (authorized English translation). June 29, 2009. Vatican: Libreria Editrice Vaticana. At http://w2.vatican.va/content/benedict -xvi/en/encyclicals/documents/ hf_ben-xvi_enc_20090629_caritas-in-veritate .html.

Buchanan, James. "An Economic Theory of Clubs." *Economica* 32, no. 125 (1965): 1–14.

Catechism of the Catholic Church. London: Geoffrey Chapman, 1994.

Charles, Rodger. *Christian Social Witness and Teaching: The Catholic Tradition from Genesis to Centesimus annus.* Vol. 1. Leominster, Mass.: Gracewing, 1998.

Chroust, Hermann, and Robert J. Affeldt. "The Problem of Private Property According to St. Thomas Aquinas." *Marquette Law Review* 34, no. 3 (1951): 152–82.

Coase, Ronald H. "The Problem of Social Cost." *Journal of Law and Economics* 3 (1960):1–44.

Costello, Christopher, Daniel Ovando, Tyler Clavelle, Kent Strauss, Ray Hilborn, Michael

"Elinor Ostrom—Facts." Nobelprize.org, August 23, 2016. At http://www.nobel prize.org/ nobel_prizes/economic-sciences/laureates/2009/ostrom-facts.html.

Francis. *Laudato si'* (authorized English translation). Vatican City: Libreria Editrice Vaticana, May 24, 2015. At http://w2.vatican.va/content/francesco/en/encyclicals /documents/papa-francesco_20150524_enciclica-laudato-si.html.

Fund for Peace. "Fragile States Index." *Foreign Policy,* June 17, 2015.

Gissurarson, Hannes N. *The Icelandic Fisheries: Sustainable and Profitable.* Reykjavik: University of Iceland Press, 2015.

"Haiti." Heritage Foundation. In *2016 Heritage Index of Economic Freedom.* 2016. At http://www.heritage.org/index/country/Haiti.

Hardin, Garrett. "The Tragedy of the Commons." *Science* 162 (1968):1243–48.

John Paul II. *Sollicitudo rei socialis* (authorized English translation). Vatican City: Libreria Editrice Vaticana, December 30, 1987. At http://w2.vatican.va/conten /john-paul-ii/ en/encyclicals/documents/hf_jp-ii_enc_30121987_sollicitudo -rei-socialis.html.

————. *Centesimus annus* (authorized English translation). Vatican City: Libreria Editrice Vaticana, May 1, 1991. At http://w2.vatican.va/content/john-paul-ii/en/encyclicals/ documents/hf_jp-ii_enc_01051991_centesimus-annus.html.

Kauppi, Pekka E., Jess H. Ausubel, Jingyun Fang, Alexander S. Mather, Roger A. Sedjo, and Paul E. Waggoner. "Returning Forests Analyzed with the Forest Identity." *Proceedings of the National Academy of Sciences* 103, no. 46 (2006): 17574–79.

Lam, Wai-Fung. *Governing Irrigation Systems in Nepal: Institutions, Infrastructure, and Collective Action.* Oakland, CA: ICS Press, 1998.

Lawson, Sam. "Consumer Goods and Deforestation: An Analysis of the Extent and Nature of Illegality in Forest Conversion for Agriculture and Timber Plantations." Forest Trends Report Series. Washington, DC: Forest Trends, 2014. At http://www.forest-trends.org/illegal- deforestation.php.

Leo XIII. *Rerum novarum* (authorized English translation). Vatican City: Libreria Editrice Vaticana, May 15, 1891. At http://w2.vatican.va/content/leo-xiii/en/encyclicals/documents/ hf_l-xiii_enc_15051891_rerum-novarum.html.

Marchand, Sebastien. "The Colonial Origins of Deforestation: An Institutional Analysis." Environment and Development Economics 21, no. 3 (2016): 318 49.

Melnychuk, C., Trevor A. Branch, et al. "Global Fishery Prospects under Contrasting Management Regimes." *Proceedings of the National Academy of Sciences* 113, no. 18 (2016): 5125–29.

Novoa, David Corderí. *Deforestation and Property Rights: A Comparison between Former British and Spanish Colonies.* Economic Analysis Working Papers no. 7, 2007. At http://www.unagaliciamoderna.com/eawp/coldata/upload/Deforestation _property_ rights.pdf.

Ostrom, Elinor. "Beyond Markets and States: Polycentric Governance of Complex Economic Systems." Nobel Prize Lecture, December 8, 2009. Stockholm University.

————. *The Future of the Commons: Beyond Market Failure and Government Regulation.* Occasional Paper no. 148. London: Institute of Economic Affairs, 2012.

Ostrom, Vincent, and Elinor Ostrom. "Public Goods and Public Choices." In *Alternatives for Delivering Public Services: Toward Improved Performance*, edited by Emanuel S. Savas, 7–49. Boulder, Colo.: Westview Press, 1977.

Pius XI. *Quadragesimo anno* (authorized English translation). Vatican: Libreria Editrice Vaticana, May 15, 1931. At http://w2.vatican.va/content/pius-xi/en/encyclicals/documents/ hf_p-xi_enc_19310515_quadragesimo-anno.html.

Schneider, Nathan. "How Pope Francis Is Reviving Radical Catholic Economics." *The Nation*, September 9, 2015.

United Nations Environment Program. "Haiti–Dominican Republic Environmental Challenges in the Border Zone." Nairobi: United Nations Environment Program, 2013. At http://postconflict.unep.ch/publications/UNEP_Haiti-DomRep _border_zone_EN.pdf.

United Nations Food and Agriculture Organization. "World Deforestation Slows Down as More Forests Are Better Managed." September 7, 2015. At http://www .fao.org/news/story/ en/item/326911/icode/.

U.S. Environmental Protection Agency. "National Air Quality: Status and Trends of Key Air Pollutants." August 1, 2016. At https://www3.epa.gov/airtrends/aqtrends .html#comparison.

7

The Family Economics of Pope Francis
Allan C. Carlson

ALONGSIDE ISSUES OF capitalist organization, property rights, poverty and social justice, wealth creation, charity, income distribution, and environmental health lies the micro-economy of the family. The distinct questions involved here include:

- What is the primary economic unit of society? The individual? Or the household?
- What is the value and meaning of home production, relative to the market?
- How ought men and women relate economically within the family?
- How should children be viewed? Are they, in economic terms, a consumption choice? Or do they hold a unique status?
- How should the Malthusian quandary, positing a tension between fertility within each family and national or global sustainability, be understood and resolved?
- What social values should animate the economy, as a whole?

Since his accession to the throne of St. Peter, Pope Francis has provided answers to all of these questions. While they do not form a fully developed and consistent family economics, they come close and suggest a coherent vision. The major surprise is the relationship of Francis's encyclical, *Laudato si'* ("On Care of Our Common Home") to his apostolic exhortation, *Amoris laetitia* ("On Love in the Family"). Commentary on the former has emphasized Francis's embrace of a strong, even radical environmentalism. Attention to the latter has focused on his more "pastoral" (critics say "weaker") approach to the status and treatment of civilly divorced and remarried laity. Largely ignored has been the fundamental unity of these two documents on matters of the family economy.

Theological Foundations

As would be expected, Francis's understanding of the home economy grows out of his retelling of the rich Catholic theology of the family. At the most important level, Francis emphasizes the direct relation of the family to the Godhead, or the Trinity of Father, Son, and Holy Spirit. As he writes in *Laudato si'*, "The Trinity has left its mark on all creation."[1] He elaborates: "The triune God is a communion of love, and the family is its living reflection." Using even more potent language, Francis adds: "The family is thus not unrelated to God's very being." Similar concepts include attention to "the icon of the Holy Family of Nazareth," most especially to its "daily life." In his ministry on earth, Francis explains, Jesus "restored marriage and the family to their original form . . . in the image of the Holy Trinity, the mystery from which all true love flows."[2]

In this manner the family—understood as one man bound to one woman in a sacramental indissoluble union and their children—rests at the center of the whole of Creation. As Francis declared before a gathering of American bishops in September 2015: "the family is . . . the joyous confirmation of God's blessing upon the masterpiece of creation." It is "the fundamental locus of the covenant between the Church and God's creation."[3] In this way, "the Gospel of the Family spans the history of the world, from the creation of man and woman in the image and likeness of God" to the very "end of time," described in *Revelation* as consummated in "the marriage of the Lamb."

During the interim (in which we now live), the Son of God gives to married couples "in the joys of their love and family life" a "foretaste" of that very

---

1. Francis, *Laudato si'*, 239.

2. Francis, *Amoris laetitia*, 11, 30, 63.

3. Francis, Address for the Meeting with Bishops Taking Part in the World Meeting of Families, 1.

wedding feast. Through their biological fruitfulness, married couples also become co-creators with God.[4]

Because of this, the family directly participates in the salvation process. The "incarnation of the Word" occurred in a human family in Nazareth. Francis underscores that the "ability of human couples to beget life is the path along which the history of salvation progresses." Indeed, the "welfare of the family is decisive for the future of the world and that of the Church."[5] The family is "an integral part" of God's "loving plan for humanity."[6] A couple's desire to create a family "is to resolve to be a part of God's dream, to choose to dream with him, to want to build with him. . ."[7] Accordingly, the faithful family "is the salt of the earth and the light of the world, it is the leaven of society as a whole."[8] Indeed, adopting language once used exclusively by the Protestant Reformers, Francis declares that the Roman Catholic Church "is a family of families, constantly enriched by the lives of all those domestic churches."[9]

Given the bonds of the family to the very nature of God, to the created world, to the pageant of salvation, and to the consummation of history, any disorder within Creation leads to disorder within the family, and vice versa. Accordingly, Francis holds that "the crisis of the family has produced a human ecological crisis."[10] On the obverse side, the environmental crisis "cannot be separated from the analysis of human, *family*, *work-related*, and *urban* contexts."[11] The "social degeneration" harming the family begins "when human beings tyrannize nature, selfishly and even brutally ravaging it."[12] Given a wonderful world by God, humans—"since we are not too smart"—"are now in the process of destroying" it, including the "most beautiful thing which

---

4. Francis, *Amoris laetitia*, 50, 73, 166–69.

5. Ibid., 63, 22, 31.

6. Francis, Homily for the Holy Mass for the Opening of the Extraordinary Synod on the Family, 1.

7. Francis, Address for the Prayer Vigil for the Festival of Families, 3.

8. Francis, Homily for the Holy Mass for the Family Day on the Occasion of the Year of Faith, 2.

9. Francis, *Amoris laetitia*, 87.

10. Francis, Address to Participants in the International Colloquium on the Complementarity Between Men and Women, 2.

11. Francis, *Laudato si'*, 141, emphasis added.

12. Francis, *Amoris laetitia*, 26.

God made . . . the family."[13] Mary, the Mother of God and Queen of Creation, grieves for a world "laid waste by human power."[14] And she grieves especially for damage to the family.

The Building Block of Society . . . and Economy

On the matter of defining the fundamental economic unit of society, Francis strongly favors the family household. His critique of individualism is relentless. He underscores the perils of considering ourselves as "autonomous" beings. Proper social order comes only "[i]f we can overcome individualism."[15] In *Amoris laetitia*, he describes the desire by some lay folk to remain unmarried as "adolescent individualism." Elsewhere, he equates a false "personalism" with "fear of commitment, self-centeredness, and arrogance." Francis condemns "an extreme individualism which weakens family bonds and ends up considering each member of the family as an isolated unit." In blasting "ideologies which devalue marriage and family," he implicitly includes liberalism with its grounding in individualism.[16] And he sternly corrects those who "believe that they are free as long as they have the supposed freedom to consume."[17] "Freedom is not the ability simply to do what I want."[18]

On the positive side, the pope insists that "the People of God [is] composed, for the most part, of families." Indeed, he declares it "impossible to quantify the strength and depth of humanity contained in a family." Found therein are the economic tasks of "mutual help," education and sharing. Families are the very "bricks" for "the building up of society."[19] In the family, unlike in the marketplace, "love is free!" And here "true freedom" can be found: *"the gift of being able to choose the good."*[20]

---

13. Francis, Address for the Prayer Vigil for the Festival of Families, 1.

14. Francis, *Laudato si'*, 241.

15. Francis, *Laudato si'*, 208, 224.

16. Francis, *Amoris laetitia*, 131, 33, 40.

17. Francis, *Laudato si'*, 203.

18. Francis, Homily for the Extraordinary Jubilee of Mercy—Jubilee for Boys and Girls, 2.

19. Pope Francis, Homily for the Holy Mass for the Feast of the Exaltation of the Holy Cross, 1.

20. Francis, Homily for the Extraordinary Jubilee of Mercy—Jubilee for Boys and Girls, 2, emphasis in original.

Francis is also relentless in his critique of the vast urban-industrial revolution. "Consumerism" draws his strongest rebukes. In *Laudato si'*, expectedly, the pope rejects "[a] consumerist vision of human beings, encouraged by the mechanisms of today's globalized economy," for levelling the "immense variety" of human cultures. He argues that "the market tends to promote extreme consumerism" and "a whirlwind of needless buying and selling." Indeed, it is "the highly effective workings of the market" that feeds the destructive "paradigm of consumerism" threatening the globe.[21] Unexpectedly, the same themes animate *Amoris laetitia*. "Consumerist propaganda"—his term for advertising—"presents a fantasy that has nothing to do with reality." In "a consumerist society," Francis writes, "the sense of beauty is impoverished and so joy fades." He continues: "Everything is there to be purchased, possessed or consumed, including people." As examples, he condemns surrogate maternity as "the exploitation and commercialization of the female body" and the "spread of pornography" as the fruit of capitalism.[22]

In Francis's view, consumerism has infected all of human life, "[c]onsuming relationships, consuming friendships, consuming religions, consuming, consuming. . . . Whatever the costs or consequences." This economic system "does not favor bonding"; it "has little to do with human relationships." Rather, under industrial capitalism, human contacts are a "mere 'means' for the satisfaction of 'my needs.'" In this system, the neighbor is lost, along "with his or her familiar face, story, and personality."[23]

Marriage is affected as well. Francis despairs over consumerist cultures that pressure young people "not to start a family" by simultaneously denying them stable economic "possibilities for the future" while presenting them with too many other options.[24] Francis notes that in the past, Buenos Aires mothers often complained about their sons "who were 30, 32, or 34 years old and still single." His response as a young priest had been: "Well, stop ironing their shirts!"[25] His implication is that such simple answers no longer suffice.

---

21. Francis, *Laudato si'*, 144, 203, 215.

22. Francis, *Amoris laetitia*, 101, 127, 54, 41.

23. Francis, Address for the Meeting with Bishops Taking Part in the World Meeting of Families, 2.

24. Francis, Address to the Joint Session of the United States Congress, 6.

25. Francis, Address for the Meeting with Bishops Taking Part in the World Meeting of Families, 3.

This criticism carries over into a fairly dark vision of the industrialized city. Francis points to "the disproportionate and unruly growth of many cities," adding: "We were not meant to be inundated by cement, asphalt, glass and metal, and deprived of physical contact with nature." Cities take an even deeper toll through their "constant noise, interminable and nerve-wracking distractions," and "the cult of appearances."[26] In "big cities," the "roar of traffic," "smog," and a "deafening anonymity" lead to the depersonalization of all humans, especially foreigners, children, the homeless, and the elderly.[27]

In contrast, Pope Francis gives praise to the simple, albeit "economic" tasks of the home. He describes the active home as "the domestic pilgrimage of daily family life."[28] Referring to Psalm 128, he praises the work of the husband and father, who "shall eat the fruit of the labor" of his hands and "shall be happy," and of his wife who "will be like a fruitful vine within your home." For both, "your children will be like olive shoots round your table," promising the faithful that they might see their "children's children." For the early Christians, the home was also a "domestic church," "a setting for the Eucharist, the presence of Christ seated at its table." The Bible, Francis relates, describes the family home as the place where children are raised in the faith, where parents become "their children's first teachers in the faith." More broadly, the sacrament of marriage invests the spouses "with a true and proper mission, so that, starting with the simple ordinary things of life they can make visible the love with which Christ loves his Church. . . ." As a "friendship marked by passion," marriage leads the couple into an "all-encompassing" union, "permeating their entire lives," where they "share everything in constant mutual respect."[29]

Francis provides concrete examples of how the Christian home economy properly relates to a healthy economic order. Drawing from the bishops of Paraguay, he holds that every farmer "has a natural right to possess a reasonable allotment of land where he can establish his home, [and] work for subsistence of his family and a secure life."[30] Alongside this advocacy for the

---

26. Francis, *Laudato si'*, 44, 205.
27. Francis, Homily for The Holy Mass at Madison Square Garden, 1–2.
28. Francis, Homily for the Holy Mass for Families, 1–2.
29. Francis, *Amoris laetitia*, 7–10, 15–16, 121, 125.
30. Francis, *Laudato si'*, 94.

subsistence family farm, Francis praises the small "neighborhood store," where business is conducted "on the basis of trust" and people know one another and are "all neighbors." He contrasts such family-held and operated shops with the megamarkets and superstores where business "is no longer conducted on the basis of trust."[31]

The Beauty of Complementarity

In the absence of other values, the market economy welcomes the competitive labor of women, children, and men alike. Modern equity feminism aims for the full movement of all able women into paid employment.

Pope Francis rejects this form of feminism. True, he says favorable things about "the recognition of women's rights and their participation in public life." He welcomes an end to the old patriarchy and "false" forms of "male chauvinism."[32] However, his primary emphasis is on the differences between men and women, distinctions that carry over into the world of work.

For example, Francis quotes John Paul II on sexual differentiation, seeing it as "a source of fruitfulness and procreation" and as possessing "the capacity of expressing love: that love precisely in which the human person becomes a gift."[33] In contrast to the secular, levelling ideology of feminism, Francis raises up the Virgin Mary, "the one who opens the way to the Church's motherhood and constantly sustains her maternal mission to all mankind."[34] Francis holds that "[t]he weakening of this maternal presence with its feminine qualities poses a grave risk to our world." He rejects a feminism that demands uniformity or negates motherhood. The special feminine abilities—"motherhood in particular"—actually impose duties on women, "because womanhood also entails a specific mission in this world, a mission that society needs to protect and preserve for the good of all."[35]

---

31. Francis, Address for the Meeting with Bishops Taking Part in the World Meeting of Families, 2.

32. Francis, *Amoris laetitia*, 54.

33. Ibid., 151.

34. Francis, Homily for the Holy Mass on the Solemnity of Mary, Mother of God, XL-VIII World Day of Peace, 2.

35. Francis, *Amoris laetitia*, 173.

This rejection of equity feminism carries into a strong denunciation of contemporary gender theory, the idea that maleness and femaleness exist on a continuum, with no intrinsic relationship to one's biological body. As Francis writes, ". . . valuing one's own body in its [biological] femininity or masculinity is necessary if I am going to be able to recognize myself in an encounter with someone who is different."[36] He deplores the "ideology of gender" which "denies the difference and reciprocity in nature of a man and a woman" and seeks a society without sex distinctions, "thereby eliminating the anthropological basis of the family." This explains his forceful rejection of "same sex marriage," for "only the exclusive and indissoluble union between a man and a woman has a plenary role to play in society as a stable commitment that bears fruit in new life."[37]

Instead, Francis praises the complementarity of men and women, with spiritual and human equality conditioned by a celebration of differences. He finds in complementarity a dynamic harmony which lies "at the heart of all Creation" and serves as "the foundation of marriage and the family."[38] This "profound harmony," involving "a closeness both physical and interior," is "evoked not only in its sexual and corporal dimension, but also in its voluntary self-giving in love."[39]

Indeed, Francis holds that "biological sex and the socio-cultural role of [sex] can be distinguished but not separated." Put another way, there are feminine and masculine "roles" grounded in human nature. Mothers, Francis tells us, find their primary task in *Proverbs* 31, which "presents the labor of mothers within the family; their daily work is described in detail as winning the praise of their husbands and children." Another distinctive female task drawing praise from Francis is breast feeding, "a delicate and tender intimacy between mother and child." In these ways, mothers serve as "the strongest antidote to the spread of self-serving individualism," including certainly its economic expressions.[40]

---

36. Francis, *Laudato si'*, 155.

37. Francis, *Amoris laetitia*, 56, 52.

38. Francis, Address to Participants in the International Colloquium on the Complementarity Between Men and Women, 1.

39. Francis, *Amoris laetitia*, 13.

40. Francis, *Amoris laetitia*, 56, 24, 28, 174.

For their part, fathers naturally serve as workers and breadwinners, to provide "for the sustenance, stability, and fruitfulness" of their families. Francis praises men who "are conscious of the importance of their role in the family and live their masculinity accordingly." Where mothers introduce their children into a "good and welcoming" world, he says that fathers help their children "to perceive the limits of life, to be open to the challenges of the wider world, and to see the need for hard work and strenuous effort."[41]

Pope Francis insists that marriage amplifies the differences between men and women, "wherein the husband helps his wife to become ever more a woman, and wherein the woman . . . [helps] her husband to become ever more a man."[42] Such language implies that Francis would join several of his predecessors in endorsing a "family wage." Calling maternal employment "an intolerable abuse . . . to be abolished at all costs," Pope Pius XI urged that "[e]very effort must therefore be made" to insure "that fathers of families receive a wage large enough to meet ordinary family needs adequately."[43] And John Paul II concurred, arguing that "society must be structured in such a way that wives and mothers are not in practice compelled to work outside the home, and that their families can live and prosper in a dignified way even when they devote themselves full time to their own family."[44] Still, by avoiding direct commentary on a "just wage," Francis leaves the issue hanging.

On Children

Pope Francis leaves no doubt, however, regarding the valuation of children. He joyfully embraces them as gifts from God, as "living stones" of the family. Drawing from the Psalmist, Francis affirms that "[l]ike arrows in the hand of a warrior are the sons of one's youth. Happy is the man who has his quiver full of them!" As among the ancient Hebrews, "the presence of children is a sign of the continuity of the family throughout salvation history, from generation to generation." Furthermore, each new life "allows us to appreciate the utterly

---

41. Francis, *Amoris laetitia*, 24, 55, 175.

42. Francis, Homily for the Holy Mass for the Feast of the Exaltation of the Holy Cross, 2; *Amoris laetitia*, 221.

43. Pius XI, *Quadragesimo anno*, 15.

44. John Paul II, *Familiaris consortio*.

gratuitous dimension of love . . . . It is the beauty of being loved first: children are loved even before they arrive." Francis concludes that "[l]arge families are a joy for the Church," because they affirm "the fruitfulness of love."[45]

Predictably, Pope Francis denounces the view of children as merely a consumption choice, a contention held by many liberal economists especially when they approach tax policy. For the pope, children are, in a way, the means of the salvation process, the very purpose of human history! His list of hostile forces that deter people from having children includes industrialization, economic woes, "consumerism," the sexual revolution, and "fear of overpopulation."[46]

The latter two of these forces point toward the Malthusian quandary: the contention that unregulated human sexuality leads to overpopulation and poverty. The standard "neo-Malthusian" answer has been to praise and welcome any and all birth control techniques that would limit human numbers. Many Protestant denominations followed this path in the twentieth century.[47] Roman Catholic leaders, however, soundly rejected "all positive methods of birth prevention" for violating the moral order, the sanctity of nature, and the natural law. This position received strong reaffirmation in the encyclical of Pope Pius XI, *Casti Cannubi* (1930). How then should Catholics respond to the Malthusian challenge? The usual answer has been—adopting words from the American theologian John A. Ryan—to advocate a "reasonable and just" redistribution of "the good things of life," through a pro-family tax structure, wage policy ("the family wage"), and welfare state.[48]

Pope Francis agrees with this tradition. He affirms, for example, that "the family has a right to decent housing, fitting for family life and commensurate to the number of members." He affirms this as part of a larger "family right" to "an adequate family policy on the part of public authorities in the judicial, economic, social, and fiscal domains."[49]

---

45. Francis, *Amoris laetitia*, 14, 166, 167.
46. Francis, *Amoris laetitia*, 42.
47. Carlson 2012, 79–112.
48. Ryan 1916, 684–96; Ryan 1906.
49. Francis, *Amoris laetitia*, 44.

However, Pope Francis's primary response to the Malthusian challenge is different, even unique. Where the twentieth century Catholic hierarchy essentially welcomed the cornucopia of industrial goods produced by the capitalist economy, *subject to its proper (re)distribution*, Francis focuses instead on *simplicity*: "the capacity to be happy with little"; the need to learn and accept that "less is more"; a "simplicity which allows us to stop and appreciate the small things"; a "sobriety" which, "when lived freely and consciously, is liberating."[50] Living with "less," living simply: these behaviors will bring human numbers into a balance with existing goods.

Francis emphasizes the vital importance of the family in achieving this moral and economic revolution. As he argues in *Amoris laetitia*, "the family is the principle agent of an integral ecology."[51] Intentionally expanding his family imagery to a global scale, Francis states that "the urgent challenge of protecting our [common] home includes the effort to bring the entire human family together in the pursuit of a sustainable and integral development."[52] More poetically, he preaches: "Dear families, always live in faith and simplicity, like the Holy Family of Nazareth!"[53]

Precursors?

Most obviously, the inspiration for this economics of "simplicity" and "less" is the current Pontiff's namesake, St. Francis. In a way, the current Francis can be understood as trying to give a system, an historical context, and a contemporary program of action to the messages of that venerable Saint. As Pope Francis remarks in *Laudato si'*, a "change in lifestyle could bring healthy pressure to bear on those who wield political, economic and social power."[54]

Are there other precursors? For example, does the family economics of Pope Francis echo the Distributist campaign of the early twentieth century? This ef-

---

50. Francis, *Laudato si'*, 222, 223.

51. Francis, *Amoris laetitia*, 277.

52. Francis, Homily for the Closing Mass of the Eight World Meeting of Families, 2.

53. Francis, Homily for the Holy Mass for the Family Day on the Occasion of the Year of Faith, 2.

54. Francis, *Laudato si'*, 206.

fort to achieve family and social justice is properly identified with two English Catholic journalists, Hilaire Belloc and G.K. Chesterton. They claimed that their whole economic, social, and political program was an effort to implement the principles of Pope Leo XIII's 1891 encyclical, *Rerum Novarum.*[55] Indeed, there are many convergences between Francis and the Distributists: a rejection, implicit or open, of globalist capitalism; the denunciation of advertising; a preference for the family farm and the small shop. However, Belloc and Chesterton placed their strongest emphasis on the widest possible distribution of *property*: the ownership by each family of a house, a few acres of land, and small scale tools.[56] However, Francis gives very little attention to property ownership of this sort as part of his program. The phrase rarely appears in *Laudato si'*, *Amoris laetitia*, or related homilies and speeches.

The family economics outlined by Pope Francis does resemble that offered in much greater detail by the contemporary American agrarian, Wendell Berry. Like Francis, Berry links an often profound description of the failures of contemporary marriage and family life to the "destructive" excesses of "The Economy." Both hold to a stark appraisal of the current global environment, while rejecting any turn to population control. Moreover, as prescription, Berry agrees with the current Pope that each family must learn to live with less: "We must achieve the character and acquire the skills to live *much poorer* than we do," understanding that authentic economy "exists by the willingness to be anonymous, humble, and unrewarded."[57] However, there is no evidence that Francis is familiar in any way with Berry's work.

Another, more religiously relevant, but also most surely unknown predecessor may be the American Jesuit, John C. Rawe. Active in the 1930s and early 1940s, he was in almost all respects the Catholic precursor to Wendell Berry.[58] Like Francis, he held that industrialization of land would "bring death to living things [and] barrenness to its soil."[59] Within the consumerist economy, "a

---

55. Chesterton, "Forty Years On," 2; Belloc, *The Servile State*; Chesterton, *The Outline of Sanity.*

56. Belloc, *The Restoration of Property.*

57. Berry, *What Are People For?*, 200, emphasis added.

58. Hamlin, "The Greening of America: Catholic Style, 1930–1950," 464–66, 484, 489.

59. Rawe, "The Home on the Land," 25.

workman had better be 'free' from a home, because if he had a home he would not be sufficiently mobile"; "above all, he had better be free from children."[60] The stripping of the land through industrialized agriculture, Rawe held, paralleled the disappearance of mothers and children in the sterile city.[61] On the positive side, Rawe yearned for "a balanced life for all, grounded in subsistence agriculture" and "lived out in a definite social tradition, a life in which religion, the arts, good manners, conversation, hospitality, sympathy, family life, and all the other social exchanges can reveal and develop . . . in an equitable economy founded on the right relations of man to nature."[62]

Father Rawe has been criticized by his sympathizers for failing to draw on the Franciscan tradition.[63] Without being aware of it, Rawe's fellow Jesuit, Pope Francis, has begun to fill in and amplify their common arguments.

Criticisms of the broad economic vision of Pope Francis are found elsewhere in this volume. Relative to the family, I would add doubts over his frequent conflation of the very small economy of each distinct home with the economy of "the entire human family." Even within an "agrarian" matrix, the two are very different; equating them can only create confusion. In addition, and assuming his own framework and goals, Francis gives too little attention to the importance of private property as a guarantor of family security and basic wellbeing. As noted earlier, he would find a useful corrective here in the arguments of the Distributists. Finally, he largely avoids the political implications of his call for living more simply and with less. His summons is for voluntary action by his flock, and sympathetic others. However, his solution to the Malthusian challenge would only work if most of humanity concurred. Is "fallen man" really capable of the sweeping renunciations that Francis's plan would require? Would not the coercive force of law need to come into play? He does not say.

Pope Francis does, however, offer a fairly unique and largely consistent economic vision resting on the family economy. Its implications are, at once, simple and sweeping, traditional and radical, small and vast.

---

60. Rawe, "Agriculture and the Property State," 3.
61. Rawe, "Agriculture—An Airplane Survey," 1, 24–25.
62. Rawe, "Agrarianism: The Basis for a Better Life," 182.
63. Hamlin, "The Greening of America: Catholic Style, 1930–1950," 481.

References

Belloc, Hilaire. *The Servile State*. Indianapolis, Ind.: Liberty Classics, [1977] 1912.

———. *The Restoration of Property*. New York: Sheed and Ward, 1936.

Berry, Wendell. *What Are People For?* San Francisco: North Point Press, 1990.

Carlson, Allan. *Godly Seed: American Evangelicals Confront Birth Control, 1873–1973*. New Brunswick, N.J.: Transaction, 2012.

Chesterton, Gilbert Keith. "Forty Years On." *G.K.'s Weekly*, [May 23] 1931.

———. *The Outline of Sanity*. Norfolk, Va.: IHS Press, [2001] 1926.

Francis. Address for the Meeting with Bishops Taking Part in the World Meeting of Families. September 27, 2015.

———. Address for the Prayer Vigil for the Festival of Families. Philadelphia, Pa. September 26, 2015.

———. Address to Participants in the International Colloquium on the Complementarity Between Men and Women. November 17, 2014.

———. Address to the Joint Session of the United States Congress. Washington, DC. September 24, 2015.

———. *Amoris laetitia*. Post-Synodical Apostolic Exhortation of the Holy Father, Francis, on Love in the Family. 2016.

———. Homily for the Closing Mass of the Eight World Meeting of Families. Philadelphia, Pa. September 27, 2015.

———. Homily for the Extraordinary Jubilee of Mercy—Jubilee for Boys and Girls. April 24, 2016.

———. Homily for the Holy Mass at Madison Square Garden. New York, N.Y. September 25, 2015.

———. Homily for the Holy Mass for Families. December 27, 2015.

Francis. Homily for the Holy Mass for the Family Day on the Occasion of the Year of Faith. October 27, 2013.

———. Homily for the Holy Mass for the Feast of the Exaltation of the Holy Cross. September 14, 2014.

———. Homily for the Holy Mass for the Opening of the Extraordinary Synod on the Family. October 5, 2014.

———. Homily for the Holy Mass on the Solemnity of Mary, Mother of God, XLVIII World Day of Peace. January 1, 2015.

———. Homily for the Holy Mass with Bishops, Clergy and Religious of Pennsylvania, Philadelphia, Pa. September 26, 2015.

————. *Laudato si'*. Encyclical Letter of the Holy Father, Francis, on Care for Our Common Home. 2015.

Hamlin, Christopher and McGreevy, John T. "The Greening of America: Catholic Style, 1930–1950." *Environmental History* 11, July 2006.

John Paul II. *Familiaris Consortio*. Apostolic Exhortation of the Holy Father, John Paul II, on the Family. 1981.

Pius XI. *Quadragesimo Anno*. Encyclical Letter of the Holy Father, Pius XI, Forty Years After *Rerum Novarum*. 1931.

Rawe, John C. "Agrarianism: The Basis for a Better Life." *The American Review* 6, December 1935.

————. "Agriculture and the Property State." In *Who Owns America? A New Declaration of Independence*. Edited by Herbert Agar and Allen Tate. Wilmington, Del.: ISI Books, [1999] 1936.

————. "The Home on the Land." *Catholic Rural Life Bulletin* 2, February 1939.

————. "Agriculture—An Airplane Survey." *The Catholic Rural Life Bulletin* 3, February 1940.

Ryan, John A. *A Living Wage*. New York: MacMillan, 1906.

————. "Family Limitation." *The Ecclesiastical Review* 4, June 1916.

Conclusion

Robert P. Murphy

HISTORICALLY, THERE HAS been an undeniable tension, if not outright conflict, between religion and economics. In the hands of enthusiastic partisans, accusations of heartlessness and ignorance abound, while writings from "the other side" are interpreted in the most uncharitable light. Theologians with little training in economics have often been wary of the pronouncements of a discipline that seems uncomfortably suited to justifying the moneychangers. Agnostic economists, for their part, have dismissed what they view as paternalistic moralizing from an institution that is always playing catch up to the findings of science.

This traditional impasse is unfortunate. Economics *is* a science—albeit a *social* science, not a natural science such as physics, notwithstanding the feelings of inadequacy that this difference causes for many professional economists. As such, economists have an understanding of *how the world works*, which those who lack training in the subject simply lack.

There are plenty of cases—which have been documented in this book, and some of which we will review below—where a religious writer, even one from the Vatican, makes pronouncements about the *application* of Church doctrine that are misguided, simply due to ignorance of matters of cause-and-effect. (For an analogy, imagine someone who had no understanding of modern medicine opposing the use of needles on children because of the pain they cause.) In cases such as these, economists have a role in *educating* Church officials on the unintended consequences of their recommendations.

Followers of Christ should not resent such efforts at education. If the critiques from economists are right, and (for example) some of Pope Francis's ideas on aiding the vulnerable in our society would actually hurt the very people he is trying to assist, then it is crucial for the pope and/or his advisors to acknowledge this awkward fact and adjust accordingly. Before the Church can effectively serve as salt and light for the world, its members—and particularly the leadership—must take every effort to ensure that they are not contributing, even unwittingly, to any of the problems they seek to address. Jesus warns us to first clear out the beam from our own eye before removing the speck from our brother's.

At the same time, I plead with my fellow economists to take seriously the faith-based critiques of "capitalism" issuing from Pope Francis and others. I put the term in quotation marks because part of the misunderstanding is a simple matter of terminology; as this volume has addressed and I highlight below, some critics use "capitalism" to mean *the present system as practiced in many societies*, and in that light, their critiques make perfect sense. It is not enough for economists to say "that's not pure capitalism" and move on; real people are suffering, often under reforms that were billed as "privatization" or "liberalization."

Moreover, the dispute is not one of mere nomenclature. Jokes abound concerning the heartlessness and *amorality*—which is not the same as *immorality*—of economists, at least as economics is often taught. Whether it's recommending a market for kidneys, or advocating a minimum wage of $0, economists often puncture sacred cows with counterintuitive analysis, and many of them relish the role of "shocking" their classes and the public with their cold efficiency. (As the author of *The Politically Incorrect Guide to Capitalism*, I speak from a position of authority on this matter.)

Economists too often try to have it both ways. On the one hand, they stress the value-free, *scientific* nature of their pronouncements: "Hey, don't shoot the messenger, here's why your proposal will backfire." Yet on the other hand, they often smuggle in value judgments using economics as a Trojan horse. For example, an economist might start with a standard (and objective) evaluation of the effects of drug prohibition, conclude that drugs should be legal, and then go further and suggest that drug use is unobjectionable even from a moral perspective so long as it doesn't violate others' rights. For a different example, an economist might oppose state welfare programs for reasons of both efficiency and the proper role of government, but then extend this attitude to dismissing even *private* charities as ruining initiative and "subsidizing" indolence.

In sum, the Church and the economics profession have different areas of expertise. All Christians have a duty to help the poor and other unfortunates, and Catholics in particular have a long tradition of social teachings that work toward restoring justice in this fallen world. Economists, for their part, have inherited a scientific discipline that studies the institutional mechanisms with which humans grapple with material scarcity.

To collapse the matter into a pithy if somewhat simplistic statement: The Church, guided above all by the words and actions of Jesus, should teach people the ends to pursue, while economists can offer guidance on the best means of achieving them.[1] Religious authorities and economists have much to offer each other; there are "gains from trade" in the parlance of economists. But this mutually beneficial discussion can only occur amidst a foundation of mutual respect and acknowledgement that there is always more to learn.

A Foundation of Mutual Respect

It is our fervent hope that the present book has contributed to such a foundation of mutual respect. To be sure, some of the essays are forceful in their criticism of certain statements from Pope Francis, though hopefully any Catholic reader would appreciate the earnestness of the arguments. Furthermore, other essays—in particular, those from Samuel Gregg and Gabriel X. Martinez—explicitly seek to defuse hostility to Pope Francis's writings and to

---

1 Catholic author Thomas E. Woods takes this approach in his 2005 book *The Church and the Market: A Catholic Defense of the Free Economy* (Lexington Books). More generally, members of the Austrian School of economics use the value-free, objective science of economics in order to persuade the public that they will achieve popular goals (such as prosperity and longer life spans) by embracing the market economy; see my book *Choice: Cooperation, Enterprise, and Human Action* (Independent Institute, 2015) for an elaboration. Catholic readers in particular should investigate the writings of the Austrian School, as its roots can be traced to the natural law tradition of Aquinas and the Spanish scholastics. Alex Chafuen's book *Faith and Liberty* (Lexington Books, 2003) is especially helpful in demonstrating this connection.

explain that they are not the "attack" on market economies that many casual observers believed.

The contributors to this book took Pope Francis sincerely when he gave an invitation to a dialogue, and we look forward to any future replies made in the same spirit.

In the balance of this concluding essay, I reiterate and amplify several of the themes running throughout the book. My aim is to neither berate economists nor to lecture religious readers, but instead to highlight areas where members of each "camp" could benefit from a more thoughtful reading of the other's perspective.

Understanding Pope Francis in Context

In the present volume, essays from Andrew M. Yuengert and Gabriel X. Martinez provide a very useful explanation of the *context* of Pope Francis's writings. Especially for economists who may have no prior familiarity with the current Pope, it is important to understand the long tradition of the Catholic Church's positions on social and economic issues, and also Francis's experience with the failures of economic "reforms" and how they often ravage society's most vulnerable members.

I am sure that many free-market economists will consider Pope Francis's experiences and conclude, "Well *that's* not capitalism, that's cronyism!" And this is certainly correct. However, it's not enough to *merely* dismiss these objections by an appeal to definitions. After all, the proponents of a market economy presumably have little sympathy for Marxist scholars who dismiss the record of atrocities under Stalin and Mao by saying, "That's not true communism." No, in these cases, reasonable people conclude that the communist system *unavoidably* places "the worst on top." It is naïve to think that a move toward government ownership of the means of production would result in a regime that eschews personal power and treats all subjects with justice.

In that context, then, it is understandable that Pope Francis (and other critics) are very skeptical of proposals to "liberalize" the economy. There have been many examples of alleged "privatization," "deregulation," and "pro-growth reforms"—whether in the former Soviet Union, South America, or even the United States—that did not turn out as advertised. It's certainly valid for free-market economists to explain after the fact (although prefer-ably *before* the fact) why the proposals were not actually representative of the market economy, but they should not berate outsiders for taking these labels at face value.

Furthermore, free-market economists should engage in deep reflection to see whether any of these "failed reforms" were due to *inherent* weaknesses in their worldview or policy approach. If indeed there is scope for improve-ment, then reading outside critiques—such as those of Pope Francis—may be a source of discovery.

The Limitations of Economic Analysis

As a value-free science, in principle economics does not presuppose value judg-ments. However, in practice this often means that economists eschew value judgments *period*. In libertarian circles, this habit manifests itself in an atti-tude that no one should even *criticize* heroin use, prostitution, pornography, and so forth because "it's all voluntary." Regardless of whether these activities *are* in fact morally blameless, it should be clear that economic analysis and even libertarian political theory have no say on the matter: one of the standard points in a (coherent) objection to the Drug War, for example, is that immoral acts shouldn't necessarily be illegal.

We see what are (in my opinion) other examples of overreach in the free-market economist community in its treatment of human vices. Adam Smith famously observed that an individual "*intends only his own gain, and he is in this, as in many other cases, led by an invisible hand to promote an end which was no part of his intention.*"[2]

As a Scottish moral philosopher who believed in God (though scholars argue about the exact nature of his views, as criticism of orthodoxy at that time could have career consequences), Smith saw Providence at work in the social arena. Note in particular that Smith did *not* say—even though many often misquote him—that the individual is led "as if" by an invisible hand. No, Smith says that the individual is led "by an invisible hand."

---

2. Smith, *The Wealth of Nations*, Part IV, Chapter I, 184–5, para. 10.

Adam Smith's discussion of an invisible hand may remind some readers of Genesis 50:20, when Joseph tells his brothers (who had sold him into slavery), "You intended to harm me, but God intended it for good to accomplish what is now being done, the saving of many lives." The point of Smith's analysis was not to *praise* selfishness, but instead to remark on the wonders of a peaceful social system that transforms vice into virtue.

Yet look at how some have carried the baton. Ayn Rand (with Nathaniel Branden) released a collection of essays (1964) literally titled, *The Virtue of Selfishness*, which contains much valuable economic analysis, but the entire premise of which could understandably offend any disciple of Christ. Or for a more modern example, many libertarians quote the fictitious character Gordon Gekko's speech on why "greed is good," without any irony. Here again, one could translate much (though not all) of Gekko's remarks into unobjectionable economic analysis, but nonetheless he chose to summarize his view as "greed is good," which is *prima facie* incompatible with the Sermon on the Mount.

When many self-described fans of the free market choose icons such as these, it is understandable why a devout Catholic might recoil. Pope Francis has a very valid point when he notes our habit of saying how much a person is "worth" when we refer to the market value of a person's property. Money *can* be an idol, to adopt Biblical language, and such idolatry is a sin. I suspect there are many free-market aficionados who reject the very *notion* of sin, viewing everything through the lens of utility. This type of worldview definitely can benefit from exposure to "moralizers" from the Church.

Besides picking uncomfortable heroes and smuggling in dubious value judgments, sometimes agnostic fans of the market economy refuse to consistently apply their own principles. In casual discourse I have noticed many who endorse some version of John Locke's theory of homesteading as a basis of property rights, yet they consider the God of the Bible to be a monstrous tyrant. But this is contradictory; if we stipulate for the sake of argument that the Genesis account is correct, then God created the entire physical universe *de novo*. As such, He clearly owns everything, and thus has the perfect right (in standard libertarian theory) to lay down whatever rules He wishes to His tenants for the use of His property. To be sure, an agnostic could reject the Genesis account as fiction, but then the proper position should be, "I don't believe in this God," *not* "These rules in Deuteronomy are very unlibertarian!"

As my brief remarks here should indicate, I urge professional economists to seriously consider their own potential biases when evaluating criticism from outside "moralists." Yes, their objections to economic analysis may often contain imprecision due to their unfamiliarity with jargon and technical nuances, but often the *spirit* of the critiques is valid.

Pope Francis on the Family

There may be a temptation on the part of agnostic, market-friendly economists to dismiss Pope Francis's writings on capitalism and the environment as merely attempts to curry favor with fashionable progressives. However, such a suspicion is unfair and unwarranted. Francis's writings on the family demonstrate quite conclusively that he is willing to deviate sharply from progressive orthodoxy when his principles demand it.

In his essay for this volume, Allan Carlson relays Francis's politically *incorrect* views on the family. Francis declares that the "ability of human couples to beget life is the path along which the history of salvation progresses"; this is incompatible with extreme environmentalists advocating for "zero population growth" or even a shrinking number of humans. And Francis is surely not catering to feminists when he emphasizes the biological differences between men and women, and how these undergird traditional roles in the family.

The Failure of Socialism

In the introduction by Robert M. Whaples, and in the essay on charitable giving by Lawrence J. McQuillan and Hayeon Carol Park, reference was made to F.A. Hayek's "knowledge problem" and the shortcomings of top-down central planning. Inasmuch as we have stressed the *technical* nature of economic science, and how it shows the limits of mere good intentions, it will be useful to review the historical debate over socialism.[3]

In the debates of the nineteenth century, the conservative opponents of socialism typically stressed warnings about the concentration of power, and about the harmful effects on productivity if reward were no longer tied to

---

3. For a broader survey with references to the economic literature, see Murphy 2006.

effort. In other words, they warned that socialism was dangerous because power corrupts, and because workers could shirk.

The socialist writers dismissed such warnings as fear-mongering. Yes, perhaps it was true that people *who grew up in a capitalist society* would be selfish, domineering, and lazy—if they could get away with it—but that was only because of the dog-eat-dog system that surrounded them. Once the switch to socialism were effected, according to the socialist writers, people would have no need to flatten others in their race to the top. And workers would be happy to create for the sheer joy of providing for the community, since there would be no worry of where their next meal was coming from.

Into this impasse stepped the Austrian economist Ludwig von Mises. In a pioneering 1920 essay,[4] Mises stipulated for the sake of argument that a central planner would have nothing but altruistic motives for his people, and that his subjects would obey any orders issued. Mises further stipulated that all technical knowledge regarding physical, chemical, and engineering facts would be relayed to the central planner.

Nonetheless, Mises argued, the central planner would have no way of knowing—even after the fact—if his economic instructions made a sensible use of society's scarce resources. The planner's aides could tell him, for example, that such-and-such quantities of iron, rubber, glass, and labor hours went into the production of so-many automobiles in a given month. The planner might also conduct surveys and learn that his subjects *enjoyed* the new vehicles.

But that wouldn't be sufficient. The real test of *economic efficiency* is whether the cars produced were *the best possible use* of the resources consumed in the process. In other words, the central planner would need some way of determining whether the benefit of the production exceeded its (opportunity) cost. That is a fundamentally economic question, which is not directly answerable by physics, chemistry, or engineering.

In the market economy, this problem of "economic calculation" is solved day in and day out through accounting. A business owner knows if she is making "rational" use of society's resources by seeing whether customers spend

---

4. Mises's 1920 salvo against socialism was written in German. An English translation appeared in 1935 in a collection edited by Hayek. See Ludwig von Mises, [1935] 1990.

more money on the output than the business spends on the inputs. Mises acknowledged that this method of scorekeeping is not perfect, but at least it is *coherent*. In contrast, a central planner, lacking genuine market prices, would simply have no way of even beginning to answer this question.

The significance of Mises's critique of socialism is that it wasn't about intentions. Instead, it showed the limits of human reason outside of a proper institutional framework. Beyond a critique of full-blown socialism, Mises's analysis shows us the dangers of social reform that eschews the guidance of market prices. For a simple example, sending vast numbers of shoes to a poor country may be a very wasteful method of providing aid, compared to alternative strategies that cost the same "sacrifice" from the donors.

Catholic writers who are (understandably) concerned about consumerism should first familiarize themselves with Mises's work before launching broadside attacks on the market economy (or "capitalism") itself. To jettison the profit-and-loss test as unnecessary in the quest to aid the downtrodden would be akin to rejecting books as a reaction against pornography.

The Environment

To many casual onlookers, it seems obvious that whatever the merits of a market economy in the realm of conventional products, when it comes to environmental protection we need much more than the profit and loss test. Indeed, many people believe that left to its own devices, an "unregulated" capitalist system would dump toxic waste in the rivers, clearcut forests, deplete stocks of fish and minerals far too rapidly, and emit greenhouse gases that pose catastrophic risks for future generations.[5]

In their essays for the present volume, A.M.C. Waterman and Philip Booth provide a summary of Pope Francis's views on the environment—and how capitalism allegedly falls short of the mark in this regard—and excellent rebuttals. Here I will review some of their analysis and expand upon it.

Laudato si' counsels the reader that "science and religion, with their distinctive approaches to understanding reality, can enter into . . . dialogue fruitful for

---

5. For an excellent examination of the relationships among regulation, markets, and environmental protection, see the book *Nature Unbound: Bureaucracy vs. the Environment*, by Randy T Simmons, Ryan M. Yonk, and Kenneth J. Sim (Independent Institute, 2016).

both."[6] In the context of concerns about climate change and (say) the Genesis account's assignment of what might be called man's "dominion" over nature,[7] the statement is probably intended primarily to reassure agnostic scientists that the Catholic Church is willing to hear evidence on the ecological dangers of human activity. However, we can flip the statement on its head, and reassure devout Catholics that the technical findings of *economic* science will only help to achieve environmental goals that we should pursue as stewards of God's creation.

Nonrenewable Resources

For those (such as Pope Francis) wary of market forces in the context of ecology, one major concern is the shortsighted exploitation of natural resources. For example, Pope Francis warns, "Caring for ecosystems demands far-sightedness, since no one looking for quick and easy profit is truly interested in their preservation."[8]

This is not correct, or at least, it overlooks standard findings from economic science. First, some background: Friedrich Hayek stressed the role of market prices in communicating *information* among people.[9] If a tin mine collapses, then two things need to happen: (1) People in a position to bring more tin to market need to undertake efforts to do so, and (2) people who use tin in their operations should economize on it, substituting in other materials if possible. Note that a spike in the market price of tin—which is exactly the outcome profit-seeking speculators will yield in their reaction to their news of the mine collapse—achieves both ends. Moreover, as Hayek emphasized, the market price communicates the new conditions of scarcity in a very efficient manner. In particular, people around the world don't need to know *why* tin has suddenly become more scarce; they just need to know *that it has*, and by how much.

---

6. Francis, *Laudato si'*, 62.
7. Genesis 1:26.
8. Francis, *Laudato si'*, 36.
9. See for example Hayek 1945.

In this context, it is easy to see how market prices effortlessly solve a problem that at first seems quite problematic for a system of decentralized property rights. Namely, how can we ensure that unborn future generations have access to tin, copper, natural gas, and so on? If today's businesses are allowed to exploit and sell these nonrenewable resources to today's consumers, what voice do our grandchildren have in the matter? Don't we need the political system to step in, and limit consumption today in order to balance it against the needs of the future? (Note that in this discussion, we are setting aside the possible harms of fossil fuel development via climate change; we return to this subject shortly.)

The short answer is that so long as there are secure property rights—a condition that rules out the government imposing a "windfall profits" tax when resource prices rise—then normal market operations, especially in advanced economies with sophisticated futures markets, provide an elegant solution to the problem.

Before explaining the market outcome, let's first wrap our arms around the problem by considering its complexity. In the first place, the "optimal" amount of depletion (or "exploitation," to use a loaded term) of a nonrenewable resource can't be *zero*. In other words, it would be nonsensical to refrain entirely from burning barrels of oil today, in order to bequeath as much as possible to future generations. The reason is that when our grandchildren come of age, at that point they will face the same intertemporal tradeoff; are they too to keep their hands off the oil, so that this heritage passes along forever, without ever actually providing benefit to any human?

On the other hand, it also seems obvious that it would be incorrect to consume the lion's share of Earth's oil over the next decade or two, such that driving is incredibly cheap, but thereby setting up our children for a crisis in which gasoline becomes prohibitively expensive and people all over the planet must discontinue the use of any conventional combustion engines.

The market solution avoids both extremes. If we simply allow the owners of crude oil to maximize the (expected) market value of their property, we achieve a sensible balance between present and future consumption. In particular, Harold Hotelling showed in 1931 that (under simplifying assumptions) the (inflation-adjusted) spot price of an exhaustible resource would rise with the rate of interest.[10] The exponentially rising spot price of the resource would make present consumption continually shrink, but there would never be a crisis. The remaining quantity of the resource would dwindle away over time, but it would be a gradual, predictable process. Depending on the assumptions, the resource might not ever completely disappear, though its remaining quantity would asymptotically approach zero as the continually rising price gradually weaned humanity off of its use.

Hotelling's central insight was that the owner of a nonrenewable resource —such as barrels of crude oil—was effectively deciding on the margin whether to sell a given barrel today, at the spot price, or to hold it off the market and sell next year, at the expected price at that time. Suppose the current spot price is $100 per barrel, and the rate of interest is 5 percent. In this case, for the owner to be willing to hold oil off the market today, waiting until next year to sell, he would have to expect the price at that point to be at least $105. (If it were lower, he would do better to sell today, and invest the $100 in bonds yielding 5 percent.)

This logic shows that in a stable equilibrium, in which the owner sells a certain number of barrels today while carrying the remaining barrels into the future, it must be the case that the spot price rises at the rate of interest. (To repeat, we are ruling out all sorts of complicating real-world considerations, in order to isolate the pure time element in the decision.) Therefore, it can't possibly be the case that "everybody knows" a major oil crisis looms on the horizon, because if it *did*, then owners of oil today would do better to restrict current sales and carry extra barrels into the future, to fetch the much higher prices.

Thus, the "demand" of future generations shows up in present considerations of resource usage, through the expectation of future prices. So long as people today have *some* horizon of planning, that is enough to carry a substantial amount of resources forward another (say) ten years. At that point, the owners will perform similar calculations, ensuring a proper balance between (then) current consumption and carrying supplies forward an additional ten years.

At any point, if the system should somehow get locked in a rut of self-fulfilling expectations that foster excessive resource depletion, then any out-

---

10. Hotelling, "The Economics of Exhaustible Resources."

side observer is free to profit handsomely by, for example, buying futures contracts for oil to be delivered in seven years. As time passes and the rest of the market realizes that it had been too optimistic about the future, the owner of the distant futures position will profit. Beyond that, the very act of taking such a position pushes up the current price of oil, helping to alleviate the underlying problem. Just as an astute entrepreneur can perceive that the economy "needs," say, a good Thai restaurant in a certain neighborhood, so too can the concerned environmentalist perceive that humanity is consuming certain nonrenewable resources too quickly. If this observation is accurate *in the economically relevant sense*, then a profit opportunity exists. Whether through serving Thai food or carrying valuable resources through time, far-sighted individuals who correct market "mistakes" are rewarded by profits.

Deforestation, Overfishing, Strip Mining, Endangered Species

A critic might object that Hotelling's "solution" works well enough for a tangible commodity such as crude oil or natural gas, but that it clearly has *not* worked in the realm of forests, fisheries, mineral deposits in regions plagued by "strip mining," and with all endangered species. Surely the narrow pecuniary incentives discussed above are inadequate when broader issues of nature are involved.

It is true that Hotelling's analysis doesn't seem to work as well with bald eagles as it does with crude oil. However, the reason is *not* that economic incentives are inapplicable to nature. Rather, the explanation is that governments (typically) have well-defined property rights in crude oil or tin deposits, while such legal rights are lacking in the areas seemingly in need of conscious conservation efforts.

In his essay, Philip Booth explored the importance of property rights and applied them to deforestation and overfishing. We could cite other examples. Why was the existence of the American buffalo threatened, while nobody worries about running out of dairy cows? In lieu of complex historical and cultural facts, the economist can quickly answer, "Because traditionally herds of buffalo were not owned in the same way as herds of cattle." Even in the face of high beef prices, ranchers would never slaughter every last animal; that would be a reckless act, akin to farmers eating all of the seedcorn.

There are case studies of property rights solving the problem of poaching of endangered species. A prime example is South Africa's white rhino. In 1900, there were fewer than twenty animals in a single reserve, but by 2010, the population exceeded 20,000. Sustainability economist Michael 't Sas-Rolfes explains the remarkable turnaround:

> Saving the white rhino from extinction can be attributed to a change in policy that allowed private ownership of wildlife. Property rights over rhinos changed the incentives of private ranchers by encouraging breeding. Ranchers were also able to profit by limited trophy hunting.
>
> Poaching for rhino horn, which is in high demand for medicinal and ornamental purposes, had also devastated the rhino population. CITES [the UN Convention on Internal Trade in Endangered Species] banned the commercial sale of rhino horn, which caused black market sales to skyrocket and encouraged poaching. If the ban were lifted, ranchers are ready to supply the market by harvesting the horns humanely, which then regrow just like fingernails.[11]

Thus we see that it was the desire to avoid "commercialization" of the white rhino that had actually threatened its existence. By officially banning the sale of their horns, the UN was not actually stopping the transactions. Instead, it pushed the market underground, and took away the incentive to spend the resources necessary to truly protect the rhinos from poachers. For an analogy, if selling automobiles suddenly became illegal, we wouldn't expect car dealerships to spend money maintaining security on their lots.

Conventional Air and Water Pollution

The previous section dealt with the "commodification" of natural resources, including endangered species that have market value. Some environmentalists may balk at the proposal, thinking it is a cure worse than the disease. But another objection might be that such schemes have little to offer when it comes to standard ecological problems such as conventional air and water pollution. Surely *here* the notion of unbridled *laissez-faire* is inappropriate,

---

11. 'T Sas-Rolfes, "Saving African Rhinos: A Market Success Story."

and we need conscious intervention from the political authorities to rein in the natural tendency of business to ravage the environment?

As it turns out, things are more complex here as well. The fundamental problem is a lack of property rights. However, it's not merely a matter of the government failing to define and enforce rights in air and water. On the contrary, historical protections for the public—available through common law procedures—were intentionally cast aside by the courts in the name of industrial progress. Economist Murray Rothbard explains:

> Before the mid and late nineteenth century, any injurious air pollution was considered a tort, a nuisance against which the victim could sue for damages and against which he could take out an injunction to cease and desist from any further invasion of his property rights. But during the nineteenth century, the courts systematically altered the law of negligence and the law of nuisance to permit any air pollution which was not unusually greater than any similar manufacturing firm, one that was not more extensive than the customary practice of fellow polluters.
>
> As factories began to arise and emit smoke, blighting the orchards of neighboring farmers, the farmers would take the manufacturers to court, asking for damages and injunctions against further invasion of their property. But the judges said, in effect, "Sorry. We know that industrial smoke (i.e., air pollution) invades and interferes with your property rights. But there is something more important than mere property rights: and that is public policy, the 'common good.' And the common good decrees that industry is a good thing, industrial progress is a good thing, and therefore your mere private property rights must be overridden on behalf of the general welfare." And now all of us are paying the bitter price for this overriding of private property, in the form of lung disease and countless other ailments. And all for the "common good"![12]

It is also worth pointing out that air pollution, according to several metrics, was trending downward in the United States even before passage of the

---

12. Rothbard, *For a New Liberty*, 320.

Clean Air Act in 1970, as documented by American Enterprise Institute (AEI) scholars Joel Schwartz and Steven Hayward.[13] These authors argue that general economic development played a crucial role, in which cleaner air was the byproduct even if it were not consciously planned. For example, "growing affluence allowed households to switch from coal to cleaner, more efficient natural gas for home heating and cooking," while improvements in electrical transmission allowed power plants to be located near coal mines rather than cities. Along the same lines, we can mention that the shift away from horses to automobiles allowed for much cleaner roads in America's densest cities.

More generally, as people grow richer they can *afford* the luxury of a cleaner environment. For any given level of technological know-how and capital equipment, there is a tradeoff between the material standard of living and the cleanliness of the environment. As conventionally measured real GDP increases, people can choose to "buy" cleaner air and water.

As our discussion illustrates, there is no conflict between the economy and environment. If a Catholic is concerned about the integrity of our natural resources, one of the best mechanisms for protecting them is the clear delineation and enforcement of property rights, which is to say, the application of a market economy.

Climate Change

When it comes to an apparent conflict between capitalism and the environment, the obvious topic of our times is (human-caused) climate change. Earlier in this volume, A.M.C. Waterman discussed the research challenging what has come to be known as "the consensus" in this arena. I will make complementary remarks, making sure the reader understands the nature and fragility of this alleged consensus.

In the first place, the term *climate change* is nebulous. On the face of it, who could deny that the climate is changing? But of course, in the modern *political* context, people invoking a consensus on climate change have in mind strong government policies designed to mitigate greenhouse gas emissions.

---

13. Schwartz and Hayward, *Air Quality in America*.

Yet it is not obvious that this political outcome is appropriate, *even if* one endorses "the science of global warming." Consider the steps in the argument that must *all* follow, to reach the popular conclusion on the necessity for political action:

1. Human activity is causing the earth to change—in particular, to warm—relative to what otherwise would have happened in the absence of these activities.

2. This climate change / global warming poses risks of serious damages, at least to future generations.

3. Government policies have the power to significantly alter the trajectory of projected damages.

4. The costs of implementing these policies—especially the slowdown in economic growth through higher energy prices—are more than offset by the benefits in the form of avoided climate change damages.

In light of the above, four-step argument, notice the role played by the phrase "consensus on climate change." To the extent that the statement is *true*—for example, when researchers report that large percentages of published papers agree with "the consensus"—then it can only include some of the elements on the list. In particular, the *last* element is a question heavily dependent on economics; a natural scientist who is an expert on modeling hurricanes is ill-equipped to judge the appropriate size of a carbon tax, for example.

The tremendous influence of *economic* issues on the seemingly "natural" topic of climate change policy isn't merely a matter of putting dollar figures on crop losses or dam construction, although these are certainly involved. Rather, one of the most critical debates is on the proper *discount rate* to use in the analysis. That is, how should we compare changes in our welfare, today, with changes in the welfare of humans who will be living in, for example, the year 2200?

Consider: Climate change policy involves measures that make us poorer today. (If they *didn't*, then there would be no resistance to implementing them.) There are reasons, after all, that people drive gasoline-powered vehicles and rely on power plants that burn coal and natural gas. Government measures designed to wean humanity off of fossil fuels therefore come at a cost, as people use other technologies and energy sources that, disregarding greenhouse gas emissions, are less efficient.

On the other hand, the potential *benefit* of such measures is that they will spare future generations some of the damages that further greenhouse gas emissions would ostensibly entail. Stipulating this overall framework, in order to determine a sensible climate change policy, then, we must have some way of translating far-distant future benefits into present-value terms.

Note that there must be *some* discount, lest we fall into absurdity. For example, if government measures today could reduce global economic output by $1,000, in order to boost output by $1,001 in the year 2200, then with no discount applied, that would be an economically sensible policy at least from a utilitarian perspective. This would be true even though the people in 2200 will presumably be flying around in spaceships.

Because of considerations like these, economists are generally agreed that the future *benefits* of climate change policy must be discounted to the present, when contrasting them with today's *costs* of climate change policy.

But the size of the discount rate can drive the results. For example, President Obama's administration formed a task group to estimate the so-called "social cost of carbon," which is a dollar figure placed on the total future damages—measured in today's dollars—resulting from the emission of an additional ton of carbon dioxide.

Using a 3 percent discount rate—and this is the value that the media use when reporting the figures—the Obama Administration estimated that the 2015 value of the social cost of carbon was $36 per ton. However, *using the same computer simulations regarding the physical climate system and the global economy*, if we increased the discount rate to 5 percent, then the official social cost of carbon drops down to only $11 per ton.[14]

As this simple numerical example demonstrates, even seemingly slight changes in economic parameters can have huge effects. The reason the discount rate is so influential is that the bulk of severe climate change damages don't occur until many decades in the future.

Indeed, one of the three computer models used by the Obama Working Group projects that climate change will shower net *benefits* on humanity until

---

14. Social cost of carbon estimates taken from EPA's table available at: https://www.epa. gov/climatechange/social-cost-carbon. Accessed January 28, 2017.

at least 2050![15] If this sounds impossible, consider that increased atmospheric concentrations of carbon dioxide are good for plant fertilization, and that warmer temperatures mean that fewer elderly people die in the winter. To be sure, even this particular model (which is more optimistic than the other two) concludes that further emissions of greenhouse gases are undesirable, since the beneficial warming is already "baked into the cake." (They are "sunk benefits," the mirror image of "sunk costs," and shouldn't influence our decisions on the margin regarding emissions.)

To give one final example of the ambiguities in the field, and how outsiders should not be intimidated by the "consensus" terminology: As an economist specializing on climate change issues, in 2014 I relied on the most recent publication of the Intergovernmental Panel on Climate Change (IPCC) to see if it *justified* the popular climate target of limiting global warming (relative to preindustrial times) to 2 degrees Celsius. Using projections of likely global warming under "business as usual" (meaning if governments do not take further steps to limit emissions), and using the IPCC publication's summaries of the literature on the economic costs and the avoided climate change damages flowing from this target, I concluded that the most probable outcome was that such a policy would cost more than it was worth.[16]

Now to be sure, many advocates of aggressive action on climate change have been invoking an "insurance" analogy, whereby a homeowner might pay premiums for fire insurance, even though he probably will never have a fire and in that sense will have "wasted" his money. Although I don't think the numbers make this analogy a good one—in particular, nobody would pay very large premiums for a fire insurance policy that doesn't even fully indemnify you against all types of fires, and in a situation where the fire won't even occur (if at all) for at least fifty years—that's not the main point.[17]

Rather, my modest point is that the public has been led to believe that the ravages of climate change are upon us as we speak, and that it is "obvious" that

15. See the Institute for Energy Research's formal Comment submitted to the government on the Social Cost of Carbon in February 2014, available at: http://instituteforenergyresearch.org /wp-content/uploads/2014/02/IER-Comment-on-SCC.pdf, especially the table on page 6.

16. Murphy, "Using IPCC to Defeat UN Climate Agenda."

17. For a more comprehensive analysis of the insurance analogy for climate change policies, see Murphy, "Are Climate Change Mitigation Policies a Form of Insurance?"

stringent government policies are necessary to avert catastrophe. (One can understand why Pope Francis refers to our present "ecological crisis" in light of the rhetoric put forward by environmentalists.) Yet if the proper justification for aggressive climate change policies is *insurance* for unlikely events "just in case," then it should be clear that the public has been misled all this time. Nobody sells a homeowner fire insurance by saying, "We can see the ravages of the fire on your property as we speak!"

Pope Francis is right to stress the duty we have as stewards of God's creation, and I also agree that human mismanagement of the environment is ultimately due to "the violence present in our hearts, wounded by sin."[18] But this is true in *all* problems of life in this fallen world. For example, selfishness is also ultimately due to our sinful hearts. Yet most people recognize the benefits of social institutions—namely, private property rights and the rule of law—that keep the "natural" human impulses of greed and selfishness in check, and indeed harness them into service to others.

In the same way, a market economy has the ability to constrain human impulses to litter, pollute, and overdevelop, in a manner that balances competing goals efficiently. Its outcomes will not be perfect, but religious authorities should pause before rejecting its ability to help.

Pope Francis and the Caring Society

In the introduction to this book, Robert M. Whaples noted Pope Francis's call for dialogue, and stated that "the purpose of this book is to advance the dialogue at a critical juncture . . . ." By respectfully considering Francis' critiques, the authors have tried to accurately assess his position without defensiveness or evasion. To repeat, the economics profession certainly has no monopoly on moral virtue, and it could stand to be reminded of our duty to the poor and the natural world.

On the other hand, Pope Francis and other religious authorities must recognize that the market economy is an engine of growth that has lifted billions out of poverty in recent decades. Furthermore, as Lawrence J. McQuillan and Hayeon Carol Park document in their essay, the showering of benefits

---

18. Francis, *Laudato si'*, 2.

on the poor isn't *merely* a byproduct of capitalism, but is partially achieved by deliberate philanthropy. What many perceive to be the shortcomings of "laissez-faire capitalism" are, ironically, often the unintended consequences of misguided political *limitations* on the system.

Just as the Church would seek input from medical doctors to understand technical issues before making proclamations concerning stem cell research or end-of-life treatment, by the same token it should seek greater input from professional economists before issuing statements on capitalism or environmental policy.

Through an improved technical understanding of the institutional constraints on the means at our disposal, Pope Francis and his successors can better foster a caring society.

References

Chafuen, Alejandro A. *Faith and Liberty: The Economic Thought of the Late Scholastics.* Lanham, MD: Lexington Books, 2003.

Francis. *Laudato si'.* Encyclical Letter of the Holy Father, Francis, on Care for Our Common Home. 2015.

Hayek, F.A. "The Use of Knowledge in Society." *American Economic Review* 35, no. 2 (September 1945): 519–530.

Hotelling, Harold. "The Economics of Exhaustible Resources." *The Journal of Political Economy* 39 (1931): 137–175

Murphy, Robert P. "Are Climate Change Mitigation Policies a Form of Insurance?" Institute for Energy Research blog post, April 17, 2014. Available at: http://institute forenergyresearch.org/analysis/are-climate-change-mitigation-policies-a-form-of-insurance/.

————. "Cantor's Diagonal Argument: An Extension to the Socialist Calculation Debate." *Quarterly Journal of Austrian Economics* 9, no. 2 (2006): 3–11.

————. *Choice: Cooperation, Enterprise, and Human Action.* Oakland, CA: Independent Institute, 2015.

————. "Using IPCC to Defeat UN Climate Agenda." Institute for Energy Research blog post, September 23, 2014. Available at: http://instituteforenergy research.org/analysis/using-ipcc-defeat-un-climate-agenda/.

Rothbard, Murray. *For a New Liberty.* Auburn, AL: Mises Institute, Second Edition, 1973 [2006].

Schwartz, Joel, and Steven Hayward. *Air Quality in America*. Washington, DC: American Enterprise Institute, 2007). Available at: https://www.aei.org/wp-content/uploads/2014/06/-air-quality-in-america_134905535523.pdf

Simmons, Randy T, Ryan M. Yonk, and Kenneth J. Sim. *Nature Unbound: Bureaucracy vs. the Environment*. Oakland, CA: Independent Institute, 2016.

Smith, Adam. *The Wealth of Nations: An Inquiry into the Nature and Causes*. Edited by Edwin Cannan. Chicago: University of Chicago Press, [1776] 1976.

'T Sas-Rolfes, Michael. "Saving African Rhinos: A Market Success Story." PERC Case Studies Series, August 19, 2011. Available at: http://www.perc.org/sites/default/files/Saving%20African%20Rhinos%20final.pdf.

Von Mises, Ludwig. "Economic Calculation in the Socialist Commonwealth." In *Collectivist Economic Planning*, edited by F.A. Hayek. Clifton, NJ: Augustus M. Kelley, [1935] 1990.

Index

About the Editor and Contributors

About the Editor

Robert M. Whaples is a research fellow at the Independent Institute, co-editor and managing editor for *The Independent Review*, professor of economics at Wake Forest University, and book review editor and former director for EH.Net. He received his Ph.D. in economics from the University of Pennsylvania. Professor Whaples is the recipient of both the Allen Nevins Prize and Jonathan Hughes Prize for Excellence in Teaching Economic History from the Economic History Association. A contributor to numerous scholarly volumes, he is the editor of the books *Future: Economic Peril or Prosperity?* (with Christopher J. Coyne and Michael C. Munger), *Public Choice Interpretations of American Economic History* (with Jac Heckelman and John Moorhouse), *The Routledge Handbook of Modern Economic History* and *The Routledge Handbook of Major Events in Economic History* (both with Randall Parker), and *The Economic Crisis in Retrospect: Explanations by Great Economists* (with G. Page West III). He also edits EH.Net's *Encyclopedia of Economic and Business History*. He and his wife Regina are Lay Dominicans, and their daughter is Sister Mary Josefa of the Heart of Jesus at the Monastery of Our Lady of the Rosary.

About the Contributors

Philip Booth is director of research and public engagement and professor of finance, public policy, and ethics at St. Mary's University in London and editorial and programme director at the Institute of Economic Affairs. He is a fellow of both the Institute of Actuaries and Royal Statistical Society, and he has been professor of insurance and risk management in the Cass Business School at City University, associate dean at City University Business School, and adviser on Financial Stability to the Bank of England. His articles have appeared in many scholarly volumes and journals and his many books include *Catholic Social Teaching and the Market Economy, Catholic Education in the West—Roots, Reality and Revival* (with C. von Geusau), *Christian Perspectives on the Financial Crash, The Euro: The Beginning, the Middle...and the End?, Globalization and Free Trade* (with R. Wellings),

Issues in Monetary Policy: The Relationship Between Money and Financial Markets (with K. Matthews), and *The Road to Economic Freedom* (with J. Meadowcroft).

Allan C. Carlson is the John A. Howard Distinguished Fellow for Family and Religious Studies at the International Organization for the Family and editor of the book *The Natural Family: An International Journal of Research and Policy*. Carlson received his Ph.D. in Modern European History from The Ohio University. His doctoral dissertation was published as *The Swedish Experiment in Family Politics: The Myrdals and the Interwar Population Crisis*. His other books include: *From Cottage to Work Station: The Family's Search for Social Harmony in the Industrial Age*; *The 'American Way': Family and Community in the Shaping of the American Identity*; *Third Ways: How Bulgarian Greens, Swedish Housewives, and Beer-Swilling Englishmen Created Family-Centered Economies—And Why They Disappeared*; *The Natural Family Where It Belongs: New Agrarian Essays*; and most recently *Family Cycles: Strength, Decline & Renewal in American Domestic Life, 1630-2000*.

Samuel Gregg is research director at the Acton Institute and a fellow at the Center for Law and Religion at Emory University. He writes widely on political economy, moral philosophy, natural law theory, Catholicism, the Western tradition, the American Founding, and the life and thought of Sir Thomas More. He has a Doctor of Philosophy degree in moral philosophy and political economy from the University of Oxford. A fellow of the Royal Historical Society and a member of the Royal Economic Society, his many books and monographs include *On Ordered Liberty*; his prize-winning *The Commercial Society*; *The Modern Papacy; Wilhelm Röpke's Political Economy; Becoming Europe*; and *For God and Profit: How Banking and Finance Can Serve the Common Good*. He has also authored many journal articles, essays, and opinion pieces.

Gabriel X. Martinez is chair and associate professor of business and economics at Ave Maria University. He received his Ph.D. in economics from the University of Notre Dame, and he has served in the Office of Evaluation and Oversight for the Inter-American Development Bank, Central Bank of Ecuador, and the Department of Finance in the Banco La Previsora in Guayaquil. His scholarly articles have appeared in the *Cambridge Journal of Economics, Cuestiones Económicas, Journal of Business Ethics*, and *Faith and Economics*.

Lawrence J. McQuillan is a senior fellow, director of the Center on Entrepreneurial Innovation, and creator of the California Golden Fleece Awards at the Independent Institute. He received his Ph.D. in economics from George Mason University, and he has served as chief economist at the Illinois Policy Institute, director of business and economic studies at the Pacific Research Institute, research fellow at the Hoover Institution, and founding publisher and contributing editor of *Economic Issues*. McQuillan has been an advisor for the California State Assembly Judiciary Committee, Socioeconomic

Council of Madrid, Colorado Governor Bill Owens, Heritage/*Wall Street Journal* Index of Economic Freedom, Governor Arnold Schwarzenegger's task force on a constitutional spending limit for California, California State Senator Tom McClintock, Law and Judiciary Policy Committee of the Georgia Chamber of Commerce, Swedish Office of Science and Technology, Adriatic Institute for Public Policy, and elsewhere. He is author of *California Dreaming: Lessons on How to Resolve America's Public Pension Crisis.*

Robert P. Murphy is a research fellow at the Independent Institute, Research Assistant Professor with the Free Market Institute at Texas Tech University, president of Consulting by RPM, senior economist with the Institute for Energy Research, senior fellow with the Fraser Institute, and associated scholar with the Ludwig von Mises Institute. He received his Ph.D. in economics from New York University, and he was formerly visiting assistant professor of economics at Hillsdale College, visiting scholar at New York University, research analyst at Laffer Associates, and senior fellow in business and economic studies at the Pacific Research Institute. He is author of the books, *Choice: Cooperation, Enterprise and Human Action; The Primal Prescription* (with Doug McGuff, M.D.); *Lessons for the Young Economist; The Politically Incorrect to the Great Depression and the New Deal; The Politically Incorrect Guide to Capitalism; How Privatized Banking Really Works; Study Guide for Ludwig von Mises' Human Action; Study Guide for Murray Rothbard's Man, Economy, and State with Power and Market;* and *Study Guide to The Theory of Money & Credit by Ludwig von Mises.*

Michael Novak was a founding member of the Board of Advisors for the Independent Institute and distinguished visiting fellow in the Arthur and Carlyse Ciocca Center for Principled Entrepreneurship in the Tim and Steph Busch School of Business and Economics at Catholic University of America. He formerly held the George Frederick Jewett Chair in Religion and Public Policy at the American Enterprise Institute, served as Ambassador to the U.N. Commission on Human Rights, and taught at Harvard, Stanford, SUNY Old Westbury, Syracuse, Notre Dame, and Ave Maria universities. Ambassador Novak was granted twenty-seven honorary degrees (including four in Latin America and three in Europe), the Friend of Freedom Award from the Coalition for a Democratic Majority, the George Washington Honor Medal from Freedom Foundation, and the Ellis Island Medal of Honor, among numerous other honors. His selection as recipient of the 1994 Templeton Prize for Progress in Religion capped a career of leadership in theological and philosophical discourse. In addition, the Presidents of the Czech Republic, Poland, and Slovakia gave him the highest award they can bestow on a foreign citizen. Ambassador Novak led the U.S. delegation to the Conference on Security and Cooperation in Europe in 1986, and he was a member of the Coalition for a Democratic Majority. He received his B.A. *summa cum laude* in philosophy and English from Stonehill College in 1956, a Sacrae Theologiae Baccalaureus from the Pontifical Gregorian University in Rome in

1958, and an M.A. in history and philosophy of religion from Harvard University in 1966. He was the author of hundreds of articles and fifty books including the pioneering volume, *The Spirit of Democratic Capitalism*, and his books have been translated into every major Western language, as well as Bengali, Korean, Chinese, and Japanese.

Hayeon Carol Park is a research associate at the Victims of Communism Memorial Foundation. She received her B.A. from the University of Toronto, double majoring in economics and international relations, and she graduated with a M.A. in international and development economics from Yale University. She worked previously as a policy researcher at the Independent Institute and a policy analyst at both the Reason Foundation and the Asian Development Bank in Washington, D.C.

A. M. C. Waterman is a retired fellow at St. John's College, Winnipeg, Canada; professor emeritus of economics at the University of Manitoba; and senior member of Robinson College at Cambridge University. He graduated in economics from Cambridge, studied theology at St John's College, Winnipeg, was ordained to the Priesthood and proceeded to the Australian National University, where he was awarded the Ph.D. in economics. He is a contributor to many scholarly volumes and journals, and author of many books. To learn more about his life and work, see www.amcwaterman.com.

Andrew M. Yuengert is the Blanche E. Seaver Professor of Social Science and Professor of Economics at Seaver College, Pepperdine University. Before coming to Pepperdine in 1994, he was a research economist at the Federal Reserve Bank of New York. Professor Yuengert has made research contributions in several fields: economic philosophy, Catholic Social Teaching, the empirical study of religion, labor economics, and finance. He is a former President of the Association of Christian Economists, and edited its journal, *Faith & Economics*. His most recent book is *Approximating Prudence: Aristotelian Practical Wisdom and Economic Theories of Choice* (Palgrave Macmillan 2012). He is working on a book on the place of practical wisdom in Catholic Social Doctrine. During the 2015–16 academic year Professor Yuengert was William Simon Visiting Fellow in Religion and Public Life at the James Madison Program at Princeton University. He is currently a non-resident Fellow in the Institute for Human Ecology, Catholic University of America.

Independent Institute Studies in Political Economy

Independent Institute Studies in Political Economy

INDEPENDENT
I N S T I T U T E

100 SWAN WAY, OAKLAND, CA 94621-1428

For further information:

510-632-1366 • orders@independent.org • http://www.independent.org/publications/books/